TRANSITION AND STUDENTS WITH LEARNING DISABILITIES

TRANSITION AND STUDENTS

WITH

LEARNING DISABILITIES

FACILITATING THE MOVEMENT FROM SCHOOL TO ADULT LIFE

EDITED BY

James R. Patton
and
Ginger Blalock

pro·ed
8700 Shoal Creek Boulevard
Austin, Texas 78757-6897

Portions of this material previously appeared in
the *Journal of Learning Disabilities*.

pro·ed

© 1996 by PRO-ED, Inc.
8700 Shoal Creek Boulevard
Austin, Texas 78757-6897

Library of Congress Cataloging-in-Publication Data

Transition and students with learning disabilities : facilitating the
    movement from school to adult life / edited by James R. Patton and
    Ginger Blalock.
        p.   cm.
    Includes bibliographical references (p.   ) and indexes.
    ISBN 0-89079-696-3 (alk. paper)
        1. Learning disabled youth—Education—United States.   2. Learning
    disabled youth—Services for—United States.   3. School-to-work
    transition—United States.   4. Life skills—Study and teaching—
    United States.   I. Patton, James R.   II. Blalock, Ginger.
LC4705.T688   1996
371.91—dc20   95-52856
                                                                  CIP

Printed in the United States of America

1 2 3 4 5 6 7 8 9 10   00 99 98 97 96

Contents

Preface

A number of recent works have dealt with the transition of youth with all types of disabilities from school to the demands of adult life. These materials have assisted us greatly in examining, planning, and acting upon the range of challenges faced in these transitions. This book adds to that body of capacity-building literature by offering in-depth perspectives on outcomes and issues of a specific group, youth with learning disabilities, as they move from high school to adulthood. Difficulties in independent living, social and interpersonal networks, higher education, and employment are frequently ignored for this group, due to perceptions about their intellectual capabilities and other competencies. In fact, failure to address transition needs in each of the major life domains could, and does, pose very serious problems for many young adults, including those with learning disabilities.

The importance of comprehensive transition planning for this group of students was the impetus for bringing this very collaborative effort to print. The covered topics, arranged as chapters, reflect areas that have the greatest implications for these adolescents' preparation, and the authors present potent arguments for consideration regarding these topics. The contributors to this volume have been active and interested in both areas—transition and learning disabilities. Through their chapters, they address, as comprehensively and understandably as possible, the educational, employment, social, and living options available to and critical for persons with learning disabilities. The result is a collection of interrelated chapters that offer rich insights into current trends and promising practices for individuals with learning disabilities who are moving into a new stage of their lives. Because the order of the chapters attempts to mirror, more or less, an unfolding of the journey taken by the person preparing to tackle adult challenges, readers are encouraged to peruse the text in this order. We are hopeful that the material covered in this book provides a foundation to help professionals involved in transition planning become better "tour guides" for the journeys upon which students are embarking.

The philosophical approaches held by the editors of this volume have been heavily influenced by many different professionals. We would like to note specifically the work of Dr. Bob Stodden and the staff of the Hawaii Transition Project, who helped shape our thinking about the transition process. We also want to acknowledge Dr. Lee Wiederholt, who not only promoted the development of the present volume, but also helped focus our attention on the needs, issues, and achievements of adolescents with learning disabilities. This work also represents the culmination of a process that received substantial support from the publisher, PRO-ED, an organization that saw an opportunity to champion more far-reaching treatment of transitions for persons with learning disabilities than individual efforts had accomplished. The very professional staff at PRO-ED— particularly Dr. Judy Voress, Lisa Tippett, Melissa Tullos, Mindy Ahuero, and Teresa Nieto—provided uniquely focused guidance and ensured quality outcomes through an extensive external and internal review process, and gave other editorial assistance where requested. We hope you agree that this volume meets the challenge of guiding us all to facilitate the movement from school to adult life for persons with learning disabilities and others.

GB and JRP

Editors' Note. The royalties generated through the sales of this book are being shared by two entities that work to address the needs of individuals with disabilities: The Donald D. Hammill Foundation and the Division on Career Development and Transition (DCDT) of the Council for Exceptional Children.

1. Transition and Students with Learning Disabilities: Creating Sound Futures

GINGER BLALOCK AND JAMES R. PATTON

Planning for the future has long been recognized as a good idea. Financial planners lure us to seminars using this incentive; it is at the heart of what urban planners are paid to do. Yet, relatively little attention has been given to planning for the adult life of students who do not deal well with the events of everyday life. Although many students do have access to quality career counseling programs, many others do not. Interestingly, when efforts to plan for a student's future have been made, they have traditionally focused on further education or employment, ignoring other areas in which competence will be needed (e.g., daily living and community skills).

Special education and related services have been mandated for a long enough time that we would expect better outcomes for students who were eligible to receive them. Until rather recently, a key piece of the "preparation for life" puzzle had been overlooked. This missing piece involves the systematic consideration of what students need to function successfully as adults. Essentially, if students have the knowledge, skills, services, and/or supports to deal effectively with the various demands of

Reprinted, with changes, from "Transition and students with learning disabilities: Creating sound futures," by Ginger Blalock and James R. Patton, *Journal of Learning Disabilities*, Vol. 29, 1996, pp. 7–16. Copyright © 1996 by PRO-ED, Inc.

1

adulthood, then it is likely that their lives will be more enriched and satisfying.

Students acquire the knowledge and skills, or access the services and supports, required to meet everyday challenges in a number of different ways. Families often are the source of much of what young adults will need to know; but students on their own also pick up useful information and learn needed skills through incidental events. Schools should also be addressing many of the important demands of adulthood. However, none of these sources, singly or in combination, prepare youth as comprehensively as is needed.

Services that prepare students with special needs for adult life have been operative for quite some time in many locales. In the past, they may have been called something else and may not have focused too often on students with learning disabilities (LD). Nevertheless, it is important to acknowledge that many special education teachers, guidance counselors, and other personnel were very much in the business of preparing students and their families for the realities of life after high school long before the current emphasis on transition commenced. It is also useful to note that many families, to whom much of the planning for the future has fallen, have also done a splendid job of getting their adolescents ready for the big show.

It was not until the mid-1980s that we began to systematically examine the importance of formalizing the process to better prepare students for life after high school. The beginning of the transition movement is usually associated with the initiatives that came from the Office of Special Education and Rehabilitative Services (OSERS), with Will's (1984) document being the seminal work.

The transition movement was precipitated by facts that were coming to light about the adult outcomes of students who had been in special education for significant parts of their school careers. Data were emerging from various studies conducted during this time in various locations in the United States. These studies substantiated a rather bleak picture of unemployment, long-term underemployment for those with jobs, minimal participation in postsecondary education, an inability to live independently, limited social experiences, restricted participation in community activities, and inordinately high arrest rates (Affleck, Edgar, Levine, & Kottering, 1990; Hasazi, Gordon, & Roe, 1985; Mithaug, Horiuchi, & Fanning, 1985; Sitlington, Frank, & Carson, 1992; Wagner et al., 1991).

As mentioned at the outset of this chapter, the idea of preparing students for the real world after their school careers end is not new. For example, many work-study programs for students with mental retardation that were common in the 1960s focused specifically on training and employment issues that were linked to postsecondary outcomes. However, it was not until the mid-1980s that comprehensive transition services were proposed, and not until 1990 that planning for such services was mandated. Unfortunately, what is mandated is not always implemented; evidence continues to mount indicating that students' total transitional needs are not being met at the time they leave school (Benz & Halpern, 1993). The next section examines the concept of transition on a general level and chronicles the evolution of one of the many transitions individuals make: moving from school into adult life.

CONCEPT OF TRANSITION

A Life-Span Perspective

Important transitions occur across everyone's life span. Some are normative and predictable; others are time or situation specific and may not apply to everyone. Polloway, Patton, Smith, and Roderique (1991) refer to the former as *vertical transitions* and to the latter as *horizontal transitions*. A graphic representation of these two types of transitions is presented in Figure 1.1.

The life-span developmental transitions (i.e., vertical transitions) are associated with major life events, such as beginning school, leaving school, growing older. Coordinated planning for these events can minimize the trauma and anxiety that may arise, but in reality, little comprehensive planning occurs in the lives of most individuals. However, planning for two of these transitions is mandated by the Individuals with Disabilities Education Act (IDEA): transitions during the infant, toddler, and preschool years, and the transition from high school to adult life.

Horizontal transitions refer to movement from one situation or setting to another. Figure 1.1 highlights a number of such transitions for individuals who are disabled from a chronological perspective. One of the most important and frequently discussed horizontal transitions is the movement from separate settings to less restrictive, more inclusive ones. This type of transition is not age specific, as opportunities for such movement are available throughout the life span for persons with disabilities.

Even though all of the vertical and some of the horizontal transitions have merit for students with learning disabilities, this book and the remainder of this chapter will focus on the transition of these students from the school environment to any one of a number of postschool settings. The next section will highlight how the professional conceptualizations of transition have evolved.

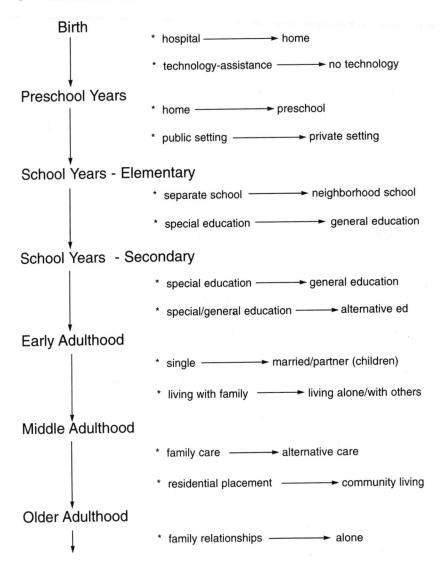

Figure 1.1. Vertical and select horizontal transitions. *Note.* From *Transition From School to Adult Life for Students with Special Needs: Basic Concepts and Recommended Practices,* by J. R. Patton, 1995, Austin, TX: PRO-ED. Copyright 1995 by PRO-ED. Reprinted with permission.

Evolution of a Professional Concept

In 1984, a policy on transition was promoted by OSERS. Transition was defined as "an outcome-oriented process encompassing a broad array of services and experiences that lead to employment...." (Will, 1984,

p. 1). This "bridge-from-school-to-working-life" model of transition emphasized employment as the primary outcome on which training and services—whether time-limited or ongoing—should be based. Halpern (1985) described Will's rationale for the seemingly singular focus on employment: "The nonvocational dimensions of adult adjustment are significant and important only in so far as they contribute to the ultimate goal of employment" (p. 480).

Recognizing the limited scope of the OSERS model of transition, Halpern (1985) offered a revision, suggesting that two other dimensions— the quality of one's residential environment and the adequacy of one's social and interpersonal networks—are as important to successful community adjustment as employment is. Halpern's revisionist model reflected the thinking of other professionals working in the area of transition who felt that additional dimensions must be considered if comprehensive transition planning and preparation were to be accomplished.

As the federally funded transition projects of the mid-1980s began to disseminate their work on transition services, and particularly transition planning, it became clear that more areas were being identified as critical to transition planning. Table 1.1 highlights the transition planning areas promoted by various sources.

The 1990 amendments to the Education for All Handicapped Children Act once again changed a number of different parts of the already twice-amended act. One of the changes involved the notion of transition services. The law now mandated that one of the purposes of the annual Individualized Education Program (IEP) meeting for students with disabilities reaching 16 years of age would be to plan for necessary transition services. The law defined transition services as

> a coordinated set of activities for a student, designed within an outcome oriented process, which promotes movement from school to post-school activities, including post-secondary education, vocational training, integrated employment (including supported employment), continuing and adult education, adult services, independent living or community participation.
>
> The coordinated set of activities shall be based upon the individual student's needs, taking into account student preferences and interests and shall include instruction, community experiences, and the development of employment and other post-school objectives, and if appropriate, acquisition of daily living skills and functional vocational evaluation. [Sec. 300.18]

Individual planning for transition services as prescribed in the legislation and accompanying regulations includes three components: assessment, family participation, and specific procedures to be followed in the development of the IEP. Since these requirements went into effect, states and school districts have developed a variety of ways to address them, ranging from quality comprehensive planning to minimal compliance.

TABLE 1.1
Transition Planning Domains

Major domains	Clark & Patton (in press)	Wehman (1995)	IA	AL	TX	LA
Advocacy/Legal				×		×
Communication	×					
Community Participation	×			×		×
Daily Living (including domestic areas)	×		×			×
Employment (including workplace readiness & specific job skills)	×	×	×	×	×	×
Financial/Income/Money Management		×	×	×		×
Health (including medical services)	×	×	×	×		×
Independent Living (including living arrangements)	×	×				
Leisure/Recreation	×	×	×	×	×	×
Lifelong Learning			×			
Personal Management				×		
Postsecondary Education	×	×	×		×	×
Relationships/Social Skills	×	×	×			×
Self-Determination/Self-Advocacy	×	×	×			
Transportation/Mobility		×	×	×		×
Vocational Evaluation				×		
Vocational Training	×	×			×	

Note. IA = Iowa; AL = Alabama; TX = Texas; LA = Louisiana. From *Transition From School to Adult Life for Students with Special Needs: Basic Concepts and Recommended Practices*, by J. R. Patton, 1995, Austin, TX: PRO-ED. Copyright 1995 by PRO-ED. Reprinted with permission.

In 1994, the Division on Career Development and Transition (DCDT) of the Council for Exceptional Children adopted a new definition of transition that arguably is the best blend of contemporary thinking on this concept. Acknowledging that as students leave school they will have to assume various adult roles in the community, the definition promotes the notion that transition education starts in the beginning levels of schooling and that students should be intricately involved in this process whenever possible. The DCDT definition reads as follows:

> Transition refers to a change in status from behaving primarily as a student to assuming emergent adult roles in the community. These roles include employment, participating in post-secondary education, maintaining a home, becoming appropriately involved in the community, and experiencing satisfactory personal and social relationships. The process of enhancing transition involves the participation and coordination of school programs, adult agency services, and natural supports within the community. The foundations for transition should be laid during the elementary and middle school years, guided by the broad concept of career development. Transition planning should begin no later than age 14, and students should be encouraged, to the full extent of their capabilities, to assume a minimum amount of responsibility for such planning. (Halpern, 1994, p. 117)

The transition planning process is multifaceted, reflecting a complexity that requires (a) a thorough understanding of this process, (b) knowledge of what must be done, and (c) a variety of skills to implement needed transition activities successfully. The model depicted in Figure 1.2 depicts the interrelated aspects of the transition process and suggests that the primary responsibility of transition efforts should be shared by the student, his or her parents/guardians, and the school; however, in reality, all three sources might not contribute to this process. It is essential that all efforts lead to the acquisition of skills, knowledge, services, and/or supports that enable the student to successfully deal with the demands of adulthood. Being reasonably successful in meeting the challenges of everyday living, whether at work, at home, in school, or in the community, can lead to personal fulfillment—an idea that relates closely to the concept of quality of life as discussed by Halpern (1993).

Transition Services and Students with LD

As Dunn (chapter 2 of this book) points out, much of the early emphasis in transition activities was directed toward individuals with more extensive needs. The common assumptions were that students with mild disabilities (e.g., learning disabilities) were able to make the transition to adult life without too much difficulty and that emphasis should be placed

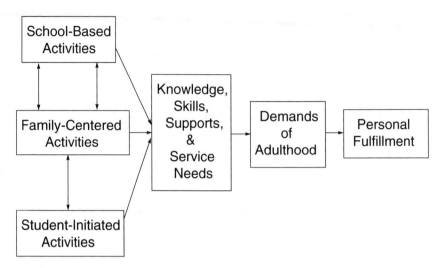

Figure 1.2. Elements of the transition process. *Note*. From *Transition From School to Adult Life for Students with Special Needs: Basic Concepts and Recommended Practices,* by J. R. Patton, 1995, Austin, TX: PRO-ED. Copyright 1995 by PRO-ED. Reprinted with permission.

on academic-related topics. The fact that many students with learning disabilities are in diploma-track programs of largely an academic orientation contributes to this dilemma.

A number of sources suggest that the transitional needs of students with learning disabilities are not entirely being met (Benz & Halpern, 1993; Karge, Patton, & de la Garza, 1992). Transition planning for students with learning disabilities must be comprehensive in nature, addressing *all* the major areas of adult functioning: employment, continuing education, daily living, health, leisure, communication, interpersonal skills, self-determination, and community participation.

A growing database of information related to the transition needs of students with learning disabilities is emerging. Select highlights are provided below.

- Students with learning disabilities receive inadequate vocational experiences—Benz and Halpern (1993) found that 25% of these students received no vocational instruction or school-related work experience.

- Students with learning disabilities are most likely to have to find a job on their own—little help is given to them by the schools or adult agencies (Halpern, Doren, & Benz, 1993).

- Relatively few students with learning disabilities go to 2-year colleges (12%) or 4-year colleges (4%) within 5 years after leaving school, and only 16% attend vocational schools (Wagner et al., 1993).

- Students with learning disabilities are less adept than their nondisabled peers at using community resources and managing various aspects of their lives (Lewis & Taymans, 1992).

The information provided above, coupled with the other adult outcome findings discussed earlier, raises a number of important issues. First, given that a limited number of individuals with learning disabilities are entering postsecondary education, transition efforts must better address employment needs. Second, other functional areas, such as daily living skills, cannot be taken for granted; transitional needs in these areas have to be identified, planned for, and acted on (see Sitlington, chapter 3 of this book).

TRANSITION PLANNING AND STUDENTS WITH LD

The grave issues cited in the prior section highlight the critical choices persons with learning disabilities must make about their lives. The transition planning process provides just the opportunity needed to shape one's future in a powerful way. Youth and young adults can participate in and even manage the individualized transition planning process, supported by a multifaceted team. The team can guide students with learning disabilities in making and acting upon their choices about further education, work, living arrangements, medical attention, physical and mental health supports, transportation options, leisure/recreation lifestyles, and other life areas.

The Roles of the Planning Team

Blalock (chapter 10 of this book) elaborates on the idea that the team should consist of the student, family member(s), critical teachers in special and general (especially vocational) education, an administrator or counselor, a postsecondary education representative, appropriate adult agency staff, and any others tied to essential transition services. Creative options for the future, and ways to achieve them, would be much more forthcoming in a group situation than if a single service provider or student were making decisions alone. Team members can help each other stay future-focused, targeting educational, vocational, and other critical goals after the student leaves high school (often 3 years or more in the future).

Cronin and Patton (1993) helped students and educators envision potential postschool or transition goals by grasping the realm of adult life demands and then working backwards. Once the postschool goals have been agreed upon, the team must identify specific activities that will get the student moving toward accomplishing those goals. Many districts are finding that a 1-page attachment to the IEP, or a section of the existing IEP form, works well for listing those activities; this serves as the individualized transition plan (ITP). Those particular objectives can then be translated into IEP annual goals and short-term objectives. Figure 1.3 provides an example of how those transformations work from one level or context to the next. By allowing the transition goals (or the ITP) to drive the instruction developed within the IEP, all involved parties (most importantly, the student and family) are clear about the overall focus, and content or skill acquisition is very connected to an outcome.

The IEP/ITP requires that present levels of performance be documented, so that the team can identify where to start and what the critical areas of instruction are. This section, which should come early on the IEP form, provides the opportunity to set the tone of the planning process. Building on the student's abilities, rather than coming strictly from a deficit perspective, is much more in concert with transition planning. Students with learning disabilities will have numerous strengths among their various functioning areas of physical/motor development, social/behavioral performance, independent living skills, and career/vocational development. Stating those abilities provides the basis for effective outcome-oriented planning. Academic areas are the ones most likely affected by learning disabilities, but present levels of performance can be stated by grade level in a straightforward fashion without focusing on deficits. In a later section, "services required" can address any particular academic or social behavior that the student needs to improve.

The Importance of Timing

Districts, cooperatives, and other school programs are working hard across the United States to develop and refine their transition services programs, to meet the mandate set forth in IDEA. In most cases, the development of a timeline for these services has been a helpful framework to guide practitioners and researchers. The timeliness of various services (assessment, planning, instruction) is an element in the career development theories (aimed at the general population) of Donald Super, John Holland, and others. Specifically, opportunities for career awareness activities at the elementary level, career exploration at the middle school/junior high level, and career education at the high school and postsecondary levels are important for all students. They are particularly

I. Transition (ITP) Goal: Attending an Appropriate College Program

ITP activities or objectives:

    A. Demonstrating self-advocacy about learning support needs

    B. Researching specific colleges' offerings

    C. Selecting a major

II. Instructional (IEP) Annual Goals

    A. Demonstrate self-advocacy about learning support needs

        Objective 1: The student will identify own learning strengths

        Objective 2: The student will identify own learning needs and related supports

        Objective 3: The student will discuss learning supports needed with high school counselor

    B. Research five colleges' academic and special support offerings

    C. Select a major for the freshman year in college

        Objective 1: Participate in career/vocational and academic assessment

        Objective 2: Review findings of all assessment results with teacher or counselor

        Objective 3: Explore five occupational directions that emerge from the assessment, in library and on computer

        Objective 4: Select one occupational area that seems most promising and match that area to major areas at the selected college

Figure 1.3. Relationship of Individualized Transition Planning (ITP) goals to Individualized Education Program (IEP) goals and objectives.

critical for students with learning disabilities, whose incidental learning outcomes across their school careers may be spotty at best; systematic, focused instruction in life areas may be required for many of these students to be able to reach their educational and vocational goals. A suggested timeline for transition planning and its requisite elements for students with learning disabilities is presented in Table 1.2.

Critical Considerations in Transition Planning

IDEA mandates that we consider students' interests and goals as primary factors in transition decision making, a requirement that is long

TABLE 1.2
Timelines for Transition Planning & Services for Students with Learning Disabilities

	Preschool	Elementary	Mid-school	High school	Postsecondary
	Developmental assessment	Academic, developmental, and informal interest surveys	Academic, adaptive, and interest assessments	9th-vocational interest aptitude, & values 11–12th—update same Ongoing Academic assessment	Formal vocational & academic
	Individualized Family Services Plan (IFSP)	Individualized Education Program (IEP)	IEP, 4-year plan for high school	Individualized Transition Planning (ITP) as part of IEP	IEP/ITP and possible Indiv. Written Rehabilitation Plan (IWRP) or other individual plans
	Developmental and other curricula	Basic skills; Work-related behaviors[a] Self-determination instruction Career awareness	Basic skills Work-related behaviors[a] Self-determination Career exploration	Basic skills (within functional context &/or college prep) Self-determination Career education	Specific academic & vocational curricula
	Chores at home	Chores, hobbies at home and in school	Rotated, varied small job tryouts, supervised experiences	Paid jobs (varied) with supervision gradually faded	Career entry placements

[a]Work-related behaviors include social skills, work ethic, reasoning/problem-solving skills, punctuality, dependability, following through on tasks, following directions, and so forth.

overdue for such critical life planning. In addition, key family members' visions, goals, and requests should drive decisions to an equal degree (Halloran, 1989); some states have even conferred families with agency status so that they can make decisions of the same weight as those of other agency representatives (Blalock et al., 1994). Differing wishes between the student and his or her family members may need to be resolved, compromised on, or even mediated, but the requests of both parties must be respectfully considered. Hopefully, earlier training in self-determination and self-advocacy (particularly appropriate for students with learning disabilities) will have prepared the student to successfully negotiate decisions that are satisfactory to all. The need to begin such instruction (as well as in the areas of work-related behaviors and career awareness and exploration) early on in school becomes evident when the demands at each age level are clarified.

Often, families will base requests, opinions, or comments on their own community or cultural values, accepted practices, or expected traditions. Linguistic differences introduce additional considerations. Rather than viewing these differences as problems, school and agency personnel are encouraged to consider language, culture, and exceptionality as gifts of diversity (Scott & Raborn, 1995); such a perspective matches the use of IEP/ITPs from a capacity-building rather than deficit viewpoint. School and adult-agency personnel must critically review, and in most cases reject, any professional recommendations that are at odds with local mores or family wishes, unless the young adult knowingly and deliberately has chosen to act differently for his or her own perceived best interest. The professionals' role at that point may need to be gathering and collecting data to indicate potential outcomes of the chosen path(s) for both the student and the family.

Recent Forces Influencing Transition Programs

Bassett and Smith (chapter 11 of this book) discuss in some depth the influence that educational reform has had (or may have) on transition efforts in the United States. The inclusion movement, teacher preparation reform, special education reform, and standards-based education serve as both a threat to and a strategy for provision of transition services. More than nondisabled students, students with learning disabilities are in a position to benefit from these reforms—as well as to lose certain options—due to the nature of their disabilities. Careful collaborative planning, as described above, should ensure that individuals' transition needs receive the attention required for successful outcomes.

A more recent educational initiative promises a much stronger imperative for transition planning for students with learning disabilities, because it mandates school-to-work transition education for *all* students in the educational system. The School to Work Opportunities Act, coupled with the Goals 2000 Education Act, prompts school-based education that is tied to employment and other adult outcomes (as in a career education model), and work-based education that provides the rationale for learning applied academic skills and information. As long as students with learning disabilities are not excluded from these general curricular options, this legislation offers many more opportunities for meaningful transition education than any singular special education or rehabilitation act has been able to muster. Families, consumers, educators, business leaders, and other interested parties are urged to ensure that the acts indeed address educational opportunities for all students. At this writing, 27 states have received implementation grants while all other states are still in planning stages.

BOOK OVERVIEW

This final section of the chapter provides background information about the book and what to expect in the other chapters. How the book originated is briefly discussed, followed by a short examination of some common themes found throughout it. Last, a short introduction to each of the chapters is presented.

Genesis

The book evolved from a symposium on the topic of transition and learning disabilities that was held in Austin, Texas, for 3 days in September of 1994. Select professionals who had an established interest in transition and learning disabilities were invited to participate in the symposium. Each symposium member received a draft of the other papers prior to the symposium. Upon completion of each participant's presentation at the symposium, immediate critical feedback was given and other discussion ensued. The book editors were part of the symposium and provided comments at this time.

After the symposium was completed, participants revised their papers based on the feedback they had received. Their revised versions were then subjected to the typical review process, and an additional review by the book editors. Final versions of the contributed pieces were worked on through the summer of 1995.

Common Themes

Certain themes are extremely important in regard to meeting the transition needs of students with learning disabilities. These themes are interwoven throughout the book and are described briefly below.

1. *Student Participation Is Crucial.* As Karge et al. (1992) noted, "it is an inherent right to be involved in one's own life planning" (p. 65). To do this effectively, students must be more than observers at their IEP meetings; they need to be provided the tools to be effective participants. At the very least, a student's interests and preferences should be determined. However, it is more desirable to have the student actively contribute to the development of his or her transition plan.

2. *Efforts Should Be Made to Get Families Involved in the Transition Process.* School-based personnel need to be sensitive to family values, needs, and situations; and families should be encouraged to participate to whatever degree possible in identifying transition needs, determining transition goals, and acting directly or indirectly on achieving those goals.

3. *Transition Efforts Should Start Early.* Various aspects of the transition process can begin easily at the elementary level. Transition education (i.e., content related to ultimate transition areas) can be initiated through the teaching of life skills and career education. Families can be introduced to the major areas of transition planning when their children are young so that they become aware of areas that will be very important for their children in the future.

4. *Transition Planning Must Be Sensitive to Cultural Factors.* Professionals involved in transition planning need to be aware of various cultural factors that can affect the nature of student and family participation in the transition planning process. The way families participate may differ from what school-based personnel desire. Futhermore, cultural factors may very well influence the priority of transition needs, again in potential contrast to what school-based individuals think is important. The goal of transition planning is to act on areas of need. Agreeing on what the most important areas are requires mediation and collaboration skills.

5. *Transition Planning Must Be Comprehensive.* As important as employment is as an outcome, it is only one of many other areas for which transition needs should be evaluated. Edgar (1988), in summarizing his thoughts (shared by others), cautioned, "In our society, employment, and the money earned from employment, plays a critical role in everyone's quality of life—hence the focus on employment. But we must remain aware that employment and jobs do not guarantee quality of life" (p. 5). The important point is that we need to reach a workable balance across all of the transition areas.

Content

The sequence of the chapters in this book on transition for students with learning disabilities deliberately follows the flow of events or practices that should take place as those students prepare for and embrace adulthood. These chapters provide critical data about this diverse group as they prepare for adulthood—about their instructional needs, promising practices, and critical considerations. The result is a collection rich in ideas for discussion, for possible implementation in schools and professional preparation programs, and for use as guideposts for evaluating collaborative efforts.

In chapter 2, Caroline Dunn describes the current status of transition programming for students with learning disabilities, to the extent that we can identify it, which can serve as a baseline marker from which to explore specific aspects of transition. An outline of myths about students with learning disabilities and their needs for transition services serves as the basis for an overview of state and federal mandates and initiatives that have influenced (and continue to drive) transition practices. Dunn describes the diversity of promising practices that currently address adolescent and adult programming and service needs. Finally, her overview of transition considerations for persons with learning disabilities sets the stage for the remaining chapters.

Patricia Sitlington's chapter also sets the tone for the book in a very significant way. She tackles the "neglected component of transition planning" for this population: community living needs and opportunities. Her compelling rationales depict for the reader the problems with major adult living roles that some individuals with learning disabilities experience. She reviews the research findings in this area in relation to these individuals' learning characteristics and then spotlights current models of career education and life skills education pertinent to those learners. Her final segment examines our instructional practices with this population and offers recommendations for more comprehensive interventions.

Many individuals with LD struggle with learning about and acting on behalf of themselves, and that subject is artfully presented by Sharon Field in her chapter on self-determination instruction. Basic terminology and model characteristics will help readers understand the importance of self-determination for persons with learning disabilities. The chapter examines existing curricula and promising strategies for promoting self-determination among this population. The final section offers important insights into issues pertinent to such intervention, such as role redefinition and the importance of taking risks.

The remainder of critical functional skills instruction is addressed in the comprehensive chapter by Mary Cronin. She conducts a thorough review of the literature in life skills education of students with learning disabilities, examining historical terminology, follow-up/follow-along studies, theoretical papers, model program descriptions, and empirical findings. Her concluding recommendations include more far-reaching and systematic research directions, curricular changes, and training with teachers and parents. The appendices to her chapter are rich summaries of the literature, including theoretical conclusions and research findings, an annotated bibliography of life skills books, and outcomes of field-based programs that have enhanced life skills development.

Vocational education for students with learning disabilities becomes the next step in life skills instruction, providing a critical arena for delivery of both broad and specific vocational development. In her chapter, Rebecca Evers analyzes the relationship of vocational/technical education to postsecondary employment and other life outcomes. Research findings related to placement and service delivery in vocational/technical programs are presented, organized into critical areas of accessibility, teacher preparation, teacher attitudes, and environmental and instructional demands. Evers also presents recommendations for future investigation.

Once the instructional models have been theorized, individual student needs must be carefully examined. Gary Clark assists us in conceptualizing our choices and recommends practices in his chapter on assessment for transition planning. He discusses the challenges involved in evaluating large numbers of students who have not yet participated in such planning. The importance of our rethinking such IEP components as "present levels of functioning" in relation to informal and formal assessment procedures is linked to understanding appropriate adult adjustment outcomes. He provides an overview of existing practices in transition-related assessment and offers recommendations for transition needs assessment at the secondary level.

The first chapters deal with secondary issues and practices in transition programming for individuals with learning disabilities, whereas later chapters examine adult needs and perspectives. Loring Brinckerhoff offers an extensive set of strategies for students to prepare for postsecondary education in any form. His organization by grade level, beginning no later than eighth grade, provides educators with invaluable guidelines and strategies that will enable students to systematically empower themselves to act upon their postsecondary education goals. His discussions of the final transition planning and the differences between high school and college serve to guide the design of appropriate intervention.

Many individuals preparing for postsecondary education or employment find that additional agency support is needed. Carol Dowdy's chapter on accessing the vocational rehabilitation system emphasizes the importance of a collaborative model, and she assists professionals in that effort by explaining terminology, policy guidelines, academic versus employment emphases, and regulations that differ across the educational and rehabilitation systems. Her case study approach readily illustrates the utility of establishing partnerships that will enhance the employment outcomes of individuals with LD.

The chapter on community transition teams brings the reader back to all of the previously described components of the transition process by placing them within the context of local strengths and needs. Ginger Blalock describes the composition, member roles, and responsibilities of community transition teams, which support transitions from school to postsecondary activities for students with learning disabilities. The evolution of these teams, their critical access to community supports and employment opportunities, and their potential outcomes are described.

The final chapter, by Diane Bassett and Tom Smith, sums up the transition needs of young adults with learning disabilities and discusses the role of educational reform in creating (or not creating) services to respond to those needs. General education reform, special education reform, inclusion, and changes in personnel preparation are analyzed in terms of their impact on appropriate transition services. Readers are encouraged to take advantage of the changes under way to help secure systematic supports for individuals with learning disabilities who are working toward their goals. The time is now; the task is ours.

2. A Status Report on Transition Planning for Individuals with Learning Disabilities

Transition was identified as a national priority in the early 1980s. Since that time, the movement's predominant focus has been on individuals with moderate and severe disabilities. Whereas the social, vocational, residential, and other long-term follow-up needs of these individuals are well documented, the transition needs of individuals with mild disabilities have received considerably less attention (e.g., Neubert, Tilson, & Ianacone, 1989; Rojewski, 1992). A major reason for this lack of attention has been the assumption that individuals with mild disabilities move from secondary to postsecondary environments with greater ease than do their peers with more severe disabilities.

That assumption, however, is now being challenged through the findings of recent studies that underscore the need for systematic transition planning for students with mild disabilities, including those served primarily in general education and resource settings (Lichtenstein, 1993; Sitlington, Frank, & Carson, 1992; Wagner, 1990). Such studies indicate that compared to their nondisabled peers, individuals with mild disabili-

Reprinted, with changes, from "A status report on transition planning for individuals with learning disabilities," by Caroline Dunn, *Journal of Learning Disabilities*, Vol. 29, 1996, pp. 17–30. Copyright © 1996 by PRO-ED, Inc.

ties experience (a) a higher unemployment and/or underemployment rate, (b) more restricted participation in community activities and leisure activities, (c) lower pay, (d) more dependency on parents or others, (e) more dissatisfaction with employment, and (f) higher academic failure rates in postsecondary settings.

Within the group of individuals with mild disabilities, transition planning for students with learning disabilities (LD) has probably received the least attention of any other facet of their lives and "is just beginning to receive serious consideration" (Reiff & deFur, 1992, p. 239). The purpose of this chapter is to provide an overview of transition as it relates specifically to this group of individuals.

TRANSITION PLANNING FOR INDIVIDUALS WITH LD

Transition planning for individuals with LD has lagged behind that of other groups for several reasons, the primary one being the inaccurate assumptions often made about individuals with LD that contribute to special and general educators' reluctance to consider transition planning for them. Another reason concerns the appropriateness of the transition model employed for individuals with LD. Finally, the wide range of characteristics exhibited by this group make transition planning challenging. Each of these factors will be discussed below in more detail.

Myths About Individuals with LD

Reiff and deFur (1992) identified several pervasive myths that contribute to special and general educators' reluctance to consider transition planning for such students. The first myth relates to the perception that persons with learning disabilities do not encounter difficulties with employment. Although adults with learning disabilities may achieve success more readily than individuals with other kinds of disabilities, they still experience higher rates of unemployment, underemployment, and part-time employment than their peers without disabilities (Peraino, 1992). A second myth is that most individuals with learning disabilities can achieve basic academic competencies, consistent with those of their nondisabled peers, because they graduate from high school. The reality is that a significant number of students with LD (27% to 29%) drop out of school with minimal academic skills and little vocational training (Reiff & deFur, 1992; Wagner, Blackorby, Cameto, Hebbeler, & Newman, 1993).

A third myth concerns intellectual functioning. Many definitions suggest that individuals with learning disabilities have average to above-average ability; therefore, it is assumed that most will be able to pursue higher education. In reality, individuals with LD have a wide range of intellectual abilities. Wagner et al. (1993) reported a mean IQ score of 87.1 for secondary students with LD, with 13.1% of the students having an IQ score below 75 and 52.8% having an IQ score in the 75 to 90 range.

Finally, the hidden nature of learning disabilities leads many to discount their seriousness. Consequently, they often are viewed as only a school-related problem. Such is not the case. In fact, many individuals with learning disabilities experience difficulties in multiple aspects of their lives, including social and interpersonal relationships, independent functioning, and employment, both during and after high school (Lewis & Taymans, 1992; Minskoff, Sautter, Sheldon, Steidle, & Baker, 1988).

Appropriateness of Transition Models

Many transition models were developed for students with more severe disabilities, individuals with more limited postsecondary options. Blalock and Patton (chapter 1 of this book) provide a discussion of the models that have emerged over the years. The majority of these transition models (e.g., Halpern, 1985; Will, 1984) define transition services in terms of type and intensity of the services (i.e., no special services, time-limited, ongoing) needed for an individual to reach selected goals (often, employment). It is frequently assumed that individuals with learning disabilities take the "no special services" path (Reiff & deFur, 1992) or require only time-limited services (Rojewski, 1992).

Rojewski (1992) advocated that transition be viewed in terms of the *processes,* or pathways, required to transition from school to postschool environments, rather than the services, and he suggested an alternative transition model that has direct implications for students with LD (see Figure 2.1). The reason for the emphasis on processes rather than services is the greater diversity in postsecondary training and education options available for this group. The model encompasses four main paths to employment and adult life that take into account the variety of possible postsecondary options.

1. *Direct path from high school to employment.* The direct path involves moving from high school to employment. Because the individual does not participate in any postsecondary training or education, most of his or her postsecondary/career/vocational preparation must occur before exiting high school.

2. *Path from high school to postsecondary education/training.* Support for postsecondary education and training can be provided in several ways, one of which would occur at the secondary level, ceasing after high

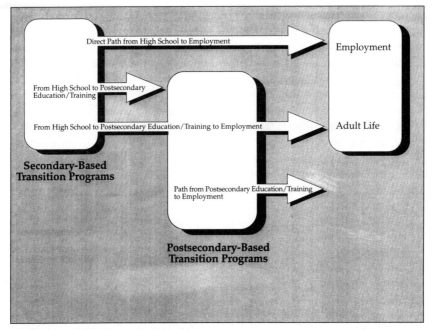

Figure 2.1. Transition options available for students with learning disabilities. *Note.* From "Key Components of Model Transition Services for Students with Learning Disabilities," by J. A. Rojewski, 1992, *Learning Disability Quarterly, 15,* p. 140. Copyright 1992 by Council for Learning Disabilities. Reprinted with permission.

school. Examples of the kinds of transition services provided in this path include the formal transfer of responsibility to adult service providers and assistance in identifying and enrolling the individual in postsecondary education or training.

3. *Path from high school to postsecondary education/training to employment.* Support for postsecondary education and training can also begin in high school, continue through postsecondary training and education, and then end with employment.

4. *Path from postsecondary education/training to employment.* Finally, services can be initiated after a student enters a postsecondary environment. Such services include academic support, career development, and job placement.

The specific kinds of services an individual needs are determined, then, by the processes required to reach individual goals. One important aspect of this alternative transition model is that it allows consideration of a wide array of postsecondary training and employment options. Furthermore, it helps to address the heterogeneity of the group of individuals with learning disabilities to ensure that transition planning and programming will be based on individual skills and goals.

Population Characteristics

An examination of the characteristics of adolescents and adults with learning disabilities reinforces the need for transition planning for them (Sitlington, chapter 3 of this book). At the secondary level, the learning difficulties that children with learning disabilities experienced during the elementary years persist and are often compounded as students confront increasingly complex academic and social demands (Mercer, 1991). Difficulties in reading, mathematics, and writing continue, and often interfere with learning of content in other areas, such as social studies and science. As instructional techniques rely more and more on many of the basic skill areas affected by a learning disability, and greater independence in work habits is expected, many students with learning disabilities experience increased failure.

Problems in areas other than academics may become more apparent at this time. For example, individuals may experience difficulties in independent decision making and problem solving (Alley, Deshler, Clark, Schumaker, & Warner, 1983; Cronin & Gerber, 1982; Getzel & Gugerty, 1992), experience problems related to social skills, exhibit poor social perception, and have difficulties maintaining interpersonal relationships (Ariel, 1992).

Adolescents must also refine their ideas about the world of work and begin to direct their attention toward possible career choices during this time. With regard to career attitudes and awareness, Bingham (1978) reported that many adolescents with learning disabilities demonstrate immature responses to demands associated with career choice and have unrealistic perceptions of basic job requirements and the "world of work" expectations.

Another issue concerns dropout rates. Levin, Zigmond, and Birch (1985) documented the progress of students with learning disabilities who had entered ninth grade in the 1977–78 school year. They found that by 1981, 47% of the initial group with learning disabilities had dropped out of school. This was significantly higher than the 36% dropout rate reported for their nondisabled peers. Edgar (1988) reported similar findings for a group of students in Washington state; he indicated that some 50% of the students with learning disabilities who entered secondary programs never finished.

The problems associated with learning disabilities during the school years persist into adulthood. In fact, as these individuals become older, their problems may become more magnified or manifest themselves differently as the demands of work, home, school, and community living increase and become more complex (Polloway, Smith, & Patton, 1984). Academic problems persist, and social skills continue to be an area of concern (Hoffman et al., 1987; Patton & Polloway, 1982). In the psychological domain, memory appears to be a major problem (Hoffman et al., 1987). Other difficulties include impulsivity, restlessness, hyperactivity (Patton & Polloway, 1982), short attention span, and distractibility (Texas Rehabilitation Commission, n.d.).

With regard to personal characteristics, these adults appear to exhibit a wide range of behaviors that are present along a continuum ranging from mild to severe. Typical problems include disorganization, sloppiness, carelessness, difficulty following directions, and poor decision-making skills (Patton & Polloway, 1982). In addition, some have limited independent-functioning skills (e.g., difficulty handling money, banking; Hoffman et al., 1987). Blalock (1981) reported orientation problems (i.e., getting around the community) and difficulty in such everyday tasks as setting alarm clocks, packing boxes, and handling new situations.

Difficulties are also present in the vocational domain. In a study on the vocational adjustment of young adults with learning disabilities, White et al. (1983) found that these individuals held approximately the same number of jobs as their nondisabled peers; however, they reported more dissatisfaction with their jobs and were more likely to be underemployed. Edgar (1988) reported on the employment status of 600 high school graduates who had been out of school from 1 to 5 years. He indicated that the majority went on to low-paying jobs that provided few, if any, benefits.

Although general characteristics of this group have been identified, one must remember that secondary students and young adults with learning disabilities constitute an extremely diverse group, which can present challenges to appropriate transition planning. Unfortunately, the variety of abilities, disabilities, and programming needs they bring to the educational process are sometimes masked by the single label of learning disabilities (Wagner, 1990). Several researchers have proposed using the concept of severity of disability to attain more homogeneity within the group and to guide educational programming for these students. For example, Minskoff and DeMoss (1993) suggested classifying students with learning disabilities at the mild, moderate, or severe level. Students classified as *mild* have above-average intelligence, adequate psychological adjustment and vocational/employability skills, high academic achievement, and limited processing and language deficits. Programming for these students would likely be characterized as college preparatory, with mainstreaming in general education classes and resource support.

Students at the *moderate* level have average intelligence, some cognitive and language deficits, one or more academic disabilities, some psychological adjustment problems, and difficulty with vocational/employment skills. These students would benefit from a combined academic and vocational curriculum. It is also likely that they would be mainstreamed into general academic and vocational classes when appropriate.

Individuals classified as having *severe* LD display below-average intelligence, significant cognitive processing and language deficits, low academic achievement, a lack of psychological adjustment, and a lack of vocational/employment skills. These students need a *functional* and *vocational* secondary program. Programming would include life skills curricula in special education offered along with mainstream vocational education or special vocational education.

Polloway, Patton, Epstein, and Smith (1989) advocated a similar approach for students identified with mild disabilities. They argued that the students who constitute this group have variant needs, making it necessary to focus on subgroups with different curricular needs. They identified four subgroups, three of which could include students with learning disabilities. The College Preparatory Track group includes students who have a reasonable opportunity to attend and complete a postsecondary school. The curriculum for these students should include maximum participation in the general high school program so that students can earn the credits necessary for a high school diploma as well as participate in content requisite for college success. Additionally, Polloway et al. stressed the importance of academic and career advising and attending to skills necessary in the targeted postschool environment for these students.

Students with more significant learning and behavior problems who are not likely to attend academic postsecondary programs belong to the Functional Track A group. The needs of these students include access to functional data-based curricula in independent living and vocational preparation, as well as social development. The third group, Tough-to-Call Track, includes students who do not fit easily into the other groups. These are students with "unconfirmed interests, marginal academic achievement, and absence of commitment to particular career directions" (Polloway et al., 1989, p. 10). These students need continuing basic skills remediation, career education, learning strategies, and adult outcomes.

The application of the Minskoff and DeMoss (1993) and Polloway et al. (1989) models may assist in curriculum planning and implementation for individuals with learning disabilities. Not all individuals, however, will fit neatly into the existing groups. Thus, transition planning must ultimately be based on each individual's needs, abilities, and preferences.

Although many students with disabilities have reaped benefits from the transition movement since its commencement, the fact remains that the emphasis has been on those with moderate and severe functioning levels. Yet, the population of students with learning disabilities must not be ignored. Consider, for example, that of the 132,192 students with LD (ages 14 through 21) who exited from the school system in 1992, only 60.5% graduated with either a diploma or certificate (U.S. Office of Special Education Programs, 1994). The remainder of this chapter provides a review of transition as it relates to students with LD. Presented first are state and federal transition initiatives and guidelines.

FEDERAL AND STATE GUIDELINES

Federal and state initiatives and mandates have had a significant influence on the provision of services to secondary students with disabilities. Several of the most important efforts at these two levels are highlighted here.

Federal Initiatives

The Office of Special Education and Rehabilitative Services, U.S. Department of Education, identified the transition from school to work as a federal priority in the early 1980s. Initially, transition programming and planning were encouraged through discretionary funding of demonstration projects (P.L. 98-199, P.L. 99-457). The National Transition Institute at the University of Illinois was established to provide national leadership with regard to the transition initiative.

In 1990, transition planning was mandated for all students with disabilities ages 16 years and older (P.L. 101-476). The new federal regulations, which became effective in November 1992, contain several regulation sections that guide the provision of transition planning and services. Four important regulation requirements are (a) notification (Section 300.345), (b) participation in meetings (Section 300.344), (c) content of the IEP (Section 300.346), and (d) agency responsibilities (Section 300.347).

Notification. With regard to parent notification of the IEP meeting, regulations require that if the purpose of the meeting is to consider transition services for a student, the parent(s) must be notified of this intent. Additionally, they must be informed that the student, as well as any appropriate agency representatives, also are invited to the meeting. The intent of this regulation is to provide the parents with the opportunity to (a) prepare for this aspect of the IEP meeting, (b) discuss transition goals and activities with their child, (c) request that additional or alternate agencies be invited, and (d) request information about the services and policies of the other agencies (National Transition Network, 1993).

Participation in Meetings. In the IEP meetings in which transition is discussed, IDEA participation is expanded to include the student and representatives of other agencies that are likely to be responsible for providing or paying for transition services. The student's participation is particularly important. IDEA regulations require that the activities identified for the IEP be "based on the individual student's needs, taking into account the student's preferences and interests" (300.18(b)(1)). If the student does not attend, this must be documented, and measures must be taken to have student input considered. The values of self-determination, enablement, and shared responsibility are reflected in this mandate for student involvement. Furthermore, the values of long-term, person-centered planning; coordination; and shared responsibility are reflected in the requirement to involve agencies responsible for providing or paying for services (National Transition Network, 1993).

Content of the IEP. Transition service areas that each IEP team must address in transition meetings include, at a minimum, instruction, community experiences, and development of employment and other postschool adult living objectives. If the IEP team determines that services are not needed within any of the four designated areas, the IEP must include a statement to that effect and the basis upon which the decision was made. Additionally, if appropriate, activities could include acquisition of daily living skills and functional vocational evaluation. The delineation of these areas ensures that the IEP team addresses all areas critical to successful postschool outcomes (National Transition Network, 1993).

Agency Responsibility. The successful transition from school to postschool environments must be the responsibility of many individuals, due to the complexity and long-term nature of the process. IDEA seeks to ensure the involvement of an array of members in the transition process (e.g., students, families, school and outside agency personnel). IEPs must include statements of each participating agency's responsibilities or linkage, if any, before the student leaves school, as well as a commitment by these agencies to meet financial responsibilities associated with the provision of services. This increases the likelihood of a more coordinated transition from school to adult services and postschool settings.

Another federal initiative has been making federal funds available to help 5-year state systems change projects on transition and establish a center to provide technical assistance and evaluation services to states implementing the systems change projects. Thirty states (12 states in 1991, 12 in 1992, and 6 in 1993) have entered into cooperative agreements with OSERS to undertake these projects. The goals of these systems change projects are as follows:

1. Increase the availability of, access to, and quality of transition assistance for youth with disabilities.

2. Improve the ability of professionals, parents, and advocates to work with youth with disabilities in ways that promote the understanding of, and the capability to successfully make, the transition from student to adult.

3. Improve working relationships among those who are, or should be, involved in the delivery of transition services, in order to identify and achieve consensus on the general nature and specific application of transition services to meet the needs of youth with disabilities.

4. Create an incentive for accessing and using the existing, or developing, expertise and resources of programs, projects, and activities related to transition. (National Transition Network, n.d., p. 2)

In 1992, a cooperative agreement was finalized between the University of Minnesota and OSERS to establish the National Transition Network. The purpose of the Network is to provide technical assistance and evaluation services to states implementing systems change projects. More specifically, the role of the Network is to

> strengthen the capacity of individual states to effectively improve school-to-work transition policies, programs, and practices, by providing technical assistance and consultation in essential areas of state project implementation. Further, the network operates to generate and disseminate policy-relevant information for the purpose of improving state and local policy and program structures and achieve higher levels of intergovernmental cooperation to benefit individuals with disabilities and their families as they transition from school to work and community. (National Transition Network, n.d., p. 1)

In summary, the federal government has influenced transition practices through several means. Initially, funds were made available for demonstration projects, and the National Transition Network was established to provide leadership in the area. Later, transition planning was mandated for all students with disabilities ages 16 years and older. Finally, federal funds have been made available to states for state systems change projects on transition.

State Efforts

State policy and initiatives are also influencing transition practices. Prior to 1990, there was no mandate for providing transition services, and no mechanism for funding transition other than through federally funded model demonstration projects. Consequently, transition services for secondary youth with disabilities were provided at the discretion of the state or local education agency, resulting in considerable heterogeneity with regard to state responses to the transition initiative (Halloran,

1993). DeStefano and Wermuth (1992) described the pattern of transition services that emerged in the nation as inconsistent, with "areas of excellence mixed with areas of great need" (p. 539). For some states, the lack of a federal prescription resulted in the creation of highly effective transition service delivery systems based on those states' education, adult service, economic, and employment contexts. Conversely, little occurred in other states toward development of transition service delivery systems in the absence of a federal mandate. This inconsistency should diminish as a result of federal mandates requiring the provision of transition services (DeStefano & Wermuth, 1992).

Although states must now meet the minimal criteria specified in IDEA, they have some flexibility with regard to *how* they meet the mandates. Some of the dimensions on which states vary are (a) the age at which transition services are implemented, (b) the nature of interagency cooperation, and (c) the assistance provided to local education agencies (LEAs).

Age at Which Transition Planning Is Initiated.   The law requires that students' IEPs contain a statement of necessary transition services beginning no later than age 16 (and beginning at age 14 or younger if deemed appropriate for the individual). Many states' administrative codes reflect this requirement exactly. However, some states (e.g., Minnesota, New Jersey, Illinois, Kansas) require that transition planning be initiated no later than age 14. Several other states are considering the age 14 requirement.

Interagency Cooperation.   IDEA requires that interagency linkages be established to increase the effectiveness of service delivery while the student is in school and to support the movement to postsecondary settings. Although the public agency (usually the school) is primarily responsible for the provision of transition services, IDEA clearly signals that preparing students to move from school to postschool environments is not the *sole* responsibility of public education. The responsibilities or linkages of participating agencies for a given student needing such linkages must be designated before the student leaves school.

Stowitschek (1992) conducted a survey that examined policy and planning in transition programs at the state agency level. He received and analyzed transition documents from 52 of the 60 states, territories, and protectorates. Ninety-four percent of the states addressed interagency planning and cooperation. In the majority of the cases, this was represented through formal agreements. The most common agreements were dual agreements between vocational rehabilitation and special education. Also fairly common were dual agreements between vocational rehabilitation and developmental disabilities offices, and three-way agreements among vocational rehabilitation, vocational education, and special education state offices.

Some states' interagency activities are quite sophisticated. Minnesota's legislation, for example, requires that community transition interagency committees be established in all communities and that an interagency office on transition services be established within the state's department of education. Minnesota has a State Transition Interagency Committee comprising individuals representing many agencies and programs (e.g., Department of Education, Department of Human Services, Department of Jobs and Training, Division of Rehabilitation Services, State Job Training Office Job Training Partnership Act, Parent Advocacy Coalition for Educational Rights). Service activities, such as outreach, assessment, eligibility determination, responsibility for individualized planning, vocational programming, and independent living programming, have been delineated and the agencies responsible for each service activity identified.

As another example, Illinois has developed an integrated system for providing transition services. That state's transition legislation is modeled after Minnesota's; the primary difference is that in the former, responsibilities for specific activities are shared among agencies (Bates, 1993). In other words, the educational agency has the primary responsibility for transition planning in conjunction with the IEP meeting. The Department of Rehabilitation Services is responsible for organizing local transition planning committees, while the Transition Coordinating Council has the responsibility for coordinating the overall state initiative.

Support to Transition Service Providers. Another dimension that varies substantially from state to state is the amount and kind of support provided to transition service providers. In general, those states that have received the state systems change grants demonstrate a wider variety and more comprehensive array of supports. New Jersey, for example, has developed training workshops and materials for different service providers, such as case managers and guidance counselors. Additionally, they sponsor a summer institute that focuses on recommended practices.

Iowa has developed a number of training materials and conducted numerous train-the-trainers sessions. Wisconsin has developed multiple documents that address transition planning, including materials addressing the development of IEPs that incorporate transition services; vocational experience programs (including labor laws, program guidelines, and vocational assessment); collaborative transition planning; and transition information for parents. Minnesota also has developed multiple documents. Additionally, their Interagency Office on Transition Services sponsors Project Invest, a resource bank of parents and professionals from an array of social services, such as rehabilitation, independent living centers, higher education, vocational education, special education, and other school service providers who have received training to conduct technical assistance in various areas of transition. Utah has developed a set of guidelines for transition service providers at the preschool, elementary, middle/junior high school, and high school levels. The goal of these guidelines is the development and implementation of a seamless transition process from birth to 22. These are but a few of the efforts being made by states to assist in the development of a comprehensive system of transition planning.

TRANSITION PRACTICES

The needs of secondary students with disabilities have been a national concern for the past 30 years (Browning, Brown, & Dunn, 1993). It was not until the 1980s, however, that the field began to develop a menu of "best practices." Practices frequently cited in the literature include interagency cooperation and collaboration, vocational assessment, vocational skills training, social skills training, career education curricula, paid work experience during high school, written transition plans, and parent or family involvement in the transition process (Kohler, 1993).

Kohler (1993) examined the extent to which practices recommended in the literature are actually substantiated. She reviewed 17 follow-up studies, 11 theory-based or opinion articles, and 20 quasi-experimental studies. Evidence supporting particular practices was classified as either (a) substantiated or supported in the literature by results of a study, or (b) implied as desirable or effective by the publication's author. In total, there were 272 literature citations for 21 identified practices. Of these, there was substantiated evidence for only 24 (8%) of these citations.

Table 2.1 delineates the practices identified in Kohler's literature review. Included in the table are the total number of times each practice was cited, as well as the kind of evidence (i.e., substantiated or implied) supporting its use. The most frequently cited practices, which appeared in more than 50% of the documents analyzed, were vocational training, parent involvement, and interagency collaboration. Social skills training, paid work experience, and individual transition plans and planning were cited in at least one third of the documents.

What is interesting about Kohler's (1993) findings is that most of the practices lacked empirical support. In fact, no practice was substantiated more than five times. Peters and Heron (1993) cautioned that the way in which professionals in special education use the term *best practices* is misleading, because measurable criteria have not been systematically applied. Kohler concluded that many of the practices that have been

TABLE 2.1
Frequency of Literature Citations for Best Practices

Transition components	Total citations	Substantiated by study results	Implied by authors
Vocational training	28	5	23
Parent involvement	25	3	22
Interagency collaboration/ service delivery	24	0	24
Social skills training	17	4	13
Paid work experience	17	5	12
Individual plans/planning	17	0	17
Interdisciplinary transition teams	14	0	14
Follow-up employment services	13	1	12
Employer input	13	1	12
Integration/LRE mainstreaming	12	2	10
Community-based instruction	12	0	12
Vocational assessment	11	0	11
Community-referenced curricula	10	0	10
ID vocational, residential/social and social outcomes	9	0	9
Daily living skills training	9	1	8
IEP reflects transition	8	0	8
Career education curricula	8	0	8
Employability skills training	7	2	5
Formal interagency agreement	6	0	6
Early transition planning	6	0	6
Academic skill training	6	0	6

Note. From "Best practices in transition: Substantiated or implied?," by P. D. Kohler, 1993, *Career Development for Exceptional Individuals, 16,* 107–121. Copyright 1993 by Division on Career Development and Transition. Adapted with permission.

identified as "best" have not been substantiated through empirical means, although she acknowledged that they have, to some extent, been socially validated and now must be subjected to empirical validation. Even though most of the components of transition planning that have been identified in the literature need further validation through research, there is some evidence for their utilization. In essence, she suggested that these practices be the foundation for future transition programs that are developed. By carefully describing and incorporating these practices into transition programs, professionals can begin to develop the empirical evidence needed to support or refute their usage (Kohler, 1993).

The transition practices discussed so far are generic in the sense that they are applicable with *all* youth, regardless of type of disability. However, modifications to meet the unique needs of individuals with learning disabilities also must be considered. Again, early efforts at identifying critical variables focused on programs for individuals with moderate and severe disabilities. The particular challenges and needs of individuals with learning disabilities have only recently been recognized. The remainder of this chapter discusses transition as it relates specifically to individuals with learning disabilities in terms of (a) secondary programming and adult service needs and (b) recommended practices.

Secondary Programming and Adult Service Needs

The secondary school programming and transition experiences of individuals with learning disabilities have been examined as part of the Congressionally funded National Longitudinal Transition Study (NLTS), which was based on a nationally representative sample. Specifically, data were collected in 1987 and 1990 for a sample of more than 8,000 youth who represented the national population of secondary special education students aged 13 through 21 in the 1985–86 school year. Several different reports have been generated from the data bank (e.g., Wagner, 1990; Wagner et al., 1993). A description of the kinds of services and programs typically provided to individuals with learning disabilities, as well as of their adult service needs, is included in the reports. That information is summarized below.

Secondary Transition Programming.   Numerous transition demonstration projects funded through federal grant competitions have focused on transition programming for students with learning disabilities. In general, these programs differ in several variables: the agency with primary responsibility, the age students access services, the scope of the program, and the length of program services (Rojewski, 1992). Programs that are secondary-based can begin as early as ninth grade or as late as graduation. These programs can be integrated into the special education program or exist separately. Postsecondary-based programs usually begin shortly before or after students exit school. The scope of the programming for both types of programs varies from highly specialized (e.g., vocational training) to comprehensive, emphasizing among other things the academic, vocational, and social/personal domains.

One of the reports of the National Longitudinal Transition study addressed the secondary-based programming and school performance of adolescents with learning disabilities (Wagner, 1990). The report indicated that despite the skill deficiencies and learning problems of secondary students with LD, the general education class was considered appropriate for most of them and was the setting in which most of these students spent the majority of their time. Students were more likely to be mainstreamed for nonacademic or vocational courses than for academic classes. Approximately 64% of the students took vocational classes, and, of those, 85% were in general education. Student support services beyond special education instruction (e.g., tutoring, life skills training) were rarely provided. Secondary general education teachers with mainstreamed students received support primarily through consultation, special materials, and inservice training. Rarely were classroom aides or reduced class sizes an option for mainstream teachers.

With regard to secondary school performance, the NLTS examined grade-point average (GPA) and failing course grades. The average GPA for students with learning disabilities was 1.94. GPA was significantly lower for general education courses (1.89) than for special education courses (2.18). Seventy-three percent of the students with learning disabilities were at least 1 year older than the typical student for their grade. Retained students were at a significantly greater risk for later academic failure and early school leaving.

Dropping out of school is a serious concern for students with LD (Wagner, 1990). Thirty-two percent of these students who exited school in the 1985–86 or 1986–87 school year left voluntarily without graduating. An additional 3% of the students left because they had exceeded the age limit for attendance, and 4% left because they were suspended or expelled. The graduation rate for this group of students was markedly lower than for the general population—61% versus 71%, respectively.

The NLTS study also examined functional skills. Parents were asked to rate their children's ability to perform tasks that involved applying basic mental functions. The tasks included the ability to (a) read common signs, (b) tell time on a clock with hands, (c) count change, and (d) look up telephone numbers and use the phone. Most youth in the general population have mastered these skills by the ages of 15 to 23. Only 46% of the students with learning disabilities, however, were rated as being able to perform all four functional skills very well, and without help.

A more recent NLTS report described aspects of the transition planning process for students with learning disabilities in the 12th grade, focusing on transition goals, the individuals involved in ITP planning, and contacts with other agencies (Wagner et al., 1993). Table 2.2 reports the kinds of transition goals written for students with LD, and Table 2.3 reports the participants who were primarily involved in transi-

TABLE 2.2
Transition Goals for Students with LD

Transition goal	Percentage
Competitive employment	58.6
Vocational training	32.4
College attendance	27.8
Supported employment	3.5

Note. From *The secondary school programs of students with disabilities. A report from the National Longitudinal Transition Study of Special Education Students* by M. Wagner, J. Blackorby, R. Cameto, K. Hebbeler, & L. Newman, 1993, Menlo Park, CA: SRI International. Copyright 1993 by SRI International. Adapted with permission.

TABLE 2.3
Participants in ITP Planning

Participant	Percentage
Special education teacher	81.5
Student	76.0
School counselor	71.5
Parent/guardian	57.4
General education vocational teacher	28.8
Vocational rehabilitation counselor	22.0
General education academic teacher	21.3
School administrator	13.8
Other	0.3

Note. From *The secondary school programs of students with disabilities. A report from the National Longitudinal Transition Study of Special Education Students* by M. Wagner, J. Blackorby, R. Cameto, K. Hebbeler, & L. Newman, 1993, Menlo Park, CA: SRI International. Copyright 1993 by SRI International. Adapted with permission.

tion planning. Table 2.4 identifies interagency contacts in the transition planning.

Wagner et al. (1993) concluded that for most students with learning disabilities, transition planning was conducted unilaterally by the secondary schools; nonschool personnel were not involved in the development of ITPs; and secondary schools were not making contacts with employers, adult service agencies, or postsecondary institutions on behalf of students with disabilities. Because the subjects involved in the study received services prior to significant changes in federal legislation, it is likely that future studies would yield different results, reflecting compliance with new laws.

TABLE 2.4
Interagency Contacts in Transition Planning

Agency	Percentage
State vocational rehabilitation	57.2
Job placement programs	38.1
Colleges	35.4
Postsecondary vocational training	33.7
Military	19.0
Other vocational training	15.2
Supported employment	10.6
Social services	9.3
Mental health	2.4
Sheltered workshops	2.3
Group homes	1.7

Note. From *The secondary school programs of students with disabilities. A report from the National Longitudinal Transition Study of Special Education Students* by M. Wagner, J. Blackorby, R. Cameto, K. Hebbeler, & L. Newman, 1993, Menlo Park, CA: SRI International. Copyright 1993 by SRI International. Adapted with permission.

Adult Service Needs. In the same NLTS study (Wagner et al., 1993), parents were asked to report whether their youth with disabilities who had been out of secondary school up to 5 years had received or needed services since exiting school. Sixty-four percent of the parents indicated that their child needed services in at least one area. The percentages of parents reporting a need in the following areas were as follows: vocational assistance, 56%; life skills training, 33%; tutoring/reading/interpreting, 27%; and personal counseling, 26%. The percentages actually receiving services in those areas were much lower: vocational assistance, 33.6%; life skills training, .17%; tutoring, reading, or interpreting, 19.1%; and personal counseling, 17.6%.

Special Transition Considerations

Transition programming for students with learning disabilities must take into account some of the distinctive traits of that population. Comprehensive analyses of transition programming for individuals with LD have been presented by Rojewski (1992) and Okolo and Sitlington (1988). Rojewski reviewed nine model demonstration transition programs for students with learning disabilities and identified key components. Okolo and Sitlington analyzed the transition needs of students with learning disabilities and identified vocationally relevant activities that should be included in secondary special education programs. Other additional transition components relevant to students with learning disabilities can be found in the literature. Usually, these components are the sole focus of the article (e.g., self-determination) or a component of a specific program (e.g., understanding one's disability); as transition programs for individuals with learning disabilities have evolved, such activities have emerged as critical for students with learning disabilities. A discussion of special considerations in transition planning for individuals with LD is provided below.

1. *Individualized Planning.* It is not safe to assume that all individuals with LD will need the same kind of transition programming. Because individuals with LD constitute a heterogenous group, the nature of transition planning will vary substantially from individual to individual. Comprehensive, individualized planning and programming based on the individual's needs, interests, and preferences is essential. The development of the individual plan should be supported by data from a variety of sources and should serve as a coordinating mechanism within and across services (Rojewski, 1992).

2. *Vocational Preparation.* Vocational training and career development have been the primary foci of transition planning. A wide range of services and activities, including systematic vocational assessment, exploration, and job training, should be available (Rojewski, 1992). In-depth career/vocational assessment forms the basis for appropriate individualized planning and includes the identification of academic, interpersonal, and vocational skills and current and future employment interests (Okolo & Sitlington, 1988).

Because many adolescents with LD hold unrealistic or uninformed career aspirations, vocational counseling is essential (Okolo & Sitlington, 1988). Instruction in work habits and attitudes is also important.

Although many programs emphasize vocational skills training, sometimes the variety of programs available to individuals with LD is limited. Vocational training programs should reflect the diversity in occupational roles filled by individuals without disabilities (Cummings & Maddux, 1987; Rojewski, 1992). A wide range of training methods (e.g., cooperative vocational education; individual and work-crew job coaching; on-the-job training; structured job tryouts; supported, transitional, or competitive employment) that build appropriate work habits and allow students to develop work histories prior to completion of high school is also necessary.

3. *Job Seeking and Placement.* A key component of many transition programs for students with LD is a structured job-seeking curriculum (Rojewski, 1992). Activities related to such a curriculum are resume writing, locating jobs through local resources, filling out applications, practicing job interviews, and learning strategies for contacting potential employers. Some individuals may not need assistance with securing employment, while others may need supported job searching (i.e., assis-

tance is provided on an as-needed basis) or direct job placement (i.e., job is secured by a placement specialist).

4. *Follow-up and Support Services.* Rojewski (1992) cautioned that many professionals believe that individuals with LD do not need transition services or, if they do, require only time-limited services. As discussed earlier, the results of follow-up and follow-along studies reflect the ongoing service needs of some individuals with LD. Sitlington (1981) further argued that follow-up services may be necessary for further training and career advancement. Potential support services include independent-living training, case management and service coordination, resource and agency referral, campus support at postsecondary institutions, and arrangements for transportation (Rojewski, 1992).

5. *Academic Remediation and Support.* Numerous professionals have identified academic remediation and support as an area needing attention for individuals with learning disabilities (Aune, 1991; Karge, Patton, & de la Garza, 1992; Minskoff & DeMoss, 1993; Rojewski, 1992; Smith, Finn, & Dowdy, 1993). Unfortunately, this area often is neglected in transition planning (Rojewski, 1992). The nature of the remediation and support will depend on the students' postsecondary goals.

Approximately 18.1% of adults with learning disabilities enroll in a 2- or 4-year college program (Wagner, 1993); however, many of these individuals have difficulties completing their postsecondary education (Aune, 1991). They often are ill prepared for the academic demands in postsecondary settings due to skill deficiencies, or because they did not participate in college preparation classes during high school. A weakness of many school-based transition programs is that academic skill deficiencies are addressed in isolation from the rest of the program, or, if they are integrated into the program, the focus is limited to those academic skills that affect vocational performance (Rojewski, 1992).

Academic skill remediation and support are also critical to success in vocational education at both the secondary and the postsecondary level, as well as in employment. The majority of individuals with learning disabilities do not attend college; thus, continued tutoring in academic subjects and remediation in basic reading and math skills may not be appropriate (Okolo & Sitlington, 1988). For these students, academic skill instruction should be oriented toward the kinds of skills that will be needed in vocational education and employment settings (Greenan, 1983, 1984; Ryan & Price, 1992).

6. *High School Curriculum.* The focus of the high school curriculum is another important consideration. The previous discussion on the heterogeneity of the population illustrated how the curricular focus can vary depending on the severity of the disability, as well as on numerous related factors, such as background experiences, support systems, and motivation. Two issues relevant to this discussion include the emphasis on *functional skills* and *mainstream classes.*

Many assume that individuals with learning disabilities do not need help in acquiring independent living skills. However, the NLTS study (Wagner, 1990) and Sitlington (chapter 3 of this book) suggest that many of these individuals are not able to perform some basic functional skills without help. Much of the focus in the transition preparation of these individuals has been directed toward postsecondary education or employment. The focus of transition efforts must be expanded to include the acquisition of critical life skills (Chelser, 1982; Cronin & Patton, 1993; Ryan & Price, 1992; Sitlington, this issue).

Another issue relates to participation in mainstream classes. Students with learning disabilities may be tracked into lower level mainstream classes or take academic classes in the resource room. However, college preparatory course work is essential for those students who appear to have the potential for postsecondary education. Aune (1991) emphasized that these students must have the opportunity to experience the nature of college demands by including mainstream classes, and they must have access to content and concepts critical to college success.

Seidenberg and Koenigsberg (1990) stressed that if individuals with learning disabilities are to be adequately prepared for postsecondary education, the secondary education program must reflect the skills and competencies critical to success in those environments. Additionally, students need to develop compensatory strategies and have the opportunity to practice using accommodations in mainstream classes.

7. *Understanding One's Disability.* The importance of understanding one's disability is particularly relevant to students with learning disabilities, but the task of helping students to understand their disabilities is frequently ignored in secondary settings. As a consequence, many postsecondary transition programs have found the need to address this area in their programs (Aune, 1991; Dalke & Franzene, 1988).

A clear and realistic understanding of one's learning disability is instrumental in empowering the individual in many areas of his or her life, including social, familial, academic, and vocational situations (Ryan & Price, 1992). Without an understanding and acceptance of one's abilities, students are not able to select appropriate goals and advocate for themselves (Aune, 1991). In addition, a lack of knowledge about one's disability can lead to a lack of acceptance of self and an inability to communicate one's needs and abilities to others (Getzel & Gugerty, 1992).

8. *Self-Determination.* Self-determination, which is emerging as a priority in the transition movement, refers to individuals with disabilities learning to make choices, set goals regarding their lives and the services they receive, and initiate actions to achieve those goals (Browning et al.,

1993). In spite of its philosophical, empirical, and practical importance, however, self-determination has received limited attention in secondary-based programs.

The importance of addressing self-determination for individuals is now being underscored (e.g., Durlak, Rose, & Bursuck, 1994; Martin, Marshall, & Maxson, 1993; Schloss, Alper, & Jayne, 1993; Ward, 1988; Wehmeyer, 1992, 1993). Reiff and deFur (1992) suggested that because the goal of transition is adult independence, it is critical, not optional, that students with learning disabilities participate in the decision-making process about their own futures. Ryan and Price (1992) further stressed the need to help such individuals learn how to make informed choices by providing specific experiences that promote the development of this ability. Training programs designed to directly teach these skills are now being developed and validated (e.g., Aune, 1991; Durlak et al., 1994; Valenti, 1989). See Field (chapter 4 of this book) for a comprehensive discussion of self-determination.

9. *Transition From Postsecondary Settings.* Ryan and Price (1992) suggested that one of the new frontiers of transition training for individuals with learning disabilities is the successful transition from postsecondary settings into the real world. They noted that most efforts have been directed toward getting students into appropriate postsecondary education or employment. Additionally, it is often assumed that if individuals can successfully complete postsecondary training or education, they do not need further support in the areas of career counseling, job placement, or independent living skills.

Siperstein (1988) proposed a transition model for students pursuing postsecondary education in a college setting. One unique aspect of his model is that it addresses post–graduation from college, which few programs do. He argued that the same issues that affect transition from high school to work are relevant in the transition from college to work.

10. *Psychosocial Issues.* Services for individuals with learning disabilities have focused primarily on academic skill development or remediation, while the emotional aspects of having a learning disability have been ignored (Price, Johnson, & Evelo, 1994). Understanding one's disability is certainly related to this consideration. Additionally, literature has reported that many individuals with learning disabilities display low self-esteem, feelings of incompetence and inadequacy, frustration, shyness, immaturity, social skills deficits, and lack of motivation (Geist & McGrath, 1983; Hoffman et al., 1987; Houck, Engelhard, & Geller, 1989; Saracoglu, Minden, & Wilchesky, 1989). In contrast, certain positive characteristics, such as persistence and creativity, have also been identified (Gerber, Ginsberg, & Reiff, 1992; Lichenstein, 1993).

One way to address psychosocial needs is through counseling, but this intervention strategy is infrequently used (Aune, 1991; Miller, Snider,

& Rzonca, 1990). Self-help groups, another strategy, is one that is more often available in postsecondary settings than in secondary settings (Aune, 1991). The goals of these approaches are to increase self-esteem, improve social skills, enhance assertiveness and self-advocacy, identify learning and coping skills, explore the nature of learning disabilities, and develop good communication skills and the ability to work in a group (Rhoades, Browning, & Thorin, 1986; Rojewski, 1992; Ryan & Price, 1992).

11. *Problem Solving.* Although the academic curriculum may emphasize basic skills within a functional context, general problem-solving strategies are equally important (e.g., Browning & Nave, 1993; Reiff & deFur, 1992). Individuals with learning disabilities often experience difficulties with problem solving (Getzel & Gugerty, 1992). Inadequate problem-solving skills can affect all facets of an individual's life—personal, social, and vocational (Izzo, Pritz, & Ott, 1990).

Cronin and Patton (1993) argued that even with the best curriculum imaginable, it is not possible to prepare students for every possible adult situation. Thus, students need to learn problem-solving strategies that will enable them to handle new and challenging situations throughout their adult lives.

SUMMARY

Transition policies and activities initially were directed toward individuals with moderate and severe disabilities because it was assumed that individuals with learning disabilities and other mild disabilities did not need special services to achieve successful postsecondary outcomes. This assumption has been challenged by the results of follow-up and follow-along studies reporting that individuals with learning disabilities experience higher rates of dropping out, unemployment, underemployment, and community adjustment problems than their peers without disabilities. The components of effective transition planning for individuals with learning disabilities have only recently begun to be articulated.

Certainly, transition practices for individuals with learning disabilities have been influenced by state and federal mandates and initiatives and the menu of recommended practices that has emerged over the last decade. What we are now finding, however, is that individuals with learning disabilities have some unique considerations that have not been addressed through traditional transition models and general practices. Practices that seem to be important to this population were identified and discussed in this article. Although future research should evaluate the relationship between these practices and adult outcomes, the practices that have emerged provide a solid foundation for the future transition planning for individuals with learning disabilities.

3. Transition to Living: The Neglected Component of Transition Programming for Individuals with Learning Disabilities

Transition planning for individuals with disabilities has become a major priority of the Office of Special Education and Rehabilitation Services. The Individuals with Disabilities Education Act (IDEA; P.L. 101-476) currently requires that Individualized Education Programs (IEPs) include a statement of necessary transition services beginning no later than age 16. "Transition services" are defined as

> a coordinated set of activities for a student, designed within an outcome oriented process, which promotes movement from school to post-school activities, including post-secondary education, vocational training, integrated employment (including supported employment), continuing and adult education, adult services, independent living, and community participation. (Section 602(a)(19))

Even with this federal mandate, a number of barriers exist. First, many professionals do not feel that adolescents with learning disabilities

Reprinted, with changes, from "Transition to living: The neglected component of transition programming for individuals with learning disabilities," by Patricia L. Sitlington, *Journal of Learning Disabilities*, Vol. 29, 1996, pp. 31–39, 52. Copyright © 1996 by PRO-ED, Inc.

(LD) require systematic transition planning. Second, although a number of studies have documented the need for transition planning related to *all* aspects of adult life, the transition planning that does occur often focuses primarily on transition to employment. The final complicating factor is the thrust to include all individuals with disabilities more fully in the general education program and curriculum. Although many positive effects of this approach have been demonstrated, the general high school curriculum into which our students are being integrated places a very low priority on life skills.

The Division on Career Development and Transition (DCDT) of the Council for Exceptional Children recently published a position statement on transition (Halpern, 1994). The definition of transition included in this statement begins as follows:

> Transition refers to a change in status from behaving primarily as a student to assuming emergent adult roles in the community. These roles include employment, participating in post-secondary education, maintaining a home, becoming appropriately involved in the community, and experiencing satisfactory personal and social relationships. . . .

The purpose of this chapter is to document the need to prepare young adults with LD for life in the community, with particular emphasis on aspects of adult life other than employment and postsecondary education. Maintaining a home, becoming appropriately involved in the community (including recreation and leisure activities), and experiencing satisfactory personal and social relationships are the elements of adulthood on which this chapter will focus.

The first section will review the results of major studies of the adult adjustment of individuals with LD and discuss these individuals' learning characteristics. The second component of the chapter will briefly highlight existing models of career education and life skills education that may be used in preparing individuals with LD to function effectively in adult life. The third section will focus on describing current practices in programming for adolescents with LD; and the final section will propose steps that must be taken if we are to more effectively assist individuals with LD in their transition to *all* aspects of adult life.

THE ADULT ADJUSTMENT OF INDIVIDUALS WITH LD

The adult adjustment of individuals with mild disabilities has been examined in a number of studies (Edgar, 1987; Halpern, 1990; Hasazi, Gordon, & Roe, 1985; Sitlington, Frank, & Carson, 1993); However, few of these studies focused on aspects of adult adjustment other than employment or postsecondary education. Halpern reviewed 41 major follow-up and follow-along studies. Career and employment variables were addressed in 100% of the studies; citizenship was never addressed; social responsibility was covered in 15%; leisure and recreation in 24%; relationships and social networks in 44%; food, clothing, and lodging in 24%; and personal satisfaction in 32% of these studies.

Darrow and Clark (1992) assembled a panel of 22 special education professionals from 18 states who had been closely involved with follow-up and follow-along studies. The panel was asked to rate 74 research questions from the original General Transition Follow-Along Model (Halpern, 1990) in terms of the importance of particular information for follow-along. Two of the four items ranked highest involved nonemployment aspects of adult life—proportion/age of individuals living independently or semi-independently and financial security and sources of income. A number of the other items that were ranked at the moderate level also dealt with life skills. However, when this panel was asked to identify items they believed ought to be considered for measurement in a common format across all statewide follow-up and follow-along studies, only three of the eight items receiving 75% or higher agreement related to life skills areas.

This section will report the results of studies that focused primarily on individuals with LD and that did address aspects of adult life other than employment and postsecondary education. Information will be provided on the individuals' level of functioning, with specific emphasis on maintaining a home, becoming appropriately involved in the community, and experiencing satisfactory personal and social relationships.

Maintaining a Home

This area includes such skills as selecting appropriate living arrangements, paying living expenses, preparing meals, and conducting basic cleaning and maintenance activities. A number of studies have specifically addressed living status (Edgar & Levine, 1987; Edgar, Levine, Levine, & Dubey, 1988; Haring, Lovett, & Smith, 1990; Roessler, Brolin, & Johnson, 1990; Schalock et al., 1986; Scuccimarra & Speece, 1990). These studies, usually conducted when the individual had been out of school for 1 year, found that between 54% and 70% of the individuals studied were living with parents or relatives, and 22% to 39% were living independently. Approximately 8% to 10% were married.

Sitlington and Frank (1990, 1993) found that 49% of their statewide sample was living independently 3 years after leaving school—a substantial increase from the 27% figure for the same subjects 1 year after their class left school. Of these same subjects, 40% were living with parents or relatives 3 years after leaving school (down from 64%). A substantial increase was also observed in the marriage rate: from 8% to 23%. The authors also found that 3 years out of school, 53% reported paying all of their living expenses, compared to 26% 1 year out of school.

The National Longitudinal Transition Study (Wagner, D'Amico, Marder, Newman, & Blackorby, 1992; Wagner et al., 1991) also found an increase over time in independent living for a national sample of individuals with LD. Forty-four percent of individuals out of school 3 to 5 years were living independently, compared to 15% out of school less than 2 years. Three to 5 years out of school, 52% were living with parents or relatives, compared to 84% 1 year out. Of their comparison group of youth in the general population, 56% were living independently 3 to 5 years out of school, whereas 32% were living independently less than 2 years out of school.

Community Involvement

Scuccimarra and Speece (1990) constructed and administered a social activity index (i.e., a percentage of seven listed activities, such as watching television, going to church, going to the movies, participating in sports). All of the 56 subjects surveyed indicated they watched television; 28% engaged in two or fewer of the remaining activities. Only one of the respondents participated in all seven activities, and 15% participated in six. A majority (66%) were satisfied or very satisfied with their social lives. Nearly all of the respondents were able to name at least one friend, and 84% were able to name two. White et al. (1982) found that nondisabled youth were more active than their peers with LD in social or fraternal groups, recreational activities, and the community, and had fewer problems with the law.

Sitlington and Frank (1990, 1993) found that 3 years out of school, 62% of their participants with LD were involved in from one to three leisure activities, an additional 17% were involved in four to six activities, and 10% participated in more than six leisure activities. Eleven percent reported not participating in any leisure activity. These numbers were not substantially different from those reported 1 year out of school. The National Longitudinal Study (Wagner et al., 1992) found that 21% of those individuals with LD out of school 3 to 5 years participated in an organized social group, compared to 31% of those out of school less than 2 years.

Researchers have also examined the rate of criminal behavior among individuals with LD. White et al. (1982) concluded that the criminal conviction rate for young adults with LD was much higher than that for nondisabled adults. The National Longitudinal Study (Wagner et al.,

1992) found that 31% of the individuals out of school 3 to 5 years had been arrested at some time, compared to 20% of those out less than 2 years.

Sitlington and Frank (1990, 1993) constructed a composite of "success" for 1 and 3 years after school. For 1 year out of school, a high level of success meant (a) employment in the community; (b) living independently (buying a home, living with a friend, or living alone); (c) paying at least some of their living expenses; and (d) involved in more than three leisure activities. Eight percent of the subjects met these criteria. A low level of success entailed: (a) employment in the community, (b) living independently or in a supervised living arrangement, (c) not necessarily paying any of their living expenses, and (d) involved in at least one leisure activity. Twenty percent met these criteria.

The high-level criteria for 3 years out of school consisted of (a) full-time employment, earning at least minimum wage; (b) living independently; (c) paying more than half of their living expenses; and (d) involved in more than three leisure activities. Eleven percent met these criteria. The low-success criteria for 3 years out were (a) employed at least half time and earning at least minimum wage, (b) living independently or in a supervised living arrangement, (c) paying at least some of their living expenses, and (d) involved in at least one leisure activity. Twenty-seven percent of the group met these criteria.

The National Longitudinal Study (Wagner et al., 1992) also constructed life profiles of individuals with LD related to the following domains: (a) engagement in work or education-related activities outside the home, (b) residential arrangements, and (c) social activities. Of individuals with LD out of school 3 to 5 years, 27% were independent in all three domains, 50% were independent in two domains, and 7% were independent in only one domain. Of individuals out of school less than 2 years, 10% were independent in all three domains, 38% were independent in two domains, and 16% were independent in only one domain.

Personal and Social Relationships

Few data exist regarding social adjustment, and the information that is provided is reported inconsistently. Hartzell and Compton (1984) rated students with LD on a 3-point measure of social success: High social success was defined as having many friends, leadership qualities, and a facility with interpersonal relationships. Medium social success was considered to be having a few friends but being uneasy in groups. Low social success was defined as having feelings of loneliness, isolation, and social awkwardness. Of the sample, 53% fell into the medium category, and

31% were rated as having high social success. In an analysis of qualitative data, Haring et al. (1990) found that the average number of activities listed per person was low (i.e., two for men and one for women). Nonetheless, 75% of the women and 80% of the men reported being satisfied with their social lives.

The National Longitudinal Study (Wagner et al., 1992) found that for youth with LD out of school 3 to 5 years, 41% interacted with family and friends 4 or more days a week, 50% 1 to 3 days a week, and 9% less often than weekly. For those youth out of school less than 2 years, 56% interacted with family and friends 4 or more days a week, 39% 1 to 3 days a week, and 5% less often than weekly. Four percent of the group 3 to 5 years out of school reported being socially isolated, compared to 3% of the group out of school less than 2 years.

White, Schumaker, Warner, Alley, and Deshler (1980) reported that individuals with LD had difficulty making friends and relating to parents and relatives. These individuals also expressed more social dissatisfaction with their employment and expressed significantly lower aspirations for further education or training.

The Learning Disabilities Association sponsored an adult adjustment study (Chesler, 1982) that included a report on the areas of life that individuals with LD indicated required the most assistance. The rank order list was as follows:

1. Social relationships, social skills;

2. Career counseling;

3. Developing self-esteem, confidence (tied);

4. Overcoming dependence, survival (tied);

5. Vocational training;

6. Getting and holding a job;

7. Reading;

8. Spelling;

9. Managing of personal finances; and

10. Organizational skills.

Two studies included control groups of individuals without learning disabilities (Hartzell & Compton, 1984; White et al., 1982). Hartzell and Compton found that nondisabled youth were more satisfied with their social success; White et al. found that both individuals with LD and those without learning disabilities reported approximately the same number of friends. Those without learning disabilities, however, reported having more friends with whom to go places and share activities.

Okolo and Sitlington (1988) found consistent results across the follow-up studies they reviewed. Adults with LD had secured employment at nearly the same rate as their nondisabled age-mates; however, their jobs carried less social status, lower wages, and fewer regular hours than those of the nondisabled groups. Moreover, most of the adults with LD reported having received little vocational counseling in high school, and they were less satisfied with their jobs than were their nondisabled peers. Okolo and Sitlington pointed out three main reasons for unemployment or underemployment among youth with LD: (a) a lack of interpersonal skills, (b) a lack of job-related academic skills, and (c) a lack of specific vocational skills to perform more than entry-level personal service jobs.

CHARACTERISTICS OF ADOLESCENTS AND ADULTS WITH LD

In addition to the previous information on the adult adjustment of individuals with LD, there is also a great deal of evidence related to the specific *characteristics* of adolescents and adults with LD that create the need not only for transition planning, but also for a focus on the areas of maintaining a home, becoming appropriately involved in the community, and experiencing satisfactory personal and social relationships. Many of the needs of adolescents with LD persist into adulthood. Comprehensive surveys of adults with LD, their advocates, and the providers of services to these adults show that adults with LD have major academic, social, personal, and vocational needs that must be addressed if they are to attain adult competence (Ariel, 1992).

According to Hoffman et al. (1987), the second most critical area for adults with LD (after vocational competency) is their ability to acquire a positive self-concept, self-understanding, and self-acceptance. Gray (1981) proposed the following approaches for working with the young adult with LD: (a) The content of diagnostic and assessment devices and of educational services should be specific to life needs, (b) assessment and intervention should be directly related to adult life goals, (c) developmental and remedial instruction in basic skills should be made available for those who desire such training and for those for whom such programs are appropriate, and (d) views of appropriate content for adult services should be expanded beyond traditional literacy requirements and vocational training.

Rosenthal (1985) named five major cognitive, affective, and motivational characteristics of individuals with LD: (a) deficits in the areas of cognition and attention; (b) poor reality testing—lacking insight and the ability to learn from prior experience; (c) poor sense of self, often stemming from failure in school and the creation of maladaptive defensive behaviors that are unacceptable in society; (d) poor visual imagery, which prevents many individuals with LD from realistically imagining themselves as competent, self-sufficient adults; and (e) learned helplessness, which manifests itself in passivity in learning and a crippling lack of independence.

Other research indicates that adolescents with LD may exhibit a general delay in abstract thinking and hypothetical reasoning, which stems primarily from production deficiencies (e.g., Torgesen, 1980; Wiens, 1983) rather than from deficiencies in cognitive abilities. Many also do not structure or organize their thoughts (Wiens, 1983). In addition, individuals with LD may exhibit deficiencies in executive-control functions, which involve such activities as planning and organizing (Deshler, Schumaker, Alley, Warner, & Clark, 1982).

Individuals with LD are continuously thwarted by an inability to achieve success in school, to meet parental expectations, and to interact or behave appropriately in other interactive environments (Ariel, 1992). In addition to developing a negative self-concept that directly affects their approach to new learning situations and new experiences, they develop poor social perception and have difficulties maintaining interpersonal relationships. Social/emotional maladjustment thus accompanies learning disabilities (McKinney, 1984; Thompson, 1986). In addition, such adolescents may develop passive learning patterns (Torgesen, 1980) and learned helplessness.

Bryan, Werner, and Pearl (1981) found that persons with LD are more likely than nondisabled persons to succumb to peer pressure, less likely to consider moral issues on a broader basis, and less likely to adopt principles of moral reasoning that involve consideration of the impact of decisions on others. This results in a high rate of antisocial acts. Derr (1986) concurred with these conclusions. The 25 adolescents with LD in Derr's study were insensitive to the social aspects of a verbal encounter and they reasoned at a significantly lower level. The nondisabled youth were concerned with norms and community and societal values, but those who had learning disabilities utilized egocentric judgments and attempted to promote their own needs and desires. They would follow rules only when doing so was in their self-interest. Youths with LD were less able to understand conventional group processes, such as negotiation and compromise.

In addition, because of their poor interpersonal relationships, their low self-esteem, and the restrictive nature of their interpersonal relationships and peer interactions, adolescents with LD have more difficulty forming a peer identity and fitting into peer groups than do other adolescents. This lack of appropriate social skills has been viewed by parents, teachers, and other professionals as a very serious deficit (Wanant, 1983). Fine and Zeitlin (1984) contended that such adolescents often learn maladaptive coping behaviors to protect themselves from the stress of failure. These maladaptive academic coping strategies include lack of organization skills, passivity in learning situations, excessive reliance on external cues for feedback, lack of flexibility, inability to generalize, difficulties in sustaining attention, low tolerance for frustration, and inadequate social skills.

MODELS

A number of theoretically sound and validated models for developing the competencies needed to function independently as an adult. These models and their major components are highlighted in Table 3.1. They emerged first from the career education movement and later from the more recent life skills emphasis. The focus and content of these models, however, are very similar.

The emphasis on all aspects of an individual's adjustment can be traced back to the concept of "career education," which emerged during the 1970s. Kokaska and Brolin (1985) defined career education as the "process of systematically coordinating all school, family, and community components together to facilitate each individual's potential for economic, social, and personal fulfillment and participation in productive work activities that benefit the individual or others" (p. 43). The first two models listed in Table 3.1, Brolin (1991) and Clark and Kolstoe (1990), are the most closely related to the career education movement.

A number of other authors have argued for the need to focus on much more than employment in planning for the adult adjustment of individuals with disabilities. In response to Will's (1984) call for programming for transition to employment, Halpern (1985) proposed a model that emphasized transition to community adjustment. The underpinnings of this adjustment were employment, social and interpersonal networks, and residential environments. The remaining models listed in Table 3.1 emanated from the life skills movement.

There is a great deal of agreement across these career education and life skills education models over the fact that maintaining a home, becoming appropriately involved in the community (including recreational and leisure activities), and experiencing satisfaction in personal and social relationships are major skills needed in adult life. Each of these models also provides a solid framework for preparing individuals to function effectively in these life roles.

TABLE 3.1
Career Education and Life Skills Education Models

Source	Major components
Life-Centered Career Education (LCCE) (Brolin, 1991)	Three major areas: • Daily living • Personal–social • Occupational guidance and preparation
School-Based Career Development and Transition Education Model (Clark & Kolstoe, 1990)	Four major areas: • Values, attitudes, and habits • Human relationships • Occupational information • Acquisition of job and daily living skills
Hawaii Transition Project (1987)	Four major areas: • Vocation/education • Home and family • Recreation/leisure • Community/citizenship
Community-Referenced Curriculum (Smith & Schloss, 1988)	Five major areas: • Work • Leisure and play • Consumer • Education and rehabilitation • Transportation
Community Living Skills Taxonomy (Dever, 1988)	Five major areas: • Personal maintenance and development • Homemaking and community life • Vocational • Leisure • Travel
Life Problems of Adulthood (Knowles, 1990)	Six major areas: • Vocation and career • Home and family living • Enjoyment of leisure • Community living • Health • Personal development
Domains of Adulthood (Cronin & Patton, 1993)	Six major areas: • Employment/education • Home and family • Leisure pursuits • Community involvement • Physical/emotional health • Personal responsibility and relationships

Table continues

TABLE 3.1 (cont.)

Source	Major components
Post-School Outcomes Model (National Center on Educational Outcomes, 1993)	Seven major areas: • Presence and participation • Physical health • Responsibility and independence • Contribution and citizenship • Academic and functional literacy • Personal and social adjustment • Satisfaction
Quality of Life Domains (Halpern, 1993)	Three major areas: • Physical and material well-being • Performance of adult roles • Personal fulfillment

APPROACHES TO TRAINING ADOLESCENTS WITH LD

This final section will discuss what is currently happening in programs for adolescents with LD. Suggestions will also be provided for steps that need to be taken if we are to assist these individuals in making an effective transition from school to *all* aspects of adult life.

Curricular Orientations

Zigmond and Sansone (1986) reviewed program options that have been implemented for adolescents with LD in public schools. They stated that the models identified tended to differ along two broad dimensions: (a) the amount of time that students with LD are assigned to receive instruction from the special education teacher, and (b) the extent to which the curriculum for these students is "special," that is, different from the curriculum offered to general education students.

These authors identified six models operating at that time in our nation's schools.

1. *Resource Room Model—Novel Curriculum.* This model emphasizes basic skills remediation, survival skill lessons, or instruction in learning strategies, or a combination of all three.

2. *Resource Room Model—Tutoring.* This model is geared to assist students with LD in mainstreamed content subjects. The instructional goals and materials are those defined by the general education teacher.

3. *Self-Contained Class—Novel Curriculum.* This model emphasizes a functional curriculum approach in order to equip students with LD with the skills necessary to function in society after graduation.

4. *Self-Contained Class—Standard High School Curriculum.* This approach involves changing the conditions and settings of learning rather than changing the curriculum or the competencies of the learner. This is also referred to as the *parallel alternate curriculum.*

5. *Consultation Model.* In this model, consultation services are provided to general education teachers in order to facilitate the academic progress of adolescents with learning disabilities in the mainstream.

6. *Work Study Model.* This model emphasizes instruction in job skills and supervised on-the-job experiences as part of the school day. (Many would argue that this is not a separate model, but content that could be delivered through any of the five previously listed models.)

Polloway and Patton (1993) identified the following curricular themes and orientations that can be found in special education programs:

1. *Remedial Programming.* This theme includes an emphasis on developing academic skills and addressing academic deficits and student needs. Some curriculum models also include an emphasis on social competence and social adjustment.

2. *General Class Support.* This orientation includes providing tutorial assistance; compensatory strategies (such as recording lectures, taking written tests in oral form); instruction in learning strategies; and cooperative teaching.

3. *Academic Content Mastery.* This approach involves teaching the same (or slightly modified) content in the special education class as is taught in the general education classroom.

4. *Adult Outcomes Programming.* This theme encompasses vocational training and preparation in life skills.

What Should Be Happening

According to Deshler, Schumaker, and Lenz (1984), the goals of secondary programs for adolescents with LD should include education in the least restrictive environment, a high school diploma, independence through acquisition of learning strategies, social skills training, and preparation for a career after graduation from high school.

Wiederholt and McEntire (1980) presented a thoughtful perspective of how the field of special education should approach the education of individuals with disabilities. They cited three dominant philosophies for programs: (a) Fit the system, (b) change the system, and (c) ignore the system. The "fit the system" rationale holds that current models are appropriate and that the student should be changed to better fit the existing learning environment. Advocates of this system would stress instruction in learning and coping strategies and would argue that if individuals with disabilities can be made more proficient in meeting the expected academic and social norms of behavior in the general education classroom, then they will also be more proficient in meeting the demands of adult life.

Advocates of "change the system" believe that current models in general education need improvement, and that general education programs are inappropriate but can be made appropriate for many individuals with disabilities. Proponents of the "ignore the system" rationale reject past practices in special and general education. They recommend the development of alternative programs to meet the needs of individuals with disabilities.

The Division on Career Development and Transition of the Council for Exceptional Children (Clark, Field, Patton, Brolin, & Sitlington, 1994) took a strong stance on the appropriateness of life skills instruction for students with or without disabilities. They argued that life skills should be taught in general education settings and in the community. As with any other instructional content area, it should be assumed that unless the student is unable to learn within the general education setting, with the provision of needed support, no move to a separate program should be made.

Clark et al. (1994) also stated that it is the responsibility of general educators at the elementary, middle school, and secondary levels to ensure the applicability and generalizability of subject matter areas to the functional demands of independent living. The authors also believe that it is the responsibility of both general and special educators to advocate for the functional needs of all students with disabilities. Finally, the authors stated that it is the responsibility of special educators to provide the specialized instruction needed to meet the student's needs. They concluded with the following statement:

"A clear commitment to a life skills approach in both general and special education is an appropriate long-term goal for achieving both curriculum and inclusive education goals for students with special needs" (p. 132).

RECOMMENDATIONS

A number of studies of the adult adjustment of individuals with LD point to the need for life skills programming and comprehensive transition planning, particularly in areas other than employment and postsecondary education. The abundant data on the learning characteristics of these individuals also point to the need for systematic instruction in the basic concepts of maintaining a home, participating appropriately in the community, and experiencing satisfactory personal and social relationships. The Individuals with Disabilities Education Act (IDEA) mandates planning for transition to *all* areas of adult life. Issues related to quality of life for individuals with LD reinforce the need for this planning. We also have a number of conceptually strong and validated models for life skills programming.

Why then are we still discussing the need for curriculum development and transition planning in life skills? What do we as a field need to do to ensure that we will not be discussing this need 10 years from now? The following suggestions build on the work of my colleagues and my experiences as a classroom teacher, state department staff member, and university professor. The first three recommendations focus on future research; the remaining recommendations focus on practices and curricular revisions based on current and future research.

1. Continue to examine and document the major approaches currently being used in educating adolescents with disabilities and the effectiveness of these approaches. Professionals must identify the most effective interventions and determine how life skills programming and transition planning can be integrated into those models or approaches. Educators can no longer take the approach of life skills *or* other options. Life skills and transition planning need to be fully integrated into all instructional and curricular approaches used with individuals with LD.

2. Incorporate variables related to transition to *all* aspects of adult life into follow-along studies. Researchers must also address these variables more consistently, although they are often difficult to quantify. This will allow the field to document the need for laying the foundation and providing the support for transition to *all* aspects of adult life.

3. Focus follow-along studies not just on the current adult adjustment status of individuals with disabilities, but also on the individuals' educational experiences and degree of competency while in school, as well as the degree of transition planning. This information should then be combined to help determine the effectiveness of interventions and transition planning in relationship to adult adjustment. Halpern (1990) proposed major components of a follow-along model, including specific research questions within each component. The Iowa Transition Initiative developed a Post-School Follow-up Instrument and In-School Data Form (Frank & Sitlington, 1994) in an attempt to collect these same type of data. Other states are obviously involved in the same type of activity. State and federal groups need to share information and data-collection instruments so that data from statewide samples can be aggregated and used to support efforts to infuse life skills curricula and transition planning into the educational process for all students.

4. Focus on integrating life skills training and transition to *all* aspects of adult life into general education programs. The thrust to include individuals with disabilities more fully in general education has much data to support it (e.g., Hunt, Farron-Davis, Beckstead, Curtis, & Goetz, 1994; Kennedy & Itkenen, 1994). Whether professionals believe in this movement or not, most would agree it is here to stay. Because of this, the focus must be on "changing the system." Transition planning is critical for all individuals, with or without disabilities, and this planning should focus on laying the foundation and providing the support for transition to *all* aspects of adult life. The School to Work Transition Act and the current emphasis on outcomes-based education are general education initiatives that will assist professionals in changing the system.

5. Examine more closely what drives the system in secondary education. Once this is determined, professionals need to work within the system for change. Special educators have been notorious for talking among ourselves, rather than educating those who can make change happen. The target audiences for these change efforts should include parents, school board members, superintendents, principals, legislators, and state departments of education.

6. Develop models for assessing the present level of educational performance of individuals with disabilities in the life skills areas discussed in this article. Techniques should include not only formal and informal assessment instruments, but also curriculum-based assessment measures. A number of validated instruments and assessment approaches currently exist; practitioners must be made aware of these. See Clark (chapter 7) for more information on assessment techniques.

7. Fight the prevailing attitude that life skills and transition programming are needed only for those labeled with mental retardation and severe disabilities. Again, the evidence is clear that this is not true, but that evidence is not reaching those who are making decisions and those who are working directly with adolescents with LD.

8. Infuse transition planning and life skills content into the college and university programs preparing teachers to work with individuals with LD of all ages. The Division for Learning Disabilities of the Council for Exceptional Children compiled a list of competencies for teachers of students with LD (Graves et al., 1992). The Division is to be congratulated in that 2 of the 10 competency areas contain competencies related to life skills. Competency Area II is entitled "Academic Support Areas: Study Skills, Consumer Skills and Career/Vocational Skills." Competency Area III is entitled, "Curriculum for Support Areas and Modification of School Core Curriculum."

As encouraging as this may seem, however, of the 209 competencies identified (in all 10 competency areas), only 27 relate to any type of life skills programming. The 27 competencies that are identified are grouped under the competency areas of "academic support" and "curriculum for support areas and modification of school core curriculum," which conveys the message that life skills education is a "support" to the primary focus of academic instruction.

Of those 27 competencies, only 16 are devoted to life skills other than employment. There is no formal mention of the transition planning process, and content from these two competency areas is not integrated into the other eight competency areas. It would have been particularly appropriate to infuse content related to life skills education into Competency Area VII: "Specialized Instructional Strategies, Technologies, and Materials," where 65 competencies are devoted to knowledge and skills related to traditional academic areas, such as listening and written language. For example, Competency 46, "skill in relating academic content to career/vocational skills" (along with the other competencies under the subheading "Career/Vocational Curricula"), could have been listed as a specialized instructional strategy along with strategies for listening and oral language, rather than being listed as "curriculum for support areas."

The Division for Learning Disabilities competency listing is, I feel, reflective of current practice in the majority of our college and university programs preparing teachers of individuals with LD. If life skills and transition planning issues are addressed at all, they are addressed in an isolated course (usually only for those preparing to work with adolescents) or in isolated presentations, and account for little of the instructional time in methods or foundations courses.

9. Finally, make a commitment to continue "to fight the good fight." Many professionals in the field have been advocating for life skills programming and transition planning for a number of years. Career education and other life skills initiatives have burst strongly onto the scene, and then slowly died. It is easy to become pessimistic and lessen our efforts. I believe, however, that we are at a crossroads for change in all education. If we lessen our efforts now, we could lose the battle. If we work more efficiently at presenting our case, I feel that we have a better chance than ever of affecting what happens to adolescents and adults with disabilities.

Education has never had a mandate such as that created by the transition component of IDEA and the School to Work Transition Act. We must work now with the federal government, state departments of education, universities, parent groups, individuals with disabilities, local school boards, administrators, and teachers to ensure that the spirit of IDEA and its rules and regulations are implemented. Transition planning must truly *drive* the Individualized Education Programs of all students with disabilities. As a student with LD (or any disability) begins to receive special education services, the emphasis must always be on the skills and support needed for successful transition to the next environment and to the ultimate environment—adulthood. As this planning occurs, the emphasis must remain not only on employment and postsecondary education, but also on the roles of maintaining a home, becoming appropriately involved in the community, and experiencing satisfactory personal and social relationships.

These efforts must be fully integrated into ongoing systems change efforts in the overall educational system, such as outcomes-based education, the National Education Goals, and overall efforts to blend special education and general education services. Life skills education is critical for adolescents with and without disabilities. It is imperative that our educational system incorporate this concept into its goals and delivery systems to ensure that *all* students achieve the ultimate outcome of education—preparation for adult life.

4. Self-Determination Instructional Strategies for Youth with Learning Disabilities

SHARON FIELD

The concept of self-determination has recently taken on increased importance in the disability community. Many have begun to question the lack of opportunity some persons with disabilities have to make determinations about their futures. According to Ward (1992), "self-determination, which includes self-actualization, assertiveness, creativity, pride and self-advocacy, must be part of the career development process that begins in early childhood and continues throughout adult life" (p. 389).

This increased focus on self-determination is particularly evident in the transition-from-school-to-adulthood movement. Typical traits of adulthood include increased self-reliance and greater control over one's destiny. This emphasis on self-determination, which includes the development of curricula and instructional strategies, is emerging as students with disabilities, their families, educators, and service providers are examining how to best help these students make the transition to adult roles.

The majority of the literature related to self-determination in the field of special education is noncategorical. Most self-determination research and model development has been conducted with students rep-

Reprinted, with changes, from "Self-determination instructional strategies for youth with learning disabilities," by Sharon Field, *Journal of Learning Disabilities,* Vol. 29, 1996, pp. 40–52. Copyright © 1996 by PRO-ED, Inc.

resenting diverse disability classifications. However, it is important to consider that students with learning disabilities face many unique barriers to becoming self-determined. First, because learning disabilities are generally hidden disabilities, and because in our culture having a disability is often viewed as stigmatizing, many adolescents with learning disabilities need not acknowledge that they have a disability, nor do they understand the implications of their disability (Sachs, Iliff, & Donnelly, 1987). An understanding of one's strengths and weaknesses and an acceptance of self form the foundation of self-determination (Field & Hoffman, 1994). The lack of self-awareness and self-esteem displayed by many adolescents with learning disabilities is a barrier to self-determination. The learned helplessness and self-deprecating attributions among students with learning disabilities have been widely documented (Smith, 1989) and also present barriers to self-determination.

In addition, many of the skills linked to self-determination are the very skills that present challenges for students with learning disabilities. For example, as further discussed later in this chapter, the abilities to plan, initiate behavior, and respond flexibly to situations are linked by several authors to self-determination. These skill areas are closely related to the executive skills (e.g., organizational and planning abilities, mental flexibility, and task initiation), which are often noted as a deficit area for many students with learning disabilities (Snow, 1992).

Although students with learning disabilities face many challenges along the way, the importance of self-determination for these students is clear. The need for self-determination skills may be especially evident for students with learning disabilities who are enrolling in postsecondary schools (Brinckerhoff, Shaw, & McGuire, 1992; Durlak, Rose, & Bursuck, 1994). Successful transitions to postsecondary educational settings are often dependent on students' ability to state their needs for supports and accommodations. For example, to maximize success in postsecondary educational settings, students with learning disabilities need such skills as (a) an awareness of academic and social strengths and weaknesses; (b) the ability to express such an awareness to faculty and staff; (c) an awareness of service needs and appropriate accommodations; and (d) the ability to request information, assistance, and accommodations when appropriate and necessary (Durlak et al., 1994).

Self-determination skills are also very important for students with learning disabilities who are planning transition directly to employment. These skills are necessary for making complex decisions, such as planning for a realistic career (Ward, 1991); moreover, employees need self-determination skills in order to be most successful in the workplace. Deci, Connell, and Ryan (1989) summarized the research on concepts related to self-determination in the organizational literature and concluded that self-determination in employees is related to more effective employee performance and is positively associated with employee satisfaction, quality of work life, and organizational effectiveness.

Recent legislation places an important emphasis on self-determination during the transition from school to adulthood. The Individuals with Disabilities Education Act of 1990 (IDEA) emphasizes self-determination in transition planning. IDEA requires that students' preferences and interests be taken into account when transition services are being planned, and that school districts include students as participants in their transition planning meetings.

This increased focus on student self-determination in the IDEA legislation is mirrored in the rehabilitation legislation. The 1992 Amendments to the Rehabilitation Act of 1973 provide the same definition of transition services as identified in IDEA. These amendments also include a very eloquent philosophical statement about disability in our society, with the following statement of rights for individuals with disabilities:

> Disability is a natural part of the human experience and in no way diminishes the right of individuals to
>
> • Live independently;
>
> • Enjoy self-determination;
>
> • Make choices;
>
> • Contribute to society;
>
> • Pursue meaningful careers; and
>
> • Enjoy full inclusion and integration in the economic, political, social, cultural and educational mainstream of American society.... (Section 2. Findings; Purpose; Policy)

The 1992 Rehabilitation Act Amendments require that individuals with disabilities have the opportunity to be active participants in their rehabilitation programs. Participation includes making meaningful and informed choices about the selection of vocational goals and objectives and the vocational rehabilitation services received. For more information on rehabilitation legislation pertinent to transition, see Dowdy (chapter 9 of this book).

Research findings add support to legislative requirements promoting self-determination. There is increasing evidence that students who are involved in the planning of, decision making about, and implementation of their educational programs perform better than peers who are not (Wehmeyer, 1992). For example, one body of evidence that supports the importance of student involvement comes from the literature on motivation. Research conducted by Koestner, Ryan, Bernieri, and Holt (1984) and by Swann and Pittman (cited in Wehmeyer, 1992) indicated that students who participate in choosing school activities show enhanced motivation to perform the tasks they select.

If, as indicated by this research, promoting self-determination can increase motivation, then self-determination is also an appropriate focus to help combat issues faced by students who are at risk for school failure. Although that population includes students with and without disabilities, research has shown that students with learning disabilities are at especially high risk for dropping out of school (Wagner, D'Amico, Marder, Newman, & Blackorby, 1992).

This chapter will provide an overview of the current state of the art of self-determination instructional practices for students with learning disabilities. First, several definitions of self-determination will be presented and discussed, followed by a description of recent models that delineate components of self-determination. The next section will provide an overview of selected instructional interventions that can be used to promote self-determination. The interventions described include curricula that are specifically geared toward increasing self-determination and instructional strategies that are consistent with self-determination principles. The final section will identify and discuss emerging issues related to self-determination.

DEFINITIONS OF SELF-DETERMINATION

Definitions of self-determination that have been offered include the following:

> determination of one's own fate or course of action without compulsion; free will (American Heritage Dictionary, 1992)

> the abilities and attitudes required for one to act as the primary causal agent in one's life and to make choices regarding one's actions free from undue external influence or interference (Wehmeyer & Berkobien, 1991, p. 305)

> choosing and enacting choice in persistent pursuit of self-interest (Mithaug, Campeau, & Wolman, 1992, p. 19)

> the attitudes, abilities and skills that lead people to define goals for themselves and to take the initiative to reach these goals (Ward, 1988, p. 2)

> the capacity to choose and to have those choices be the determinants of one's actions (Deci & Ryan, 1985, p. 38)

> one's ability to define and achieve goals based on a foundation of knowing and valuing oneself (Field & Hoffman, 1994, p. 164)

Although all of these definitions approach self-determination from different perspectives, there are common elements among them: freedom, choice, and control. In addition, the concept of action and a focus on outcomes is apparent in each definition. At a project directors' meeting for staff representing self-determination research projects in 1993, an effort was made to reach a consensus on a common working definition for self-determination among the five projects funded by the U.S. Department of Education, Office of Special Education and Rehabilitative Services (OSERS). That definition clearly reflects the commonalities in several of the definitions noted above. The following definition of self-determination was developed:

> choosing and enacting choices to control one's life—to the maximum extent possible—based on knowing and valuing oneself, and in pursuit of one's own needs, interests, and values. (Campeau & Wolman, 1993, p. 2)

Self-advocacy is a related term that is often used almost interchangeably with self-determination. Given the lack of precise definitions in the literature, it is difficult to make a clear distinction between these terms. However, self-advocacy is generally considered to be a subset of self-determination (Wehmeyer & Berkobien, 1991). Self-advocacy refers to taking action on one's own behalf; acts of self-advocacy lead to greater self-determination.

MODELS OF SELF-DETERMINATION

To promote the concept of self-determination, models are necessary; they guide the development of curricula; instructional strategies; and student supports, such as coaching, counseling, and environmental considerations (Federal Register, January 28, 1992). Models describe and simplify complex phenomena so that concepts can be applied in practical settings (Eichelberger, 1989) and make complex concepts more easily understood and, therefore, more easily applied to everyday life. Several conceptual models of self-determination that have recently been developed through OSERS' self-determination initiatives are described and compared below. These models represent some of the first attempts in the special education field to operationally define and describe the concept of self-determination.

Model Focused on Individual Beliefs, Knowledge, and Skills

Field and Hoffman (1994) modified a four-step process described by Gordon (1977) to develop a model of self-determination over a 3-year research effort. That process included the following steps: (a) reviewing the literature, (b) conducting interviews, (c) observing students in a variety of school settings, (d) considering internal expertise, and (e) considering external expertise. The model-development process included over 1,500 student observations and interviews with more than 200 individuals. The model was reviewed by panels of experts (including consumers, parents, educators, and adult service providers) in three states and revised based on their input. In addition, a National Review Panel of experts provided input on the model and oversaw the model-development process.

Field and Hoffman's (1994) model is depicted in Figure 4.1. As described in this model, self-determination is either promoted or discouraged by factors within the individual's control (e.g., values, knowledge, skills) and variables that are environmental in nature (e.g., opportunities for choice making, attitudes of others).

The model addresses both internal, affective factors and skill components that promote self-determination. The model has five major components: Know Yourself, Value Yourself, Plan, Act, and Experience Outcomes and Learn. The first two components describe internal processes that provide a foundation for acting in a self-determined manner. The next two components, Plan and Act, identify skills needed to act on this foundation. One must have both internal awareness as well as the strength and ability to act on that internal foundation to be self-determined. To have the foundation of self-awareness and self-esteem but not the skills, or the skills but not the inner knowledge and belief in the self, is insufficient to fully experience being self-determined. To be self-determined, one must know and value what one wants and possess the necessary skills to seek what is desired. The final component in the self-determination model is Experience Outcomes and Learn. This step includes both celebrating successes and reviewing efforts to become self-determined so that skills and knowledge that contribute to self-determination are enhanced.

The specific environmental variables that affect self-determination are currently being defined by Field and Hoffman and will be further delineated as a result of continuing research. The environmental variables in the school setting that affect self-determination have been identified on a preliminary basis as being (a) the availability of role models, (b) curriculum variables, (c) opportunities for choice, (d) types of response to student behavior, and (e) availability of student supports.

Model Based on Self-Determination As an Adult Outcome

Wehmeyer (1992, in press) proposed that for purposes of education, self-determination is best conceptualized as an outcome, a set of attitudes and abilities that are learned across the life span and that are associated

SELF-DETERMINATION

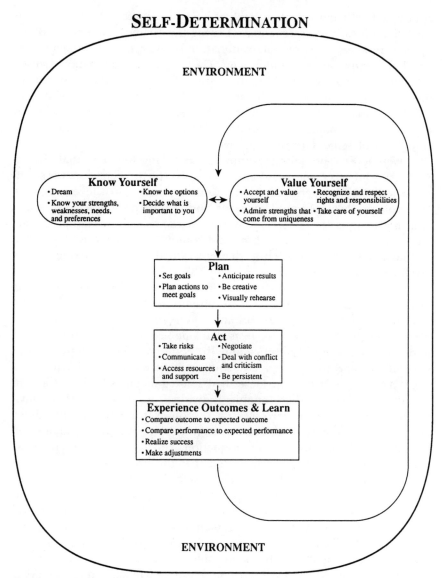

Figure 4.1. Model for self-determination. *Note.* From "Development of a Model for Self-Determination," by S. Field and A. Hoffman, 1994, *Career Development for Exceptional Individuals.* Copyright © 1994 by CDEI. Reprinted with permission.

primarily with achieving adulthood and fulfilling adult roles. A process that included two primary phases was used to develop this definitional framework (Wehmeyer, Kelchner, & Richards, 1994). First, a comprehensive review of the pertinent literature was completed and interviews were conducted with individuals with disabilities, family members of persons with disabilities, and professionals. During the second phase of the development process, an empirical examination of the essential characteristics of self-determination was undertaken. This empirical examination focused on administering and analyzing the results of several different assessment instruments that measured characteristics hypothesized to be related to self-determination. Over 400 adults with cognitive disabilities participated in the empirical validation process identifying those factors essential to the exhibition of self-determined behavior.

Wehmeyer views self-determination as having four essential characteristics: (a) The person acted autonomously, (b) the behaviors were self-regulated, (c) the person initiated and responded to the events in a "psychologically empowered" manner, and (d) the person acted in a self-realizing manner. Self-determination is viewed as a dispositional characteristic (i.e., consistent across time and context) and is a term descriptive of individuals who consistently demonstrate these four characteristics (Wehmeyer, in press).

Wehmeyer (in press) further defined each of these four characteristics. He stated that behavior is autonomous when it is based on the individual's preferences, interests, and abilities. He claimed that the term *autonomous functioning* (a) suggests that one acts independently without undue or excessive interference and (b) comprises the concept of interdependence and that others have some influence on most activities. He cited Whitman (1990), who described self-regulated behavior as a constellation of actions that "enable individuals to examine their environments and their repertoires of responses for coping with those environments to make decisions about how to act, to act, to evaluate the desirability of the outcomes of the action, and to revise their plans as necessary" (p. 373). Wehmeyer stated that the final two essential characteristics of self-determination (i.e., psychological empowerment and self-realization) emphasize the importance of considering individuals' perceptions about themselves and their environments, as well as their skill levels. He cited the work of Zimmerman when he stated that acting in a psychologically empowered manner includes (a) believing that one has control over a situation, (b) being able to behave in a way that will influence outcomes that are important to the individual, and (c) believing that such actions will produce the desired outcomes. Wehmeyer suggested that the four elements interact to define a behavioral, or dispositional, characteristic that is qualitatively different from each element individually.

Wehmeyer (in press) posited that these essential characteristics are the product of a set of related components. These related components include choice making, decision making, problem solving, goal setting and attainment, self-observation skills, self-evaluation skills, self-reinforcement skills, internal locus of control, positive attribution of efficacy and outcome expectancy, self-awareness, and self-knowledge. He claimed that instructional efforts should be targeted at these component elements to increase self-determination.

Wehmeyer (in press) emphasized the contribution of four essential characteristics of the individual that contribute to self-determination; Field and Hoffman (1994) delineated the attitudes and behaviors that lead to self-determination. A potentially valuable area for further research would be the relationship between the components identified in the Field and Hoffman model and the four basic characteristics identified by Wehmeyer. Although the Field and Hoffman and Wehmeyer models view self-determination from different perspectives, they appear to be consistent and complementary.

Model Based on Self-Regulation Theory

The model of self-determination developed by Mithaug, Campeau, and Wolman (1994) is rooted in self-regulation theory. It was developed through a process that included (a) review and analysis of the literature; (b) critical review, appraisal, and refinement by a panel of scholars and theoreticians who have written and conducted research in self-determination, self-regulation, and related areas (such as self-management, self-efficacy, and goal theory); and (c) ethnographic interviews and focus group interviews with students with disabilities, parents, and service providers (Mithaug et al., 1992).

Mithaug et al. (1992) claimed that persons who are self-determined self-regulate their choices and actions more successfully than others and that they are less influenced by others and their environments in setting their goals and deciding how they will accomplish them. They also claimed that according to self-regulation theory, self-determination is a special form of self-regulation; furthermore, it is a form of self-regulation that is unusually effective and free of external influence. Within self-regulation theory, person–environment interactions are described in terms of goal and choice contingencies: Goal contingencies specify what we must do, and choice contingencies delineate how we will do it.

The Mithuag et al. (1994) model is also based on Mithaug's (1993) work combining self-regulation and problem solving to meet goals. Mithaug's theory postulates four factors to explain the amount of gain actually produced toward goal attainment:

1. Past gain toward the goal;

2. Expectations for producing additional gain;

3. Choices to produce additional gain; and

4. Responses to those choices.

It is hypothesized that when all four factors are optimal, maximum gains toward goal attainment will be made.

The model for self-determination posited by Mithaug et al. (1994) includes six major steps:

1. The individual identifies and expresses his or her own needs, interests, and abilities;

2. The individual sets expectations and goals to meet his or her needs and interests;

3. The individual makes choices and plans to meet goals and expectations;

4. The individual takes action to complete plans;

5. The individual evaluates results of actions; and

6. The individual adjusts plans and actions until goal is achieved.

With a primary grounding in self-regulation theory, this model was developed from a perspective that is different from the Field and Hoffman (1994) or the Wehmeyer (in press) model. However, it is important to note that there is still a high degree of consistency among all three models in the definition and identified components of self-determination. The six steps identified by Mithaug et al. (1994) are very similar to the five steps described by Field and Hoffman. In both models, the first two steps emphasize self-awareness and belief in the value of one's desires, the third step focuses on planning, and the fourth step emphasizes action. An evaluation process is critical to the fifth step in both models. Finally, both models include an element focused on the individual's learning from his or her attempts to be self-determined and making adjustments as necessary. The models are highly complementary.

Model Developed From an Ecosystems Perspective

Abery's (1994) model of self-determination was developed through a participatory planning and decision-making process (Abery & McGrew, 1992). The model-development process began with a review of the literature. The next step involved use of a participatory planning and decision-making model as defined by Lewis, Erickson, Johnson, and Bruininks (1991). This process involved having the persons involved (i.e., children, youth and adults with disabilities, parents of persons with disabilities, education personnel, community service staff, and researchers in disability-related fields) identify and weight competencies relative to self-determination.

Abery's (1994) model posits that self-determination has a skills base, a knowledge base, and a motivational base and that it is influenced by environmental elements. It was developed from an ecosystems perspective, viewing self-determination as a by-product of interactions between an individual and the numerous environments in which he or she functions. Abery cited the work of Bronfenbrenner and Garbarino as he elaborated on the ecosystems framework upon which his model of self-determination is based. In the ecosystems framework, environments are delineated as *microsystems*—the immediate settings in which most persons function (e.g., church, home, school, peer group); *exosystems*—the external contexts in which a person is embedded (e.g., employment, local government); *mesosystems*—the impact that phenomena in one setting have on events in other settings (e.g., the impact that skills learned in school have on what takes place in employment); or *macrosystems*—the institutional and ideological patterns characteristic of a given culture (e.g., attitudes toward disability). In Abery's model, the self-determination process is at the center of this ecosystems framework.

The characteristics of the individual affecting self-determination in the Abery model are organized into a skills base, a knowledge base and a motivational base. The self-determination skills base includes personal choice/decision making, self-regulation, personal advocacy, and problem solving. The knowledge base includes declarative knowledge (the factual knowledge an individual possesses about her or his environment), procedural knowledge (knowing how to engage one's environment), and self-knowledge (an individual's awareness of and ability to accurately assess her or his competencies and skills). The motivational base includes sense of self-efficacy (the degree to which an individual expects to successfully behave in the way necessary to achieve desired outcomes), locus of control, and attributions for success/failure.

The Abery (1994) model places a stronger emphasis on the relationships and interrelationships between the individual and the different environments in which he or she functions than do the other models. The skills base and knowledge base described by Abery are very similar to the knowledge and skill components delineated by Field and Hoffman (1994). Although motivational issues are considered in the Field and Hoffman model within the "Value Yourself" component, the motivational base is more highly developed in the Abery model.

Each model described above is unique, but there are common themes throughout the literature in this area. This combination of diverse perspectives with common themes creates a rich knowledge base from which to develop instructional strategies and curricula that promote self-determination.

INSTRUCTIONAL INTERVENTIONS TO PROMOTE SELF-DETERMINATION

A number of instructional interventions aimed at promoting self-determination have emerged with the recent focus on empowerment, choice, and self-determination for persons with disabilities, and as a result of federally funded projects. These interventions include curricula and strategies to help students develop beliefs, knowledge, and skills that lead to self-determination.

Curricula

Steps to Self-Determination (Field & Hoffman, in press-b) is an 18-session curriculum based on the Field and Hoffman (1994) model of self-determination described earlier in this chapter. The curriculum is experientially based, allowing students to establish and work toward goals as they acquire the knowledge and skills delineated in the model. The curriculum was designed to be used in integrated environments (i.e., including students with and without disabilities) and in a variety of scheduling arrangements. It can be infused into an existing course or taught as a separate class or extracurricular activity. Teachers participate in the curriculum with the students to provide role models for them and to create a collaborative classroom climate. Parents or other significant persons in the students' lives also participate in the curriculum to support the students' efforts. The parents' involvement is seen as very important, as research has shown that parents are often viewed as both a support and a hindrance in the pursuit of self-determination (Field, Hoffman, St. Peter, & Sawilowsky, 1992); for further discussion of the role of parents in self-determination, please see Ward, 1991.

Ten "cornerstones" were critical to the development of the Steps to Self-Determination curriculum (Hoffman & Field, 1995). These cornerstones include establishing a co-learner role for teachers, emphasizing modeling as an instructional strategy, using cooperative learning, promoting experiential learning, using integrated or inclusive environments, accessing support from family and friends, emphasizing the importance of listening, incorporating interdisciplinary teaching, appropriately using humor, and capitalizing on teachable moments.

The curriculum was field tested in two high schools in the midwestern United States (Hoffman & Field, 1995) with students with and without disabilities (47% of the students in the sample had learning disabilities). The field test consisted of a treatment group, which received the Steps to Self-Determination curriculum, and a control group, which did not. A t test between the treatment and control groups indicated a significant increase ($p = .002$) in the correct responses on a Self-Determination Knowledge Scale (Hoffman, Field, & Sawilowsky, in press). In addition, the effect of a pretest–posttest (treatment vs. control group) of the effectiveness of the curriculum, as measured by a Self-Determination Observational Checklist (SDOC; Hoffman, Field, & Sawilowsky, 1995) scores (using the SDOC Pretest as the covariate) showed a significant increase ($p = .000$) in students' behaviors that are considered correlates of self-determination.

The Choicemaker Self-Determination Transition Curriculum (Martin & Marshall, 1994a) is targeted to help students acquire knowledge and skills that will give them a stronger voice in the Individualized Education Program (IEP) planning process. The Choicemaker curriculum includes lesson plans and videos that help students become comfortable and familiar with the IEP process, make decisions about input they would like to provide to the process, and develop skills to chair and participate in educational planning meetings. Student skills and opportunities in school that contribute to increased self-determination in three phases of the IEP process are delineated. The three phases of the process include choosing goals, expressing goals, and taking action. Specific teaching goals and objectives are delineated for each of these three major sections. For example, the first teaching goal under choosing goals is "student understanding." There are three teaching objectives for this goal: "Indicate goal-setting purpose and component"; "Identify student rights"; and "Identify goal-setting roles and timelines." There are a total of 10 teaching goals and 62 teaching objectives in the curriculum. The lessons are intended to be infused into existing course work.

The Choicemaker Self-Determination Transition Assessment (Martin & Marshall, 1994b) is a criterion-referenced assessment tool that corresponds to the curriculum. The assessment is used to rate both student skill and opportunity at school for each of the areas addressed in the curriculum.

According to Martin and Marshall (1994c), the Choicemaker Self-Determination Transition Curriculum is a socially validated curriculum. The first step in the curriculum development process was to conduct a literature review and interview process. This process resulted in a list of 37 self-determination concepts, which were grouped into seven major areas, including self-awareness, self-advocacy, self-efficacy, decision making, independent performance, self-evaluation, and adjustment. The second step in the development process was to operationalize each of these concepts and place them into a curriculum matrix format. The third step was to conduct expert appraisal. Finally, focus group input and curriculum field-test results assisted the authors in making additional adjustments in the curriculum.

The IPLAN (VanReusen & Bos, 1990) strategy is another intervention designed specifically to promote increased student involvement in the educational planning process. The strategy is designed to be taught to small groups of students over a 1- to 2-week period for approximately 45 minutes per day. Students are taught to use the following five-step strategy in the IEP conference:

1. "I"—Inventory your strengths, weaknesses you need to improve, goals and interests, and choices for learning;

2. "P"—Provide your inventory information;

3. "L"—Listen and respond;

4. "A"—Ask questions; and

5. "N"—Name your goals.

The five steps form the acronym *IPLAN*, which becomes a mnemonic tool for the students.

Research on this strategy has shown it to be highly effective with students with learning disabilities at increasing their level of participation in IEP conferences. To demonstrate the effectiveness of the IPLAN strategy, VanReusen and Bos (1990) cited a study of junior high students with learning disabilities by Bos and VanReusen. They found that students who received instruction in the IPLAN strategy made an average of 109 contributions during their conferences, whereas students who did not receive the instruction averaged only 31 contributions.

For additional information on transition planning, please see Dunn (chapter 2 of this book).

The Project PARTnership Core Course (Harris & McKinney, 1993) is a model program for encouraging self-determination through access to the arts. The course involves a total of 20 to 40 sessions, with approximately 3 to 4 sessions devoted to instruction in each arts modality— visual arts, creative movement and dance, music, drama, and creative writing. The arts activities give students opportunities to (a) establish a goal and a plan to accomplish it, (b) make choices, (c) work independently, (d) initiate plans, and (e) self-evaluate. Students have the opportunity to learn art skills, learn and practice self-determination skills, and express how they feel or what they think about something that is important to them. A set of specific activities is provided in the core course, but a curriculum framework that can be used with a variety of arts activities is also provided.

Life Centered Career Education (LCCE; Brolin, 1991) is a functional life skills curriculum based on three basic life domains: daily living skills, occupational guidance and preparation, and personal–social skills. Within each of these domain areas, specific functional competencies and subcompetencies are identified. Through a collaborative effort between The Arc (formerly The Association for Retarded Citizens) and the developers of the LCCE curriculum, the LCCE curriculum was examined for its appropriateness in promoting self-determination skills. A model was developed that included four domain areas hypothesized to move students through the processes necessary to achieve self-determination. These domain areas are self-awareness, self-confidence, choice and decision-making skills, and goal attainment behaviors. An examination of the LCCE curriculum revealed that there were four competency areas (i.e., No. 10, achieving self-awareness; No. 11, acquiring self-confidence; No. 15, making adequate decisions; and No. 14, achieving independence) and 17 subcompetency areas that matched the domain areas identified in the project's Self-Determination model. The relevant lesson plans for these competency areas in the curriculum were reviewed and, when necessary, strengthened for their use in promoting self-determination. According to Wehmeyer and Brolin (in press), "the LCCE curriculum provides a powerful, readily achievable and comprehensive means of teaching skills related to self-determination for youth with disabilities."

For more information on life skills curricula, please see chapters 3 and 5 (of this book) by Cronin and Sitlington.

A learning disabilities seminar (Sachs et al., 1987) was designed specifically for adolescents with learning disabilities to help them increase their ability to advocate for themselves. The purpose of the seminar was to help students (a) acquire accurate and realistic information regarding learning disabilities and use that knowledge to identify their own learning disabilities; (b) explore and discuss the productive behaviors of successful learners; and (c) conduct a self-analysis to develop a personal plan for more productive learning. The seminar was based on the belief that if students had a greater understanding of their disabilities and abilities, they would be empowered to set realistic academic expectations and implement appropriate compensations in their learning endeavors. The results of a follow-up questionnaire given to students who had completed the seminar indicated that 83% of the students acknowledged that they had a learning disability. The results also indicated that the seminar was effective in helping students acquire information about learning disabilities and use that information for developing a plan to address their learning difficulties.

Instructional Strategies

In addition to the curricula just described, several instructional strategies and environmental considerations have been advocated to encourage self-determination, including (a) using modeling, (b) providing opportunities for choice making, (c) providing attribution retraining, and (d) using appropriate behavioral strategies.

Modeling.   Modeling is one instructional strategy that has been emphasized throughout several of the self-determination model programs. The use of successful adult role models, in particular, has been strongly emphasized. Modeling is a very powerful instructional strategy (Bandura, 1986).

Modeling can be used as a direct instructional strategy (e.g., using role models to demonstrate a specific self-advocacy skill) or an indirect strategy (e.g., encouraging students to learn vicariously by observing teachers and other adults in the school who consistently model behaviors associated with self-determination). Several self-determination model projects have established mentorship programs to help students further develop self-determination skills by observing adult role models. For example, in the Take Charge curriculum (Powers et al., in press), students are paired with mentors who have challenges and interests similar to those of the youth with whom they are paired.

Cooperative learning has also been used with self-determination instructional efforts to increase the availability of peer role modeling experiences. The effectiveness of cooperative learning has been well established in the literature (Johnson & Johnson, 1986; Johnson, Johnson, Holubec, & Roy, 1984; Johnson, Johnson, & Maruyama, 1983). One of the benefits of cooperative learning is that it provides an opportunity for students to learn from the models provided by their peers.

Opportunities for Choice.   Providing students with ample opportunities for choice is another strategy that has been proposed for helping students acquire skills and knowledge related to self-determination (Field & Hoffman, in press-a; Lehmann, 1993). Abery (1994) summarized the work of several major theorists by describing the choice-making process as consisting of eight major steps. These steps include the following:

1) an awareness of preferences, 2) an appreciation that choices among preferences are possible, 3) recognition of decision-making opportunities, 4) definition of the choice or decision at hand, 5) setting of personal

outcome standards, 6) generation of alternative choices, 7) evaluation of alternatives, and 8) selection of the alternative that most closely meets the individual's goals. (p. 355)

Providing students with opportunities for choice allows them to receive, apply, and practice feedback on their choice-making skills. Providing students with opportunities for choice allows them to learn as they experience the natural consequences of their decisions in real environments. If opportunities for choice are not provided, students may see little benefit in developing self-determination skills, or they may lose existing self-determination skills.

Attribution Retraining.   Attributions are the assignments one makes about the cause of one's success or failure at various tasks. Adelman and Taylor (1993) described the tendency for "observers" (people in charge) to attribute behaviors to consistent personal dispositions and for "actors" (those being observed, such as students or employees) to attribute their actions to environmental factors. In contrast, students with learning disabilities often experience sufficient failure to expect it to continue, resulting in devastating effects on their self-esteem, willingness to take risks, and motivation about school (Smith, 1989). They come to attribute their failures to a lack of ability (internalizing the negative labels that the environment communicates) and to attribute their successes to luck, the ease of the task, or the fact that someone else gave them the answers (an external cause). Researchers have found that attributions can be changed, and students can be helped to understand the consequences of their active roles in the learning process. Smith outlined several facets of the retraining strategy, including:

- Emphasizing task-specificity, with discussions centered on actual performance and how to improve it;

- Teaching effective learning and academic strategies and reinforcing students for using them;

- Teaching students to task-analyze their learning tasks;

- Teaching students self-management procedures; and

- Discussing the factors that contribute to students' actual achievements.

Lovitt (1989) also offered several guidelines for, and empirical findings from, attribution retraining and stressed the importance of linking it with strategy instruction.

Behavioral Strategies.   The behavioral strategies teachers use can also have a significant impact on students' development of self-determination skills. Reinforcement techniques that foster motivation, self-esteem, and creativity and that encourage internal, rather than external, locus of control are recommended to promote self-determination (Field & Hoffman, in press-a). For example, positive reinforcement should be used to encourage positive behaviors, rather than using punishment to extinguish negative behaviors. Self-determination also has implications for how behavioral targets are established. Principles of self-determination suggest that students be included as participants in defining desired positive behaviors. Although naturally occurring reinforcers and consequences should be maintained, behavioral strategies should also include reinforcement of behaviors that help students reach goals they identify as important to them.

Reinforcement techniques should also encourage appropriate student experimentation and risk taking. Therefore, it may be appropriate to reinforce *approximations* of desired behaviors, depending on the starting level for each student.

When discussing reinforcement strategies, it is important to recognize that some research suggests that an overreliance on teacher-controlled behavioral techniques tends to decrease motivation. For example, Koestner et al. (1984) examined the role of teacher versus student control on motivation and engagement in activities. They set up three conditions: In the first condition, children were offered a reinforcer for painting pictures (contingent reinforcement). In the second condition, children were not told before they painted pictures that they would be reinforced, but they received reinforcement for painting the pictures upon completion of the activity. In the third condition, no external reinforcement for painting pictures was provided. When students were given the opportunity to paint pictures at a later time, the group that had earlier been given contingent reinforcement drew significantly fewer pictures than either of the other two groups. Although the use of reinforcement can be useful in helping students acquire and maintain behaviors, it is important to consider the potentially negative consequences of contingent reinforcement on internal motivation and, thus, on self-determination.

EMERGING ISSUES

As the concept of self-determination is defined and promoted for youth with disabilities, a number of issues emerge. These issues, which have both research and policy implications, include a redefinition of roles, the importance of taking risks, individual versus group orientation for self-determination, and the need for early experiences. Each of these issues is briefly discussed below.

Redefining Roles

Self-determination requires a fundamental shift in the relationships among the individual, her or his family, and service providers. Encouraging self-determination challenges the traditional views of educator and service-provider roles and requires that experience be viewed as a way of knowing that is just as important as the knowledge that results from training and study. A commitment to self-determination requires service providers to take on more consultative and facilitative roles. In self-determination paradigms, the service provider is no longer seen as "higher" and the individual she or he is serving as "lower." To the contrary, the role of the service provider in self-determination is to provide service and specialized expertise to individuals so they can make decisions about matters that are important to them.

Clearly, in self-determination, educators and individuals with disabilities become partners, both of whom have important roles to play. These partnership roles are in sharp contrast to the hierarchical way in which many educators and service providers were trained about how they and the people whom they serve should interact.

Self-determination also requires examination of traditional parent and child roles. The transition from adolescence to adulthood is a difficult period for many young people and their parents, as typical parent–child roles are being redefined. This issue is often magnified for persons with disabilities, including those with learning disabilities (Murtaugh & Zetlin, 1990; Shulman & Rubinroit, 1987). A compounding factor in the parent–child relationship during late adolescence for students with learning disabilities is the change they experience at the time of leaving school in service delivery systems. The educational system they are leaving is relatively organized compared to the often uncertain and complex array of adult services, whether the student is going directly into employment or on to postsecondary education (Will, 1984). The demands created by the new situation often lead to a higher degree of parental involvement at the time of transition than is typical for students without disabilities. For example, in an article on self-advocacy for college-bound students with learning disabilities, Brinckerhoff (1994) stated, "Parents are typically the ones to call LD service providers regarding the types of services being offered on campus, and they are often the ones to ask questions during the college interview" (p. 234). He also pointed out that excessive parental involvement can create resentment among university staff, especially those who do not typically work with students with disabilities.

Recent interviews conducted with adults with and without disabilities (Field et al., 1992) and with high-school–age students with disabilities (Field, Hoffman, & Sawilowsky, 1994) revealed that respondents frequently mentioned parents as both a strong support for and a major barrier to being self-determined.

According to Ward (1991):

> It is of primary importance that parents learn to share power and control
> .... As children and youth with disabilities progress through the life cycle,
> the advocacy process must become a partnership between parent and child.
> As the child learns self-determination skills, parent advocacy should eventually be transcended by self-advocacy .... During the transition phase,
> parents should begin to take a secondary but supportive role for their
> youth who self-advocates for services leading to employment and other
> postsecondary roles. (pp. 2–3)

Murtaugh and Zetlin's (1990) findings support Ward's (1991) suggestions for parents. Murtaugh and Zetlin found that autonomy for the student is achieved with the least amount of discord when parental control is gradually relaxed during adolescence.

There is a need to measure the impact of specific educator, parent, and consumer behaviors on self-determination and to develop personnel preparation and family support programs that encourage those specific behaviors. There is also a need to develop supports for individuals with disabilities and their families that facilitate this important shift from traditional roles. Finally, there is a need to demonstrate how school policy that supports student self-determination without infringing on the parents' rights can be developed.

The Importance of Taking Risks

Although the actions that lead to overprotection are often well intentioned, overprotection is often viewed as a major barrier to self-determination for individuals with disabilities (Ward, 1991).

An important concept in examining the impact of overprotection on self-determination is the value in taking risks. Ward (1991) elaborated on this point:

> A critical aspect of [self-determination] is creating a supportive environment in which children and youth with disabilities can test their abilities
> and limitations. ... Whereas it is the right of all people to have the opportunity to try all available experiences, it is also the right of all people,
> including those with disabilities, to fail in some of these experiences. It is
> through failing and finding one's own limitations that a person can under-

stand, adjust, and finally, accept the limitations imposed by the disability. By no longer dwelling on their limitations (or missed abilities), they can begin to focus and appreciate their talents. (p. 3)

One way that the issue of overprotection by others can be addressed is to help individuals learn how to protect themselves. For example, individuals who are developing self-determination skills should, as part of their instruction, be taught how to anticipate consequences of actions (Field & Hoffman, in press-b). They can then make determinations about whether they want to take a specific action or whether they would rather take steps to protect themselves by modifying their actions.

There is a need to determine the impact of disability on self-determination and, specifically, on the degree to which risk taking is encouraged or discouraged by others. There is also a need to develop, field test, and evaluate strategies that limit or reduce the effects of over-protection on self-determination. Finally, there is a need to implement policy language at federal, state, and local levels that limits overprotection and encourages risk taking.

Individual Versus Group Orientation

The degree to which self-determination is a product of environmental or personal variables is unclear in the professional literature. Some writings on self-determination, or on concepts related to self-determination (e.g., self-advocacy, empowerment), approach this issue from a perspective that is focused primarily on either the group or the individual. For example, group participation and support is viewed as essential to empowerment by the Cornell Empowerment Group (1990). They claim that

an essential part of the [empowerment] process is the positive validation, by others in the group in similar circumstances, of feelings, ideas and beliefs negatively experienced by the isolated individual. Other important aspects of group participation are subordination of individual interests to the needs of the whole, the expanded knowledge base that comes from involving more people, and the greater action potential produced by mutual support. (p. 1)

In contrast, Dyer (1976), in his book *Your Erroneous Zones*, which was on *The New York Times* bestseller list for over a year and is still in print, emphasized the role of the individual, asserting that individuals must take charge of their lives and that each person has the ability to make choices that will be best for her or him.

Many authors describe an interactive effect between internal and external factors on self-determination. For example, Field and Hoffman (1994) view self-determination as an outcome that is either promoted or discouraged by factors that are both internal (e.g., values, knowledge, skills) and external (e.g., opportunities for choice making, attitudes of others) to the individual. This view of self-determination—as an outcome that is affected by both internal and external variables—is consistent throughout each of the self-determination models described earlier in this article. Self-determination can likely be increased by making changes in the environment and/or by helping the individual to acquire knowledge, skills, and values associated with self-determination. The relationship between the individual and the environment is interactive.

The view of self-determination as an interactive relationship between the environment and the individual was also evident in the interviews conducted with adults (Field et al., 1992) and students (Field et al., 1994) mentioned earlier in this chapter. By far the most frequent barrier to self-determination cited by the respondents in both studies was other people. In contrast, two of the most frequently mentioned contributing factors to self-determination were self-confidence and self-esteem. Those interview results suggest that the internal factors of self-esteem and self-confidence are necessary to deal with others in a manner that promotes self-determination; they also underscore the concept that self-determination is promoted or hindered through the interaction of internal and external variables.

There is a need to further define the individual and group variables of self-determination and the relative impact of each in a variety of contexts. There is also a need for increased understanding of the interactive effects of internal and external variables related to self-determination. Increased understanding of the impact of specific individual and group factors on self-determination could lead to the development of more effective instructional interventions and to guidelines for choosing instructional targets in specific situations.

The Importance of Early Experiences

Self-determination is generally considered to be a developmental process that begins in early childhood and extends throughout adulthood (e.g., Field & Hoffman, in press-b; Ward, 1991; Wehmeyer, 1992). However, to date, most of the interventions and supports that have been developed to promote self-determination have targeted adolescence.

Adolescence is a critical time for the development and expression of self-determination, because it is a time when it is expected that individuals will begin to more actively engage in self-directed behavior. As the gateway to adulthood, adolescence involves defining and clarifying one's individuality and uniqueness (Erikson, 1975). Therefore, it is appropriate, and not surprising, that much of the emphasis on self-determination in special education has occurred in secondary programs. However, many of the beliefs, values, and skills that support or hinder adolescents' acquisition of knowledge and skills that promote self-determination are most strongly formed in early childhood (Ward, 1991).

There is a need to examine factors in early childhood that promote or inhibit self-determination, and develop interventions and supports accordingly. For example, what is the impact of various types of parent/child interaction during early childhood on the level of self-determination experienced by the individual, both during early childhood and in later years? Another example of a needed line of research related to early experiences focuses on play activities: Given the overwhelming evidence that exists on the importance of early experiences to later development, there is reason to believe that play activities in early childhood that provide opportunities for building self-awareness and self-esteem, making choices, and experiencing the consequences of those choices could have a significant impact on self-determination. In addition to examining the impact of play activities in early childhood on self-determination, there is also a need to determine the most appropriate developmental age to begin instruction in specific skill and knowledge areas related to self-determination.

SUMMARY

The focus on self-determination for persons with disabilities is relatively recent. The first model demonstration projects were funded by the U.S. Department of Education in fiscal year 1991 and the first research projects were funded by the same agency in fiscal year 1993. During that same time period there were several related federal, state, and local efforts. Although the study of self-determination is quite recent, models that define self-determination, and materials and strategies that support the development of self-determination knowledge and skills, are beginning to emerge. Several important issues, which have implications for research and policy development, have arisen during this brief time period. These issues include the need for a redefinition of roles, the importance of risk taking, the role of the individual versus the role of the group, and the timing of interventions and supports. The progress we make in furthering self-determination for persons with learning disabilities will be dependent, in part, on our ability to address these issues, as well as on our ability to implement and further develop appropriate environmental and instructional interventions.

AUTHOR'S NOTE

I would like to thank Dr. Michael Ward for his review and comments on an earlier version of this article.

5. Life Skills Curricula for Students with Learning Disabilities: A Review of the Literature

MARY E. CRONIN

That students with disabilities need to be taught the skills required to be successful adults has long been documented in the literature (e.g., Brolin & D'Alonzo, 1979; Clark, 1974, 1979; Clark, Field, Patton, Brolin, & Sitlington, 1994; Cronin, 1988; Edgar, 1987, 1988; Patton, Cronin, Polloway, Hutchinson, & Robinson, 1989; Sitlington, 1981; Wimmer, 1981). The essence of successful life skills acquisition cannot be weighed in terms of degrees, diplomas, or other documents; rather, it is demonstrated in their level of independent living, community adjustment, and enhanced quality of life (Dennis, Williams, Giangreco, & Cloninger, 1993; Halpern, 1990, 1993; Parent, 1993; Sitlington, Frank, & Carson, 1993). When a person's repertoire of various life skills increases, his or her independent functioning and quality of life also increase (Roessler, Brolin, & Johnson, 1990).

The Individuals with Disabilities Education Act of 1990 mandated that a statement of transition goals be included in the student's Individualized Education Program (IEP). The knowledge and skills necessary for successful transition to the student's next environment (e.g., banking skills, comparison-shopping skills, test-taking skills, job-securing skills, interpersonal relationship skills, etc.) are essential components of transition education. The specific competencies necessary for students' successful transition to their postsecondary situations are based on their likes, personal situations, interests, and abilities. This formalization of various components of transition education (e.g., life skills, among others) is important for all students with disabilities, including students with learning disabilities. However, teachers, administrators, parents, and other adults frequently assume that individuals with learning disabilities need no formal instruction in life skills, as they can learn these tasks on their own, are taught them by their parents, or can learn from peer models. In reality, as documented by many of the follow-up studies (e.g., Edgar, 1987; Halpern & Benz, 1987; Haring, Lovett, & Smith, 1990; Sitlington & Frank, 1990; Sitlington et al., 1993; Wagner et al., 1991), many students with learning disabilities *do not* learn life skills on their own. They need increased life skills content in high school and throughout their school careers. Life skills need to be part of their transition plans and, as some researchers have indicated, need to be taught throughout students' entire school programs (Brolin & D'Alonzo, 1979; Clark, 1994; Schalock et al., 1986; Sitlington, chapter 3 of this book; Weaver, Landers, & Adams, 1991).

The particular focus of this chapter is twofold. First, attention is given to a review of life skills literature as it applies to individuals with learning disabilities. This review comprises two different components: intervention and follow-up/follow-along studies. The second section of the article outlines a suggested direction for future research in life skills instruction for students with learning disabilities.

SUMMARY OF LIFE SKILLS LITERATURE

This review of the life skills literature will provide an overview of the journal articles and books available to professionals in the field. In addition, it is meant to give educators a perspective on the extent of empirical data on life skills curricula and instruction. The first section will address the terminology related to life skills used in the literature in the last two decades.

Life Skills Terminology

Since the early part of this century, many different terms have been used to convey the concept of life skills. In an attempt to be systematic in retrieval of life skills information in the literature, I completed a brief review of terminology used in the field.

In their historical review of the term *functional competency,* Wiederholt, Cronin, and Stubbs (1980) found an evolution of terms in the literature, starting with the use of the term *literacy* in the 1870s (Grattan, 1959). A literate person was one who left a "mark" (signature) on wood, stone, or paper. The progression of the definition of literacy moved from being able to read simple passages and write one's own name (1870 to 1880) to being able to correspond with others in the society and document and record events (Grattan, 1959). Starting in 1965, the U.S. Office of Education (USOE) established a national norm for literacy (Cook, 1977). The USOE's minimum requirements for being identified as literate included the satisfactory completion of 4 years of elementary school and the ability to function successfully in daily life. This concept, referred to as *functional literacy,* included math, reading, and writing abilities as well as a general understanding of everyday life. Wiederholt et al.'s analyses of terminology led to a working definition of functional competency or literacy as the ability to live independently through use of skills in reading, writing, and math.

Table 5.1 provides a selected number of terms describing tasks of daily life or functional literacy and their definitions; these terms have appeared in the literature in the last 20 years and describe what is commonly referred to today as "life skills." Clark (1991) stated that "'functional' in the context of preparation for adult living is simply a generalized term that does, in fact, mean the same thing as earlier terms" (p. 3). The common theme among all these terms is a description of a set of skills or tasks that contributes to an individual's success in adulthood.

For the purpose of consistency in the identification, retrieval, and review of studies in the present survey of the literature, the following definition of life skills was used as the criterion for articles reviewed: Life skills are those skills or tasks that contribute to the successful independent functioning of an individual in adulthood.

Three criteria were used in selecting *resources* from the life skills literature. First, only published books and articles were selected for review, due to the difficulty in retrieving other types of documents (e.g., final project reports, unpublished papers, university published reports, etc.) and to the fact that many documents were old or not readily available to the general public (records had been destroyed over time, authors left universities or retired, etc.). The second criterion was the inclusion of individuals with learning disabilities in the target population. (The generic classification used in some states refers to students with mild disabilities, i.e., students whose primary classification was learning disabilities, mental retardation, and/or behavior disorders. Such sources

---

TABLE 5.1
Select Terminology Related to Life Skills

Career education
- a curriculum designed to teach individuals the skills and knowledge necessary to have a career (Smith & Luckasson, 1995, p. 434).

Daily living skills
- those skills that individuals use in their personal self-care and occasionally in their interactions with others (Reynolds & Fletcher-Janse, 1990, p. 296).

Functional academics
- practical skills rather than academic learning (Hallahan & Kauffman, 1994).
- basic academic skills taught in the context of real life activities. A curricular emphasis on academic skills that are meaningful and useful for daily living (Hunt & Marshall, 1994, p. 162).

Functional curriculum
- a way of delivering instructional content that focuses on the concepts and skills needed by all students with disabilities in the areas of personal–social, daily living, and occupational adjustment (Clark, 1994, p. 36).

Functional literacy
- ability to read (decode and comprehend) materials needed to perform everyday vocational tasks (Miller, 1973, p. 7).
- rudimentary social literacy—that is, those skills required by a prospective employer or institution that a student is deemed likely to encounter in adult life (Buchanan, 1975, p. 73).

Functional skills
- the skills that are useful in accomplishing some activity in important environments (Wolery & Haring, 1994, p. 279).
- those skills required to operate in normal daily life (Bigge, 1988, p. 2).

Independent living skills
- preparation to function independently as adults. Must include more than just attaining a particular vocational or occupational skill (Meese, 1994, p. 385).

Life skills
- those skills that are relevant to independent, day-to-day living (Mastropieri & Scruggs, 1994, p. 320)
- those skills used to manage a home, cook, shop, and organize personal living environments (Smith & Luckasson, 1995, p. 421)

Survival skills
- everyday coping skills needed in adulthood (McClure, Cook, & Thompson, 1977, p. 26).
- skills necessary to function effectively in an environment (Bullock, 1992, p. 552).

---

were selected if they included a significant number of participants with learning disabilities.) The final criterion for inclusion was that the article must address life skills comprehensively; those focusing only on employment were excluded.

The following review is organized into two sections. The first section examines the literature addressing instruction or interventions using life skills information. The second section is an overview of the literature pertaining to follow-up/follow-along studies. A more detailed description of the literature reviewed is presented in Appendices A through D.

Intervention

Several observations and recommendations were common across the literature pertaining to intervention or life skills instruction for students with learning disabilities. Some of the findings relate to curricular issues; others are more methodological (see Appendices B–D).

1. *Life skills are appropriate for all students.* The first theme stresses that life skills and community skills should be included in the curriculum for all students K through 12. For that matter, it is possible to begin introducing many skills and concepts to students during the preschool years.

In middle school/junior high school and high school, many life skills introduced at an earlier time can be practiced. For example, in the elementary years, students could be introduced to newspapers by looking for ads for toy stores in the paper and discussing why toy stores advertise. Students at the secondary level might use the newspaper to comparison shop, find a used car, look for a job, or follow favorite sports teams. The overriding principle is to select life skills activities that are appropriate for the age and interest level of individual students.

2. *Life skills should be part of the ongoing curriculum.* Some research emphasizes that life skills should be taught throughout the school curriculum (Brolin & D'Alonzo, 1979; Cipani, 1988; Cronin, Lord, & Wendling, 1991; Lewis & Taymans, 1992; Roessler, 1988), rather than as isolated tasks that are separate from the content normally covered in school. Life skills instruction should also be formally included in all academic areas (e.g., math, writing, reading, science, etc.) as a way of emphasizing the relationship (and importance) of the academic activity (e.g., adding sums of money) to everyday activities (e.g., adding the cost of items in a store to be sure you have enough money to pay for them). Many sources stressed the fact that social skills instruction, as one type of life skills area, is critical to success in employment situations and adulthood in general (Brolin, 1983; Minskoff, Sautter, Sheldon, Steidle, & Baker, 1988; Montague, 1988).

Even though traditional academic curricula, in and of themselves, do not typically provide extensive coverage of life skills content, such curricula can be functional and relevant. Cronin and Patton (1993) proposed two techniques for increasing the relevance of existing content to life skills: augmentation and infusion. With augmentation, related life skills information is addressed in addition to the topics already being covered in the course. This can be achieved in several ways (e.g., during a portion of each class period, during one class period a week, during a special "life skills week" each quarter or semester, etc.). With this option, a portion of class time must be dedicated to life skills topics.

The second technique suggested by Cronin and Patton (1993) is the infusion approach. This is used when it is not possible to devote specified blocks of time to life skills instruction, as may be typical in a general education classroom. Infusion capitalizes on "teachable moments" that occur as part of covering existing course content. For this technique to be effective, teachers must first be knowledgeable about the life skills students will need as adults. They also must be able to identify existing topics in the prescribed content that have life skills relevance and then to infuse life skills information into this material. Although such an approach is limited to these opportunities, it nevertheless does provide a mechanism for covering important information and making content relevant.

3. *Vocational training is an important life skill to cover.* The next theme was that students at the secondary level should be exposed to both life skills and vocational training. In a global sense, the concept of life skills includes vocational skills (see Cronin & Patton, 1993); however, in many instances non–vocationally related skills are separated from skills of a definite vocational nature. The coexistence of these two concepts within a curriculum emphasizes the relevancy of everything we do in both work environments and everyday life activities (Cronin, Wendling, Lord, & Palmisano, 1991). There is great benefit for students when what is learned in school is directly related to adult life.

Programs that successfully combine life skills instruction and vocational content that provide students with opportunities to learn academics in applied situations, practice those day-to-day skills in the natural environment (in the community), and receive on-the-job training in community businesses with job-related academic instruction in the classroom on related job skills (e.g., job-related vocabulary, math, verbal skills, etc.) give students a more complete picture of expected adult skills and responsibilities. In addition, the likelihood of students' staying in school until they complete the program is greater.

4. *Life skills are best taught in natural settings.* Life skills need to be taught in natural environments (Cipani, 1988; Cronin, Lord, & Wendling, 1991; Roessler & Lewis, 1984), that is, where certain tasks occur naturally as opposed to being simulated (e.g., food shopping in a fictitious grocery store in the classroom). This type of instruction helps students understand how certain skills need to be used in real-life contexts.

5. *Life skills should be addressed daily.* Moore, Agran, and McSweyn (1990) urged teachers to make life skills instruction a priority on a day-to-day basis. Many students with disabilities continue to need assistance in generalizing and maintaining life skills beyond school settings (Miller, 1994; Roessler, 1988); thus, increased exposure on a daily basis will give students the continuous instruction and additional support in generalizing certain life skills concepts prior to leaving school. A commitment made by every teacher to teach one life skill a day would be a significant beginning.

6. *Parental understanding of life skills instruction can be advantageous.* Finally, some sources recommend providing parents with an orientation to life skills instruction. Roessler, Loyd, and Brolin (1990) and Vasa and Steckelberg (1980) were successful in teaching parents life skills concepts so the parents could better instruct their children on a day-to-day basis. Advising parents to have both structured and unstructured functional situations in the home (a) heightens the parents' awareness of the number of life skills in day-to-day tasks, (b) focuses on increasing the child's independence in as many activities as possible, and (c) increases daily positive interactions between parent and child. Structured activities could include ongoing household chores, such as retrieving and counting utensils or setting the table (for younger children), or doing the dishes (for older children). Spontaneous or unstructured simple tasks refer to those events that occur naturally in the home environment at unspecified times during the course of a day (e.g., folding towels, picking up toys or personal items, going to the store for milk and bread, making a simple meal). Taking advantage of such opportunities can be valuable experiences for both the parent and the child.

7. *Challenges to teaching life skills do exist.* The next theme was the reality that barriers do exist to implementing a life skills curriculum. Resistance can arise from teachers in both special and general education classes, school administrators, and school boards. Often this is due to a lack of communication or not understanding that academics (e.g., basic skills such as math, writing, reading, science, etc.) can be applied to real-life situations (e.g., reading the want ads to find a job, writing a letter of complaint to the city about potholes in the street, knowing how to put out a fire in the oven, determining financial options for purchases, deciding when to call the doctor when feeling ill, planning a picnic on Saturday, etc.). Additional barriers include (a) the lack of appropriate assessment techniques; (b) the lack of appropriate curricular materials; (c) poor generalization of specific life skills information to other, similar situations; (d) school systems' lack of commitment; (e) the lack of teacher/staff inservice on life skills/community instruction and curriculum development; and (f) administrators' and teachers' resistance to community instruction.

8. *Transition planning is important to overall quality of life.* Studies that have looked comprehensively at outcomes have had a significant impact on planning for the transition from high school to adult life (Halpern, 1993; Roessler, Brolin, & Johnson, 1991). Pertinent issues for the student's IEP/Individualized Transition Plan (ITP) committees (the student, his or her parents, teachers, adult service providers, school administrator, etc.) include the decisions made regarding individual transition plans and goals, the student's age, the various options for instruction and community experiences, the content and method of instruction, and the involvement of key personnel (including the parents and adult service providers) in the planning and delivery of instruction.

Follow-Up and Follow-Along

A significant number of the research studies in the literature during the mid- to late 1980s and mid-1990s examined the adult outcomes of special education graduates. One of the most important studies was the National Longitudinal Transition Study (NLTS) of Special Education Students (Wagner, Blackorby, Cameto, Hebbeler, & Newman, 1993; Wagner, D'Amico, Marder, Newman, & Blackorby, 1992; Wagner et al., 1991); it provided the most comprehensive investigation to date of young adults who were formerly in special education. The NLTS included 8,000 former special education students, ages 13 to 21, who were followed for 5 years to glean information about the transition from school to postsecondary situations. This database has provided, and will continue to provide, educators with nationwide data to guide life skills development and program revision.

The body of literature on follow-up and follow-along studies is significant to the review of life skills literature in that many of the studies address the tasks that contribute to achieving a particular level of adult success or independent living skills. Some studies examined specific tasks, such as maintaining a checking account (Kranstover, Thurlow, & Bruininks, 1989) or obtaining a driver's license (Fafard & Haubrich, 1981; Haring & Lovett, 1990; Kranstover et al., 1989); others investigated general categories of life skills, such as place of residence or living arrangement (Haring & Lovett, 1990; Haring et al., 1990; Schalock, Holl, Elliott, & Ross 1992; Schalock et al., 1986), independent living, community living skills, community adjustment (Chadsey-Rusch, Rusch, & O'Reilly, 1991; Halpern & Benz, 1987; Roessler, Brolin, & Johnson, 1990; Sitlington & Frank, 1990; Sitlington et al., 1993), or recreation activities (Haring & Lovett, 1990; Haring et al., 1990; Kranstover et al., 1989; Scuccimarra & Speece, 1990; Sitlington & Frank, 1990). These studies have attempted to provide feedback to individual schools, school systems, state offices of special education, and the federal government on the weak elements of curricula and instruction for students with disabilities, especially those with learning disabilities. One way in which educators, administrators, and school boards can improve the curriculum or specific content of courses is to find out how their graduates are performing, day-to-day, as adults. Adjustments to curricula and instruction can be made not only system wide, but also within special school programs. This type of feedback can also help guide teacher inservice and staff development programs.

Regardless of the level or depth of inquiry of the follow-up/follow-along studies, the researchers were interested in the participants' ability to perform day-to-day tasks, and how that ability contributed to their overall levels of success or independence as adults. The most frequent findings from the studies fell into eight groups:

1. Students with learning disabilities do not learn life skills on their own, as previously thought;

2. Individuals with learning disabilities still live with family members after they exit formal schooling;

3. Many of these students drop out before completing high school;

4. Gender differences in employment do exist;

5. Follow-up services are needed after high school;

6. Students with learning disabilities are employed competitively like their nondisabled peers;

7. These students are functioning at a level similar to their peers' in several social factors; and

8. Students participate in postsecondary educational experiences.

Two major recommendations—increase daily living skills in elementary and secondary classroom experiences, and revamp the curriculum to formalize the instruction of life skills at some point in the student's school experience—recurred in several studies.

FUTURE DIRECTIONS

The lack of a research database examining the acquisition of life skills by individuals with learning disabilities gives cause for concern. One must wonder if public schools are adequately preparing adolescents with learning disabilities for the demands of adulthood in general, and for the specific demands of their postsecondary settings. Results of several follow-up studies indicate that large numbers of individuals with learning disabilities are foundering. Sitlington and Frank (1990) found that 54% of the adults with learning disabilities interviewed in their study (a) met the criteria for meaningful employment and independent living, (b) paid a portion of their own living expenses, and (c) were seldom involved in more than one leisure activity. In a study of postsecondary community placement, Schalock et al. (1986) found that only 25% of students with learning disabilities were living independently. In their study of postschool vocational and community adjustment of recent graduates of learning disabilities programs, Haring et al. (1990) found that 79% of the sample lived with family members, only 16% of the participants registered to vote, and most participants participated in only one or two different types of recreational activities on a regular basis. These findings represent only a sampling of the problems individuals with learning disabilities face in day-to-day experiences.

Research addressing the successful transition and day-to-day functioning of individuals with learning disabilities during adulthood is minimal. Gerber and associates have studied various aspects of adults with learning disabilities who have achieved various levels of success (Gerber, 1994; Gerber, Ginsberg, & Reiff, 1992; Ginsberg, Gerber, & Reiff, 1994; Reiff, Gerber, & Ginsberg, 1993; Reiff, Ginsberg, & Gerber, 1995). Their work has certainly been a significant addition to the research in the field, but there is much yet to be done. A number of suggestions for future research follow.

Research Methodology

The lack of variety in the types of methodologies used in the research studies was evident, and was consistent with Swanson's (1993) review of special education literature. Many of the documents reviewed for this article were descriptions of programs or used primarily basic statistical techniques (e.g., descriptive statistics, Pearson product-moment correlations, t tests, chi square, one-way ANOVA) or intermediate statistical techniques (e.g., factorial ANOVA, one-way or factorial ANCOVA, multiple regression). Occasionally, advanced statistical techniques (e.g., MANOVAs) were used. This overreliance on more basic research methodologies mirrors Swanson's findings that "the current research programs in special education may be characterized by their general lack of methodological and statistical sophistication" (p. 19). Swanson, Wong (1994), and Halpern (1993) suggested that researchers in future follow-along studies use longitudinal techniques, include content that represents the important dimensions of transition, and use multivariate analysis techniques.

Moats and Lyon (1993) reemphasized critical points to contemplate when designing future research projects with individuals with learning disabilities. They reminded the field that "researchers ... and practitioners need incentives to design and use valid assessment strategies so that studies can be replicated from one setting to another and so that individuals can be observed over time" (p. 290). In addition, Moats and Lyon offered the following question for researchers to ponder: "What are the instructional conditions that must be in place for a child to learn, retain, and generalize concepts?" (p. 290). Attention to the assessment strategies used to measure life skills and the instructional conditions in which to teach life skills (i.e., using natural environments) are crucial to life skills research.

Wong (1994) discussed the importance of longitudinal studies of populations with learning disabilities. She suggested that longitudinal research data yield "needed information on and valuable insights into, developmental patterns and trajectories of target subjects" (p. 271) and allow us "to verify appropriate hypotheses, which results in more precise knowledge of the developmental patterns under study and ... enables us to debunk misconceptions" (p. 271). The use of longitudinal techniques in examining the far-reaching effects of life skills instruction with students who have learning disabilities will contribute invaluable information for teaching this population and for building transition programs.

Swanson (1993), Moats and Lyon (1993), and Wong (1994) have made many sound recommendations regarding research needed in special education, but this review would be incomplete if some mention were not made of other research methodologies. Researchers in special education need to be aware of the necessity to "explore and understand ... other inquiry options" (Ferguson, 1995, p. 199). Reid, Robinson, and Bunsen (1995) and Ferguson suggested widening our view of research to include alternative perspectives on gathering and analyzing data. For additional information on other research methodologies, refer to the special issue of *Remedial and Special Education* edited by Reid and Bunsen (Vol. 16, No. 3). Methods suggested include qualitative methods, discourse analysis, reflective teaching, and phenomenology. Finally, single-subject designs are another option for collecting and analyzing data and determining relationships (Alberto & Troutman, 1995). The variety of research methodologies outlined here can be applied to a number of the research priorities discussed in the next section.

Research Priorities

A number of research priorities for the 1990s can be identified to help professionals plan and prepare transition programs for students with learning disabilities in the 21st century. Two concerns mentioned frequently in the literature are the need to revamp curricula to reflect relevant skills and information, and the need to teach independent living skills. Curriculum revision was mentioned by several different authors (e.g., Brolin, 1983; Clark, 1994; Cronin & Patton, 1993; Helmke, Havekost, Patton, & Polloway, 1994) as the key component in linking school experiences to real-life situations during the transition years. Some also believed that merely including more life skills activities or making present course content more relevant was important (e.g., Lewis & Taymans, 1992; Weaver et al., 1991; Zigmond & Thornton, 1985). Empirical research is needed to verify the efficacy of these alternatives.

Many other topics were also suggested as important future research projects related to life skills, including the need for more data on:

1. Community adjustment or community integration of students with learning disabilities (Chadsey-Rusch et al., 1991; Gajar, 1992; Schalock et al., 1986; Sitlington & Frank, 1990, 1993; Sitlington et al., 1993);

2. Social skills instruction for students with disabilities in various high school and postsecondary situations (Minskoff et al., 1988; Montague, 1988; Sitlington & Frank, 1990);

3. The influence, attitudes, and involvement of parents and family (Fafard & Haubrich, 1981; Haring et al., 1990; Schalock et al., 1986);

4. The problem of underemployment and unemployment of women with mild disabilities or learning disabilities (Haring & Lovett, 1990; Kranstover et al., 1989; Scuccimarra & Speece, 1990);

5. The frequency and types of social and recreational activities (Fafard & Haubrich, 1981; Haring & Lovett, 1990; Haring et al., 1990);

6. The need for and extent of additional support in community, employment, and training situations during and after high school (Fafard & Haubrich, 1981; Siegel, Robert, & Gaylord-Ross, 1992; Sitlington & Frank, 1993; Sitlington et al., 1993);

7. The frequency with which, and reasons why, individuals with learning disabilities continue to live with parents after high school (Haring & Lovett, 1990; Sitlington & Frank, 1993; Sitlington et al., 1993); and

8. Delivery systems that are alternatives to postsecondary services for individuals with learning disabilities (Haring & Lovett, 1990; Haring et al., 1990).

Halpern (1993) discussed the concentration of interest in the employment dimension of the follow-up studies. He acknowledged the importance of employment but added that we need to look at many of the other community adjustment dimensions and present a balanced representation. One of those dimensions that are underrepresented is life skills.

The only way to assess the impact of these variables is to examine their effect on students' eventual adult lives. The need to conduct follow-up, or better still, as Halpern (1993) suggested, follow-along, studies of graduates of programs for students with learning disabilities cannot be overstated.

Because laws now mandate the inclusion of transition goals in students' IEPs (Public Law 101-476, 1990), the demand for life skills instruction should increase. The following are suggested research priorities to document the life skills competencies needed by students with learning disabilities when they formally exit secondary programs, and to provide empirical data on life skills curricula, interventions, and instructional techniques. This is meant to be not an exhaustive list of research directions, but a list of suggested investigations needed for moving us into the next level of study on this most important topic.

1. Longitudinal studies are needed to examine the effects of curriculum revision focusing on skills that will be of more benefit to students with learning disabilities in subsequent environments.

2. Research is needed to verify the long-term effectiveness of teaching life skills in the natural environment, as opposed to classroom instruction only.

3. Research is needed in teacher education at the preservice and inservice levels on the effectiveness of training future teachers in (a) the development and revision of life skills curricula for students in preschool through high school, (b) life skills and community instruction, (c) comprehensive transition planning, (d) continued follow-up of students after they leave the formal school system, (e) options for teaching life skills in a variety of service delivery systems, and (f) techniques for teaching self-advocacy/determination (see Field, chapter 4 of this book).

4. Research is needed on the effectiveness of parent training and subsequent teaching of life skills—starting in the child's early years and continuing until he or she can function independently in the community.

5. Data (including all areas of adult outcomes) will continually be required in follow-up/follow-along studies of both graduates and dropouts of special education programs, especially with regard to individuals with learning disabilities.

6. Variety of research designs and methodologies is required in research programs investigating life skills curricula and instruction.

7. Investigation of when, where, and how students with learning disabilities acquire life skills is needed.

CONCLUSIONS

This review of the literature on life skills indicates that over the past 25 years scant information has been disseminated on the teaching of life skills to individuals with learning disabilities. The vast majority of literature on life skills curricula and instruction that existed prior to the 1980s focused primarily on populations with mental retardation. Much of the existing literature has defined the specific components of life skills, the parameters of program development, community efforts, and so forth; however, much more remains to be done. Continued efforts to standardize the meaning of *best practice* are necessary (see Peters & Heron, 1993, for a discussion).

This cannot all happen overnight. In the meantime, teachers of students with learning disabilities need to make a commitment to begin (or continue) teaching life skills to the students in their classes, and must focus their efforts in the classroom toward their students' successful transition into adulthood. For many students, the reality is that this will be the last formal school experience they will encounter (U.S. Office of Special Education Programs, 1994). Each educator must remember that "it is our job to teach every student, every day as if it were the last day they will be taught by us or any other teacher" (Cronin & Patton, 1993, p. 62).

APPENDIX A: LIFE SKILLS BOOKS

Career Development and Transition Education for Adolescents with Disabilities (Clark & Kolstoe, 1995)
This new text gives an up-to-date overview of the history of career education, transition, and secondary education for students with disabilities. It also reviews aspects related to particular program elements and program supports, such as assessment; methods and materials; prevocational and occupational programming; job placement, training, and supervision; career guidance and counseling; referrals; interagency linkages; and transition from school to adult independent living.

Career Education: A Functional Life Skills Approach (Brolin, 1995)
This text features a detailed, sequential coverage of current issues and movements in the field. Each issue is then addressed by relating it to the Life Centered Career Education (LCCE) approach.

Career Education for the Handicapped Child in the Elementary School (Clark, 1979)
This book presents a model for deciding what curriculum content is appropriate for children with disabilities. It provides practical ideas for school-based personnel on how to deliver career education instruction in the general or special education classroom at the elementary level.

Career Ladders for Challenged Youths in Transition From School to Adult Life (Siegel et al., 1993)
Teachers, counselors, administrators, community agencies, and others will find detailed explanations of the three main components of the *Career Ladders* program: a supervised work experience program, a weekly seminar, and ongoing postsecondary services. Weekly lesson plans comprising the six curriculum strands and a handbook will be useful to those in the field.

Getting Started: Career Education Activities for Exceptional Children (K–9) (Lamkin, 1980)
This book contains approximately 150 career education classroom activities for students with disabilities at the elementary, middle, and junior high levels. Activities are broken down into three areas: awareness, orientation, and exploration. A brief review of materials and resources is also included.

Life Centered Career Education: A Competency-based Approach (Brolin, 1991)
This guide focuses on the three curriculum areas of daily living, personal–social, and occupational skills. The competency units and assessment instruments are helpful in the development of a student's IEP.

Life Skills Activities for Secondary Students with Special Needs (Mannix, 1995)
This is a collection of over 200 life skills lessons. The lessons are organized into the following areas: interpersonal skills, communication skills, academic and social skills, practical living skills, vocational skills, lifestyle choices, and problem-solving skills. Included are reproducible line master worksheets and parent letters.

Life Skills Activities for Special Children (Mannix, 1992)
This is a collection of 145 life skills lessons. The lessons are organized into the following areas: basic survival skills, personal independence, community independence, and getting along with others. Included are reproducible line master worksheets and parent letters.

Life Skills Instruction for All Students with Special Needs: A Practical Guide for Integrating Real-life Content Into the Curriculum (Cronin & Patton, 1993)

This guide is designed to provide teachers, curriculum specialists, and other school-based personnel with material for developing life skills content that can be used in a variety of instructional settings and with a wide range of students who have special needs or who are at risk for failure. The guide contains many different resources, including a list of major life demands on which life skills instruction is based, as well as a listing of materials. The guide will assist teachers and curriculum developers in making programs more meaningful to students while preparing them for the challenges and demands of adulthood.

Teaching Functional Academics: A Curriculum Guide for Adolescents and Adults with Learning Problems (Bender & Valletutti, 1982)

This is a curriculum guide focusing on the teaching of basic skills for everyday situations. It provides a series of instructional programs that directly promote competence as a student, worker, consumer, and participant in leisure activities. *Teaching Functional Academics* also serves as a flexible conceptual model that can be modified, expanded, and applied to a broad variety of individualized instructional needs.

APPENDIX B: THEORETICAL ISSUES

Source	Article focus	Findings/conclusions
Bingham (1981)	• Discussion of the effect of LD on student's readiness for exploratory experiences	• Students with LD appear to be more vulnerable to factors that inhibit or impede career exploratory activity • Career educators should seek interventions that reduce inhibiting factors and increase productive exploration
Brolin (1983)	• Review of major events or accomplishments of past 10 years. Also describes major features of and barriers to career education	• Career education has demonstrated its need and general acceptance • Need for educators to make career education a priority • More cooperation, caring, and commitment is needed among professionals
Brolin & D'Alonzo (1979)	• Discussion of the need for career education, significant events, and critical issues	• Definition of career education needs expansion • Career education is everyone's responsibility • Should be infused throughout school curriculum and also in home and community • Use career education as a vehicle for mainstreaming • School systems develop systematic and comprehensive plans • Changes needed in staff development training
Cipani (1988)	• Review of functional skills approach utilizing behavioral methodologies	• Skills that are functional in natural environment should be selected and targeted for intervention • Acquisition of functional skills will allow integration to the fullest extent possible in the mainstream • Teaching functional skills through behavioral technology will allow more people to live useful, productive lives
Clark (1974)	• Presentation of models of career education	• Career education is evolving into a movement with structure and definable parameters • Facilitates the process of living

Appendix continues

APPENDIX B (cont.)

Source	Article focus	Findings/conclusions
Clark (1980)	• Review of educational needs of students with handicaps	• Issue of appropriateness of education students are receiving at the secondary level • Career education is a valued educational goal • Student's personal outcomes must be included
Clark (1994)	• Discussion of concepts of functional curricula and full inclusion	• An inclusive model of functional curricula, but must also meet the functional, community-based needs of all students • Implementation of this type of planning and collaboration becomes more difficult and complex as student moves from elementary to high school settings
Drake & Witten (1986)	• Review of models for increasing cooperation between special educators and rehabilitative counselors, and discussion of the importance of functional content in school	• Counselor should encourage more functional content by providing more instructional materials • Give information on job modifications • Encourage instruction at both the secondary and the elementary level
Gillet (1980)	• Presentation of options to teach career education to students with LD	• Need to establish career education in programs for LD via development of innovative programs
Halpern (1979)	• Presentation of instructional options for students with disabilities at the secondary level	• Some adolescents and adults will benefit from functional academic instruction while others will benefit from remedial academic instruction • Work on breaking down barriers to employment training • Teach daily living skills within the mainstream

Appendix continues

APPENDIX B (cont.)

Source	Article focus	Findings/conclusions
Hittleman (1988)	• Presentation of a model for using literature to teach daily living skill development	• Daily living literature can be used effectively in instruction of students with learning difficulties • Daily living skills and activities can be used in all classrooms and subjects • By using daily-living literature, teachers help students realize that reading and writing are meaningful and relevant
Marchand-Martella, Smith, & Agran (1992)	• Review of literature on food preparation and meal planning for persons with learning disabilities	• Nutrition for persons with disabilities has been neglected in the research literature
Minskoff (1982)	• Review of a functional academic program for students with LD	• Students need an Individualized Education Program in which functional, remedial, and compensatory teaching are integrated
Roessler (1988)	• Presentation of a model program using a career education focus	• LCCE Model offers promising solutions to problems regarding career education assessment and curriculum materials • Students need assistance in generalizing and maintaining career education skills beyond school settings • Students need opportunities to apply and practice new skills in work, recreational, and independent living roles
Sitlington (1981)	• Examination of roles of special education and vocational education in effectively programming for adolescents with disabilities	• Special education and vocational education can function efficiently within career education models • Use of a career programming continuum integrating components of special education and vocational education is optimal
Trach & Rusch (1988)	• Review of adult life models and instructional strategies	• Dearth of instruction that focuses on transition to adult life • Implementation of adult-life model and future research activities focusing upon autonomy and adaptability to improve transition process

Appendix continues

APPENDIX B (cont.)

Source	Article focus	Findings/conclusions
Weaver, Landers, & Adams (1991)	• Discussion of ideas to implement a functional curriculum	• Functionality is a way of thinking about curricular content • Notion of functionality or authentic teaching requires the teacher to consciously decide how and where to teach the curriculum
Wimmer (1981)	• Discussion of how services can best be delivered to students at the secondary level	• Need to match traditional secondary curriculum and the skills and competencies needed by students with disabilities • Increased curricular relevance

Note. LD = learning disability; LCCE = Life Centered Career Education.

APPENDIX C: RESEARCH STUDIES

Source	Article focus	Participant descriptions	Findings/conclusions
Bucher, Brolin, & Kunce (1987)	• Investigation of the relationship between the competencies of the LCCE curriculum and the personal characteristics and employment status of former special education students as reported by their parents in an interview	• Parents of former graduates of special education (*N* = 132) • Former students between ages of 17 and 25 • 87 males, 51 females • Classified as MR (51) or LD (81)	• LCCE competencies related to employment level of females and EMH students • Female and EMH students have significantly less competencies than male and SLD students • When competency level of EMH students approached that of LD students, the employment rates were similar • Relatively low level of employment success was experienced by most former students • Female competency levels and employment rates were quite low
Fisher & Clark (1992)	• Validation of occupational vocabulary words	• Middle school teachers of students with mild disabilities (LD, MR, BD) (*N* = 33)	• 161 words were validated as having essential or important educational value. Only 25% of these were designed as having educational value and appropriate for Grades 6–9 • Model for validation appears to provide a way of producing the most highly valued words for an educational level
Greenan, Miller, & White (1985)	• Utilization of a survey to identify research priorities in career education	• Members of the CEC Division of Career Development (*N* = 132)	• There is a continuing need to investigate issues related to inter- and intraagency cooperation and the need to establish data-based instructional procedures • Field has not yet established a clearly delineated research agenda

Appendix continues

APPENDIX C (cont.)

Source	Article focus	Participant descriptions	Findings/conclusions
Hastings, Raymond, & McLaughlin (1989)	• Effects of training on rate and accuracy of money counting using a multiple-baseline design across subjects	• 7 students with disabilities (2 LD, 3 EMR, 2 TMR) • 10 students without disabilities • Age range: 14–20 • 6 males, 1 female	• All were trained to count money as rapidly as the average rate for normal group • One student suffered a significant loss of accuracy • Counting skills acquired during intervention were maintained across settings and over time
Heller & Schilit (1979)	• Utilization of a survey to identify future trends in area of career education	• Adults who work with people with MR, BD, LD ($N = 379$) • All college graduates • Mean age of 37 • Over 264 hold master's degrees • Includes classroom teachers to state department officials	• Of the 11 identified trends, only 4 were somewhat consistent across regions—with #1-ranked priority the only trend ranked high among all regions • Suggest the survey reflected a regional perspective
Kohler (1994)	• Investigation of the change in student skill level of work-related behaviors, generalized skill outcomes, and specific skill outcomes through pre and post assessment	• Some enrolled in alternative diploma program ($n = 58$) • Ages 16–19 • 11th and 12th grade	• Significant improvements were made in all skill categories, with greatest in specific skill category (job tasks)
Lewis & Taymans (1992)	• Utilization of a survey of parents of students with and without LD to determine community functioning	LD population • Parents of LD ($n = 100$) • Students ages 14–18 with $M = 16$ • 74 males, 26 females	• Adolescents with LD function less effectively than non-LD group in use of community resource activities and self-management activities • Adolescents with severe LD need to be taught skills and training that should be included in high school curriculum

Appendix continues

APPENDIX C (cont.)

Source	Article focus	Participant descriptions	Findings/conclusions
Lewis & Taymans (cont.)		LD population (cont.) • Family income range = $12,000 to $40,000 • 65% in two-parent families • 35% in one-parent families Non-LD population • Parents of non-LD (N = 250) • Student ages 14–18 with M = 17 • 135 males, 115 females • Family income range = $25,000 to $100,000 • 89% in two-parent families • 11% in one-parent families	
Minskoff, Sautter, Sheldon, Steidle, & Baker (1988)	• Utilization of a survey to compare perceptions of adults with LD and those of high school students with LD who might enter rehab in future	• Adults with LD (n = 381) • High school seniors with LD (N = 114) • Teachers of students with LD (N = 143) • Mean age = 23.2 • Male/female ratio of 3:2 • 54% White, 43% Black • All subjects resided in Virginia	• High schoolers reported few problems in daily living skills, with the exception of handling money (9%) • 30% of adults with LD reported problems with money and banking • 71% of teachers selected money as one of three problem areas • Other differences in living skills between high schoolers and adults were shopping, grooming, housekeeping, use of restaurants, and driving • High schoolers with LD not aware of scope of their difficulties

Appendix continues

APPENDIX C (cont.)

Source	Article focus	Participant descriptions	Findings/conclusions
Montague (1988)	• Investigation of adolescents with LD	• Adolescents with mild–moderate handicaps (LD, EH, MR) (N = 49)	• Training social skills is effective for teaching specific job-related social skills to students with mild–moderate handicaps
Moore, Agran, & McSweyn (1990)	• Utilization of a survey to determine level of vocational and career education instruction by teachers	• Elementary, middle, and junior high school teachers from Utah (N = 100) • 58% urban, 42% rural	• Teachers of younger students have been provided little in vocational and vocation-related task training and experiences within classroom curricula • Elementary, middle, and junior high school teachers seldom provide students with opportunities to take part in career exploration and career educational activities
Roessler & Lewis (1984)	• Investigation of increase in conversational skills using multiple-baseline design	• 2 males, 1 female • 2 trainees with mental retardation • 1 trainee with learning disabilities	• Participants improved their use of targeted conversational skills • Trainees experienced difficulty generalizing some target behaviors to other individuals • Need for additional in vivo practice and training
White (1983)	• Validation of content of work-related objectives in selected career-education curricula	• Small, medium, and large businesses in Kansas City metropolitan area	• Domain of occupation-related skills found in career education was content validated
Wimmer & Sitlington (1981)	• Utilization of a survey to determine research priorities by practitioners in the field	• Members of Division on Career Development (N = 306)	• 3 high-priority research areas include (a) instructional methodologies and settings for skill training; (b) delineation of essential competencies for vocational and community adjustment; and (c) attitudes that prevent entry into world of work • 11 middle-priority areas • 7 low-priority areas

Note. LCCE = Life Centered Career Education; EMH = educable mentally handicapped; LD = learning disabilities; MR = mental retardation; BD = behavior disorders; CEC = Council for Exceptional Children; EMR = educable mental retardation; TMR = trainable mental retardation; EH = educationally handicapped.

APPENDIX D: FIELD-BASED PROGRAMS

Source	Article focus	Participant descriptions	Findings/conclusions
Cooper (1988)	• Description of a bike repair business operated by students	• 7th- and 8th-grade students with learning handicaps	• Successful in terms of teaching math and communication skills in a real-life money earning situation
Cronin, Lord, & Wendling (1991)	• Description of a model outlining the development of a life skills curriculum with a community component for students with mild disabilities	• Secondary students with mild disabilities in a self-contained alternative program	• Successful implementation of a life skills curriculum with a community component for students with mild disabilities (LD, MR, BD)
D'Alonzo, Faas, & Crawford (1988)	• Description of model program to develop employment and life skills	• Exiting or recently exited high school students with LD ($N = 41$)	• An effective postsecondary transition model was developed and field tested. Results indicated a 92%-successful placement and employment rate among completers.
Field, LeRoy, & Rivera (1994)	• Description of middle school model of a functional curriculum used in general education settings	• Middle school students with mild/moderate disabilities	• Meeting functional curriculum needs in general education class requires team effort, creativity, and flexibility. Also benefits general education students.
Helmke, Havekost, Patton, & Polloway (1994)	• Description of model program to develop content course with a life skills orientation	• High school students with mild disabilities	• Importance of tying content to relevant, meaningful experiences for students • Top-down approach to curriculum development can be helpful in identifying content in a science course that is useful to adults

Appendix continues

APPENDIX D (cont.)

Source	Article focus	Participant descriptions	Findings/conclusions
Miller (1994)	• Description of model activity program for functional skills	• Adolescents with mild disabilities (BD and LD) (N = 15) • History of chronic truancy, aggression, and noncompliant behavior	• Evidence of positive gains in each of the four pre/posttests of the four phases of "On Your Own" • Skipping class reduced by 80% • Referrals to principals reduced by 72% • Points earned in token system increased by 92%
Posthill & Roffman (1990)	• Description of a model of college program	• All Lesley College students in the Threshold Program (N = 5)	• Mastery of a series of interrelated tasks allows a young adult to build self-confidence and to gain a sense of empowerment
Roessler (1991)	• Description of a program using LCCE	• 35 were enrolled in 3 special education inservice courses • 41 were employed in 9 school systems using LCCE • 68 teachers and • 8 administrators were involved (N = 76)	• Wider implementation of LCCE requires increased administrative support, teacher involvement, coordination of school and agency activities, parent involvement, and community opportunities
Roessler, Loyd, & Brolin (1990)	• Description of the implementation of LCCE curriculum in six school systems	• Teachers and school administrators • 6 school systems participated	• Recommendations to overcome contextual barriers to five operational goals (increase administrative commitment; involve teachers; increase inter- and intraschool coordination; increase parental involvement; and develop community educational, training, and work opportunities)

Appendix continues

APPENDIX D (cont.)

Source	Article focus	Participant descriptions	Findings/conclusions
Roth (1990)	• Description of an integrated approach utilizing vocational education and a life skills approach	• Mild to severe disabilities • 9th- and 10th-grade students with disabilities	• Attempts to bridge academic and vocational components
Rule, Fiechtl, & Innocenti (1990)	• Description of a survival skills curriculum for preschoolers	• Preschoolers with various disabilities, including MR, BD, CP language impairment, and learning problems • 13 boys, 5 girls ($N = 18$)	• Young children with disabilities can learn survival skills • Survival skill training is feasible
Scheibe & Tolonen (1973)	• Description of the SERVE program utilizing learning in real life situations and development of instructional materials	• Secondary students with disabilities • Students with EMR, LD, and BD	• Development of a set of materials (UNIPAC) for secondary and postsecondary students
Schirmer & George (1982)	• Description of a model to teach job and life-oriented skills	• $N = 3$ males • 2 were 15 years old, 1 was 16 years old	• All 3 students showed improvement • All goals outlined were met • No dramatic gains in math or reading on standardized achievement tests • Teachers should develop alternative curriculum for students with LD to better prepare them for entry into society

Appendix continues

APPENDIX D (cont.)

Source	Article focus	Participant descriptions	Findings/conclusions
Schumaker, Hazel, & Deshler (1985)	• Description of a Life-Planning Program that consists of a series of cognitive skills that enable the individual to develop and implement plans for future	• Secondary-age students with learning disabilities	• Program reflected in IEP • Involves input from significant people in student's life • Organized by difficulty level • Begins before graduation
Vasa & Steckelberg (1980)	• Description of a model parent education program in career education	• Parents of students with disabilities	• Parents inserviced on career education concepts can play a significant role in their child's development

Note. MR = mental retardation; LD = learning disabilities; BD = behavior disorders; EMR = educable mental retardation; LCCE = Life Centered Career Education; CP = cerebral palsy; IEP = Individualized Education Program.

6. The Positive Force of Vocational Education: Transition Outcomes for Youth with Learning Disabilities

Two factors can be associated with a dramatically lower probability of dropping out of high school in the 11th and 12th grades: concentration in vocational courses or having taken a survey vocational education class (U.S. Department of Education, 1994a). This finding gives credence to the hypothesis that vocational courses have some "holding power" over students with disabilities. Further, data from the *Sixteenth Annual Report to Congress* (U.S. Department of Education, 1994a) suggest that general academic classes are difficult environments for students with learning disabilities. Thus, students with disabilities who spent most of their time in general academic classes are significantly more likely to fail courses than other students. The loss of credit that occurs with course failure is one of the most accurate predictors of dropping out of school. Conversely, vocational courses appear to be a positive force. Students with disabilities who take vocational courses or participate in work experience programs tend to have fewer absences, succeed in their courses, and graduate.

The purpose of this chapter is to present research that supports the use of vocational education programs to improve the transition outcomes

Reprinted, with changes, from "The positive force of vocational education: Transition outcomes for youth with learning disabilities," by Rebecca B. Evers, *Journal of Learning Disabilities*, Vol. 29, 1996, pp. 69–78. Copyright © 1996 by PRO-ED, Inc.

of students with learning disabilities as they move into adulthood—specifically, their transition to employment. To this end, this review of the literature related to the vocational–technical education of secondary students with learning disabilities will focus on four major topics: (a) data from follow-up and follow-along studies illustrating the relationship between vocational–technical education and adult outcomes; (b) recent program trends in vocational education; (c) current practices in vocational education regarding placement and access, instructional and setting demands, and teacher attitudes and preparation; and (d) speculations about the effects of school reform and pending legislation. Particular attention is given to the topic of current practices in vocational education because understanding vocational education will allow for effective planning during students' secondary programs. Only then will the positive force vocational education can exert be evident in the adult outcome data of larger numbers of our youth with learning disabilities.

Relationship Between Vocational Education and Adult Outcomes

Transition Planning

The reauthorization of the Individuals with Disabilities Education Act of 1990 (IDEA; P.L. 101-476), mandates the provision of transition services for all secondary students who have an Individualized Education Program (IEP). *Transition services* are defined as a coordinated set of activities designed within an outcome-oriented process (DeStefano & Wermuth, 1992). Thus, the extent to which students access and succeed in postsecondary settings is a function of their secondary programs (DeStefano & Wermuth, 1992). Many schools incorporate these services into each student's IEP through a process of formal transition planning. When using an outcome-oriented process, educators can coordinate secondary school course work, related activities, work experiences, responsibilities at home, and community participation to maximize a student's readiness for postschool settings. (For more information regarding the transition process, see chapters 2 and 3 by Dunn and Sitlington, this book.)

Vocational Education's Effect on Employment Rates

Since the enactment of Public Law 94-142 in 1975, follow-up studies have attempted to assess the impact of educational programs on youth.

One emerging theme in studies that follow students with learning disabilities in their transition from high school to adulthood is the effect of
vocational–technical training programs on employment outcomes. "In our
society, employment, and the money earned from employment, plays a
critical role in everyone's quality of life—hence the focus on employment"
(Edgar, 1988, p. 5).

A number of studies conducted between 1985 and 1993 specifically
examined the relationship between vocational education programs and
adult employment opportunities for students with mild disabilities. A significant relationship was found between taking vocational classes or having a job while still enrolled in high school and postschool employment
rates (see Table 6.1).

In summary, the results from this group of follow-up studies suggest
that students with learning disabilities who receive some experience in
vocational education or paid outside work during high school are more
successful in the job market than those who had no vocational or work
experiences.

Low College Entrance and Completion

Data from the *Sixteenth Annual Report to Congress* (U.S. Department
of Education, 1994a) reveal that employment was the transition goal for
68% of the 12th graders who had transition plans. By comparison, only
23% cited college as a postschool goal.

Sitlington and Frank (1990) found that of the 914 college students
with learning disabilities they surveyed, only 50% had received some type
of postsecondary training, and only 21% had attended a community
college. Furthermore, only 6% of those surveyed were still students during the time of the survey, suggesting that these persons did not remain
in school for full programs.

Greenbaum, Graham, and Scales (1995) reported that, although the
number of students with learning disabilities attending college has risen
over the past 10 to 15 years, persons with learning disabilities are still less
likely to attend college than their nondisabled peers. Further, Marder
(1992) indicated that youth with learning disabilities are less likely to
attend 4-year colleges than 2-year colleges or postsecondary vocational
schools. Among students with learning disabilities in the survey who
attended postsecondary schools, only 15.9% attended full time. Further,
18.1% of the students who attended 2-year colleges pursued vocational
programs rather than academic programs. Finally, Marder found that
approximately 14.5% of the students with learning disabilities who entered
postsecondary schools completed degrees: 11.1% at postsecondary vocational schools, 2.9% at 2-year colleges, and 0.4% at 4-year colleges. (For

TABLE 6.1
Studies Reporting a Relationship Between Vocational Education
and Adult Employment Outcomes

Report	Findings
Humes & Brammer (1985)	100% of students who took vocational education were employed
Mithaug, Horiuchi, & Fanning (1985)	82% of students who took vocational education were employed
Hasazi, Johnson, Hasazi, Gordon, & Hull (1989)	Significant relationship between taking one or more vocational classes and adult employment
	Significant relationship between high school work experience and employment
Shapiro & Lentz (1991)	In sample of graduates from vocational school, after 24 months no different found between employment rates of students with LD and non-LD students
Schwarz & Taymans (1991)	78% of vocational program graduates with learning disabilities were employed
D'Amico (1991)	68% of vocational education students with LD were employed vs. 48% of students with LD and no vocational education
Sitlington, Frank, & Carson (1993)	Significant relationship between part-time high school job and adult employment

more information on postsecondary education, see Brinckerhoff, chapter 8 of this book.)

The data cited above indicate that most youth with learning disabilities have not been employed or enrolled in postsecondary educational settings at rates equal to those of their nondisabled peers. However, new trends in secondary programs may offer opportunities to increase the inclusion of students with disabilities in postsecondary training programs.

RECENT PROGRAM TRENDS IN VOCATIONAL EDUCATION

Current Vocational Education Options

The emerging trends in the field of vocational education include the school reform programs known as the Tech-Prep Act and School-To-Work Opportunities Act, both of which will be discussed below with particular focus on their impact on youth with learning disabilities.

Tech-Prep Act. The Tech-Prep Act came about when Congress amended the Perkins Vocational and Applied Technology Education Act in 1990.

Implementation of the Tech-Prep Act requires an extensive reorganization of present vocational programs. Of primary importance is the requirement that vocational programs deliver academic and job-related information to students in curricula that are clearly related to the workplace (Green & Weaver, 1994). In other words, class work must be occupationally oriented. In addition, the secondary phase of Tech-Prep includes a core of required competencies in mathematics, science, communication, and technology.

The curriculum is competency based, stressing assessment of the competencies needed by workers in realistic settings, including (a) basic skills (e.g., reading, writing, arithmetic, listening, speaking); (b) thinking skills (e.g., creativity, decision making, problem solving, reasoning, the ability to visualize abstract information); and (c) personal qualities (e.g., responsibility, self-esteem, sociability, self-management, integrity).

Another requirement of Tech-Prep programs is that students' years enrolled in secondary and postsecondary vocational or technical programs must be combined (e.g., 2 + 2 = 2 years of secondary and 2 years of postsecondary training; 4 + 2 = 4 years of secondary and 2 years of postsecondary training) to provide a smooth transition with continuity of curricula. For example, a secondary student who took 4 years of Automotive Shop (known as Transportation Technology under Tech-Prep) would be transitioned into a 2-year automotive program at the community college.

Tech-Prep programs present positive opportunities for students with learning disabilities (Brown, Asselin, Hoerner, Daines, & Clowes, 1992). Specifically, such programs could more consistently offer all students (a) a common core of math, communication, and science; (b) an emphasis on transition from school to postsecondary settings; (c) opportunities for career planning; and (d) connections between school years and the future. At the same time, these programs may present problems, particularly for students with learning disabilities. Target students suggested for Tech-Prep classes are the middle quartiles of the typical high school student body, and target occupations are midrange jobs requiring some education and training beyond high school (Schell & Babich, 1993). Targeting only these higher functioning students and higher level occupations may result in eliminating at-risk students from these programs entirely. Furthermore, Tech-Prep classes may become even more like academic classes, where students with learning disabilities are likely to encounter failure (see section on Instructional Demands, this chapter).

The School-To-Work Opportunities Act.   Signed into law on May 4, 1994, the School-To-Work Opportunities Act offers another opportunity for students with learning disabilities to participate in vocational education. One purpose of the act is to provide a school-to-work transition system that enables youth to identify and move into roles in the workplace

(Council for Exceptional Children, 1994). Through this act, funding will be provided to programs such as Tech-Prep, career academies, school-to-apprenticeship programs, cooperative education, youth apprenticeship, and business–education compacts. The act requires that the above programs include a school-based learning component, a work-based component, as well as such activities as guidance and counseling, workplace mentoring, technical assistance for employers, and coordination with employers.

The act is intended to serve "all" students and is an effort to increase opportunities for minorities to prepare for careers that are not traditional for their race, gender, or disability. In this context, "all" means male and female students from a broad range of backgrounds and circumstances, including disadvantaged students; students with diverse racial, ethnic, or cultural backgrounds (e.g., American Indian, Alaskan Natives, Native Hawaiians); students with disabilities, including students with learning disabilities; students with limited English proficiency; migrant children; school dropouts; and academically talented students.

Although Tech-Prep programs and the School-To-Work Act hold potential benefits for students with learning disabilities, special educators must be aware that these students will be competing with an extensive general population for their place in these programs. Although the potential for advantages exists, so does the potential for further limitation of access to vocational education for students with learning disabilities. If, as more academic requirements and content are integrated into vocational–technical courses, the levels of achievement required for admission are raised, Tech-Prep classes may come to be considered "elite" programs.

CURRENT PRACTICES IN VOCATIONAL EDUCATION DELIVERY

As previously noted, adult employment outcomes are significantly higher for students who participated in vocational education programs during high school. The issues of accessibility, instructional/setting demands in vocational classrooms, and teacher preparation and attitudes define how vocational education is delivered. Special educators should understand these issues in order to help students plan for transition.

Accessibility

Cawley, Kahn, and Tedesco (1989) provided an important early look at the status of students with learning disabilities in state-operated regional vocational–technical schools. The school records of 500 students in 17 regional schools operating full-day programs for Grades 9 through 12 were examined. Students with learning disabilities were enrolled in 28 career options; the top 3 were automotive, carpentry, and electrical. Grades for these students were in the C, D, and F ranges, with mathematics showing the highest percentage of failures. In the trade areas, however, the students earned higher grades, the most frequent being B and C. Rates of attendance exceeded 90% for all students.

Weisenstein, Stowitschek, and Affleck (1991) reported results from a field test of a model demonstration project. The model involved a partnership between vocational education and special education teachers using a combination of services intended to support students with disabilities in mainstream vocational classes. Data showed that when support was provided to the vocational teachers, the percentage of students with disabilities enrolled in vocational classes at the model schools increased.

The legislative support for vocational education of students with disabilities provided through P.L. 94-142 (the Education for All Handicapped Children Act of 1975), P.L. 94-482 (the Education Amendments of 1976, Title II), and P.L. 93-112 (the Rehabilitation Act of 1973) may have affected the inclusion of students with learning disabilities. Specifically, data from the *Sixteenth Annual Report to Congress* (U.S. Department of Education, 1994a) revealed that students with disabilities are taking a higher percentage of vocational courses (24% of total courses) than their nondisabled peers (18% of total courses). These data should be interpreted carefully, however, because enrollment in general has decreased for vocational education (U.S. Department of Education, 1994b). More than half of the vocational teachers surveyed indicated that the status of vocational education was a serious problem in their school, and 47% responded that maintaining vocational enrollments was also a serious problem. This may be a direct result of increased pressure on nondisabled students to take more academically oriented high school programs. As states have raised graduation requirements to include more mathematics, science, and other academic classes, and as college admission standards have increased the requirements for foreign languages, mathematics, and science, the number of elective credit hours available for high school students to select vocational education has been reduced.

However, regardless of overall enrollment rates, by the 10th grade, 79.8% of students with learning disabilities have taken at least one survey vocational education course, and 40% have concentrated in a vocational content area (U.S. Department of Education, 1994a). (Students in secondary schools become "concentrators" if they take four or more semesters in a particular area.) In comparison to other students with disabilities, students with learning disabilities begin their concentration in vocational education earlier, with 22% concentrating by 11th grade. On the other hand, students with learning disabilities are less likely (38.7%) than other students with disabilities (e.g., mental retardation; 44.9%) to enroll in work experience programs during high school.

Examining the vocational preparation opportunities of students with mild disabilities, Benz and Halpern (1986) found the most frequently available vocational classes to be (a) clerical and sales, (b) service occupations, and (c) benchwork occupations (i.e., wood, automotive, and metal shops). Further, service occupations, machine trades, and structural occupations (e.g., carpentry, plumbing) were the three areas reported to be most frequently chosen by students. More recently, Wagner (1991) reported that 85.1% of the vocational students with learning disabilities were taking occupationally oriented courses. Of these students, 29% were enrolled in courses in the construction trades and 29.1% in office occupations.

Although those data are encouraging for the students who have gained access to vocational education, not all students with learning disabilities are successful at entering to vocational programs. Benz and Halpern (1993) continued their investigations with a 3-year follow-along study of students with disabilities in transition from secondary to postsecondary settings. These authors reported that students with learning disabilities in their sample were not receiving adequate vocational and transitional services during their last year of high school. In fact, one quarter of the students with learning disabilities received no vocational instruction or work experience during their last year of school. Only one third of the students identified received both instruction and experience during their high school education.

Further, gender and ethnic background appear to have an effect on accessibility to vocational education (Wagner, 1991). Although male and female students with disabilities were equally likely to have enrolled in a vocational course, male students spent significantly more time than female students in occupationally oriented courses (85% vs. 68%; $p < .001$). These differences were apparent regardless of disability category. Similarly, White students were significantly more likely to take occupationally oriented courses than African American students (83% vs. 74%; $p < .01$).

Finally, one major factor determining the accessibility of vocational programs has to do with the structure of most secondary vocational programs. Enrollment in vocational programs at most high schools is reserved for junior and senior students (Cobb & Neubert, 1992), and in most secondary schools the vocational education classes are considered electives (P.L. Sitlington, personal communication, September 16, 1994). For example, in the National Longitudinal Transition Study, Wagner (1991) reported that only 39% of students with disabilities in Grades 7 or 8 and 67% of students in Grades 9 and 10 took vocational courses. In the 11th and 12th grades, 82% of the students with disabilities took vocational courses. If, as Zigmond and Thorton (1985) and Wagner (1991) have noted, students with disabilities who are experiencing difficulty in school have dropped out by the 10th grade (or earlier) or have no time/room in their programs for electives, these programs obviously are becoming available too late in the students' school careers to have a beneficial effect on their school progress. Certainly, the issue of improving access to vocational programs for students with learning disabilities is one that must continue to be addressed. Further, exploring the issues of teacher preparation and teacher attitudes may reveal additional reasons for the low accessibility rates for youth with learning disabilities.

Teacher Preparation

The research literature indicates that special educators have not assumed an active role as consultants to vocational educators. In fact, the available data suggest that special educators have limited experience with and knowledge about vocational education programs because most of them, including those who teach at the high school level, have been prepared to provide academic remediation (Okolo, 1988). This may be due in part to the undifferentiated preservice training and certification of special education majors as either elementary or secondary teachers (Cline & Billingsley, 1991) and the continued emphasis on elementary education in special education teacher preparation programs (Zigmond & Sansone, 1986). Not surprisingly, special educators continue to see their major responsibilities as providing basic skill remediation and direct instruction of content material (Cline & Billingsley, 1991). Teachers of students with learning disabilities, therefore, may not push vocational–technical classes to their students because they are not comfortable with the curriculum (Zigmond & Sansone, 1986).

Of major importance to the service delivery issue is the preservice preparation of vocational educators, especially those teaching technical classes or trade skills (e.g., wood, metal, automotive), whose training and educational backgrounds differ from those of the majority of public school teachers. Historically, technical and trade-skill teachers do not have baccalaureates, but earn their teaching certificates from a particular division of vocational education through their related trade experiences (Cobb & Neubert, 1992). Most recent data (U.S. Department of Education, 1994b) indicate that 12% of vocational teachers have not earned baccalaureates: Six percent hold associate's degrees, 4% have only an occupational license, and 2% have only a high school diploma.

The data for vocational teachers in dedicated vocational schools indicate lower rates of educational attainment; only 63% of those vocational teachers earned a bachelor's degree. Among teachers with college degrees, 50% hold a degree above bachelor's, and only 66% took an education major. In fact, many states maintain vocational certificate offices apart from the certification offices of state departments of education.

Despite these statistics, for the 10 years from 1982 to 1992, data collected on certification of teachers, both vocational and special education, and major policies related to the delivery of vocational education to learners with disabilities revealed minimal changes. The early investigations (Eschenmann & O'Reilly, 1980; Greenan, 1982; Greenan & Larkin, 1983; Greenan & Phelps, 1982) noted that most states either did not offer or require special education course work for persons completing vocational education programs ($n = 41$) or did not offer vocational special education certification for vocational personnel ($n = 36$).

Eschenmann (1989) conducted a study to assess changes in state certification. Data revealed no change in the number of states requiring vocational–technical teachers to complete special education course work since the earlier Eschenmann and O'Reilly (1980) study. Specifically, there continued to be a widespread lack of certification requirements mandating that nondegreed teachers receive some type of training in working with students who are disadvantaged or have disabilities. Furthermore, the common practice of assigning students who are disadvantaged or have disabilities to classes taught by nondegreed vocational–technical teachers who are unprepared to meet their specific needs continues in many secondary schools.

Rojewski and Greenan's (1992) results mirror Eschenmann's (1989) data. Specifically, these authors examined existing certification requirements, policies, and practices associated with teaching endorsements for vocational special needs education. Of particular interest were current certification options, types of course work, and required occupational work experience. The findings suggest that most states do not have comprehensive policies or practices for vocational special education certification, and that the status of such certification has remained static over the years. Fifteen states indicated that they do offer certification for vocational educators in vocational special education; however, 27 states do not. Conversely, only eight states offer certificates for special educators in the area of vocational special education.

Teacher Attitudes

One of the first surveys of teacher attitudes indicated that special education teachers were not concerned about or involved in cooperative ventures with vocational educators (Sitlington & Goh, 1984). However, an early survey of vocational teachers revealed that those who had been involved in IEP development or who used specialized materials for students tended to have positive attitudes toward students with disabilities (Claxton, 1986).

More recently, Sitlington and Okolo (1987) investigated the attitudes of vocational teachers toward students with disabilities and the effects of education, experience, and involvement with such students on those attitudes. Teachers reported having a median of two students with disabilities in their vocational programs; however, at the time of the study, 37% of the teachers did not have any students with disabilities enrolled in their classes. In general, the teachers who responded had very positive attitudes toward the inclusion of students with disabilities in their vocational classes.

Honaker and Henderson (1989) investigated the attitudes of vocational horticulture teachers toward students with mild disabilities. During the 5 years prior to the study, 44% of the teachers had received some inservice on providing instruction to students with disabilities, whereas 51% had not. Thirty-eight percent of the teachers reported having four or more students with learning disabilities at the time of the survey; 51% reported having one to three students in their classes. Teachers ranked students with learning disabilities as easier to integrate into their classes than students with behavioral or mental disabilities.

Evers and Bursuck (1993) questioned teachers concerning accommodations they were willing to make for students with learning disabilities. The vocational–technical teachers in the sample were as willing as their general education counterparts to make accommodations in test-taking situations, including (a) using calculators and dictionaries, (b) giving exams via alternate methods and in resource room settings, and (c) permitting extra time for exams and assignments.

In summary, although students with disabilities constitute approximately 10% of total student enrollment, they make up only 3.3% of the students in vocational education programs (Weisenstein et al., 1991). Thus, in spite of federal legislation mandating inclusion of students with disabilities in vocational education and the increase of those enrollments, students with learning disabilities remain underrepresented in vocational programs.

Several early studies reported that vocational educators hold positive attitudes toward including learners with disabilities in their programs (e.g., Honaker & Henderson, 1989; Sitlington & Goh, 1984). However, more recently, 55% of vocational teachers who participated in the National Assessment of Vocational Education rated the placement of students with disabilities in vocational classes as a serious problem in their school (U.S. Department of Education, 1994b). Certainly, the inadequacy of state certification and course work requirements suggests that many vocational teachers may lack experience and thus are unprepared, rather than unwilling, to accept students with disabilities or to make necessary instructional modifications. Furthermore, vocational teachers may not perceive a need for differential instruction because they have not been trained to provide such instruction. To prepare both vocational and special educators, an understanding of the current demands within vocational classrooms is required.

Instructional and Setting Demands

Instructional demands, as defined by Evers and Bursuck (1993), are the skills prerequisite for successful completion of a class. They include both academic skills (such as reading and math) and appropriate social behaviors (such as attending to task, working independently). Deshler, Putnam, and Bulgren (1985) defined *setting demands* as the teacher's expectations for students to effectively manage the information he or she presents, as well as the procedures the teacher uses to evaluate the students' academic progress.

Addressing the area of vocational education, Greenan (1983) defined *generalizable skills* as those that are "basic to, necessary for success in, and transferable or common within and/or across secondary vocational training program areas" (p. 8). The 489 vocational–technical teachers Greenan surveyed using the Generalizable Skills Importance Questionnaire (GSIQ), identified 28 mathematical skills, 27 communication skills, 20 interpersonal skills, and 40 reasoning skills as being generalizable to their vocational area. Elrod (1987), in turn, identified academic skills that were prerequisite to success in vocational courses. The most frequent included basic math skills (measurement and computation using fractions, decimals, and mixed numbers) and the ability to read at 7th- to 10th-grade levels.

While observing the first year of a 2-, 3-, or 4-year sequence of vocational education programs, Okolo (1988) found that a high level of independence (e.g., self-motivated appropriate work habits and self-monitoring of on-task behaviors) was expected of all vocational education students, especially in vocational labs or workshops. Although the provision of hands-on experience and demonstrations were the most frequently reported instructional methods in vocational labs, other activities relied heavily on reading and writing skills. To further compound this situation for students with learning disabilities, vocational teachers rarely modified the curriculum or the manner in which they presented instruction to accommodate specific needs. Further, exploratory vocational classes seemed very similar to high school academic classrooms, in that teachers provided instruction through planned activities, such as lectures and discussions; required substantial amounts of listening, reading, and writing; and delivered most instruction in large groups.

Okolo and Sitlington (1988) reported similar results regarding the instructional practices of secondary vocational education programs. Specifically, teachers reported that students worked independently in classrooms and labs where the most frequent instructional methods were lecture and demonstration and the most common materials were texts and workbooks.

Denny, Epstein, and Rose's (1992) direct-observation study provided additional information regarding the setting demands of vocational classes. Vocational teachers spent the overwhelming majority of time lecturing or demonstrating; they rarely monitored student progress or engaged in one-to-one or small-group instruction. Teachers gave very few instructional directions or critical feedback and seldom praised target students. Furthermore, teacher behaviors did not appear to differ significantly whether they were working with students with disabilities or those without disabilities. Overall, teachers did not engage in behaviors typically associated with effective instructional practices.

Few empirical studies have investigated secondary educators' grading practices, and even fewer have addressed this issue with respect to mainstreamed special needs students in vocational classes. Rojewski, Pollard, and Meers (1990) found that although vocational teachers use both norm-referenced and criterion-referenced grading procedures, they most commonly use a combination of these procedures. Further, the vocational educators in their study believed that grades should reflect the degree of success the student achieved and the quality of his or her work. Some of these educators believed that students with special needs should be required to meet the same levels of mastery (with no special considerations) as nondisabled students, whereas others allowed for a student's extra effort, giving the "benefit of the doubt" when grading. Finally, these teachers responded that they had received little or no undergraduate preparation for grading and cited a lack of inservice staff development or support on how to grade students with special needs.

In a later study, Rojewski, Pollard, and Meers (1992) continued their efforts to describe grading practices and perceptions toward grading students with disabilities in vocational classrooms. Competency-based (criterion-referenced) assessment was preferred by 69.2% of the teachers. Again, the majority (85%) reported having received no instruction on grading or evaluating special education students in their undergraduate preparation; 72.5% noted having received no instruction in graduate course work in this area, and 88% reported no inservice.

Evers and Bursuck (1993, 1994) conducted survey and follow-up interview studies to assess the instructional and setting demands of secondary technical classes. They found that vocational teachers tended to teach to whole-class groups in both classroom and workshop settings. The teachers lectured for 20 to 30 minutes at least twice each week, and most of them expected students to take notes (but they did not monitor student note taking). Vocational teachers also did not use advance organizers or graphic organizers when lecturing. Further, vocational teachers used textbooks and accompanying workbooks extensively, often for independent seatwork without teacher supervision or guided practice. These textual materials were estimated by most vocational educators to be around the 9th- to 10th-grade reading level. All vocational teachers reported using "no particular" method to teach new vocabulary words. Other basic skill demands included the basic four math computations, rudimentary geometry, and manipulation of fractions, primarily for measuring purposes. The majority of teachers gave homework that counted for up to 20% of the final grade. All vocational teachers reported using tests and quizzes that accounted for 20% to 30% of a student's total grade. Teachers preferred multiple-choice, true/false, and fill-in-the-blank formats.

Generally, results reported by Evers and Bursuck (1993, 1994) indicated that vocational education work was done in the workshop, where tools are available. Students completed work independently with minimal instructor supervision. The predominant assignment was a product of the shop in which the student was working (e.g., food in home economics, a wooden product in wood shop). Students were required to do specific projects; freedom to choose a project was only occasionally allowed and, then only to the very best students. When questioned about how they corrected student errors, vocational teachers most often responded, "I show them what is wrong and make them do it over until it's done right."

Evers and Bursuck (1993) found no significant differences in the vocational educators' responses compared to those of the general secondary education teachers on the School Survival Skills Questionnaire (SSSQ; Kerr, Zigmond, Harris, & Brown, 1985). Part 1 of the SSSQ requires teachers to rate 48 items that represent skills or behaviors associated with school success (e.g., turns in work on time, handles criticism). Part 2 requires teachers to rate 21 items that represent school problems (e.g., falls asleep in class, gets out of seat without asking). The top 10 responses were virtually the same for both general and vocational educators, that is, they required students to be on time, prepared, and compliant.

REFORM AND LEGISLATION

The issues involved in school reform have been much debated during the last decade. For example, in excess of 274 task forces were formed during the 1980s to report on the condition of America's schools. The essence of these reports was a pronouncement that our schools are in trouble and in need of "fixing." As a result, from 1983 to 1985, 700 legislative acts intended to reform and improve America's schools were passed (Orlich, 1989). According to one important report published during this decade of reform, "Workforce 2000" (Johnson & Packer, 1987), more than half of the new jobs to be created between the years 1984 and 2000 will require education beyond high school, and one third of these jobs will be held by college graduates. Further, only 4% of the new jobs created will be filled by individuals with the lowest levels of skills. The authors of "Workforce 2000" suggested that to ensure continued economic growth and reassert America's position as a world leader, current educational standards must be raised. "Workforce 2000" further warned that America can no longer tolerate high school diplomas that are merely indications of school attendance, or accept vocational training that "merely warehouses" (p. xxvii) poor academic achievers.

Goal 3 of the "America 2000" (U.S. Department of Education, 1991) policy statements developed during the Bush administration seems to be a direct response to the "Workforce 2000" data. According to this goal, "every school in America will ensure that all students learn to use their minds well, so they may be prepared for responsible citizenship, further learning, and productive employment in our modern economy" (p. 9).

As the recommendations of school reform have been reshaping schools in general, the structure of special education service delivery models and teacher preparation programs have come into question (Edgar, 1987; Gartner & Lipsky, 1987; Gersten & Woodward, 1990; Majsterek, Wilson, & Southern, 1988; Okolo & Sitlington, 1986; Schumaker & Deshler, 1988). For example, a number of reformers have called for the full inclusion of special education students into mainstream school settings (Jenkins, Pious, & Jewell, 1990; York & Vandercook, 1990), resulting in a movement known as the Regular Education Initiative (REI; Will, 1986). In addition, the long-standing tradition of legislation providing for inclusion of students with disabilities in vocational education (i.e., the 1968 Vocational Amendments of the 1917 Smith-Hughes Act; the Carl Perkins Act) has been continued under the provisions of the Individuals with Disabilities Education Act of 1992 and Section 504 of the Rehabilitation Act (1973). However, as noted below, this tradition may end if the Perkins Act is not reauthorized.

Perkins Act Reappropriation

At the time of the writing of this chapter, Congress and the U.S. Education Department were in negotiations regarding the renewal of the Carl C. Perkins Vocational Applied Technology Act (P.L. 101-392). If passed, the reauthorization law would take effect mid-1997. At the fore-front of these negotiations is the Education Department's attempt to increase the support services provided to special populations in voca-tional education classes, such as Braille tests and teachers' aides. Voca-tional education administrators, however, believe that an expansion of support services will deplete program improvement funds and reduce the overall quality of vocational education programs (*Vocational Training News,* 1994). Meanwhile, congressional Republicans are working to combine vocational education with job training programs and convert them to state block grants (*Vocational Training News,* 1995). Whatever legislation is approved, the new law would supersede the Perkins Act.

If the Perkins Act is replaced and the set-asides for students with special needs are lost, students with disabilities may lose the support services, such as teachers' aides, special materials (taped and/or Braille texts), and technological assistance (computers, talking calculators), that make it possible for them to be successful in vocational education.

Program Cuts

Finally, despite federal policy aimed at increasing the participation of students with disabilities in vocational programs, local implementa-tion has resulted in a shrinkage of programs and services (Kochhar & Deschamps, 1992). According to Kochhar & Deschamps's survey, specific program cuts at local levels include (a) the elimination of special needs positions at state and local levels, (b) the shifting of vocational education dollars to academics, (c) the elimination of vocational assessment and evaluation services, and (d) the shifting of secondary vocational educa-tion funds to postsecondary programs (where there is no legal require-ment to provide special education services under IDEA). This trend is all the more alarming in view of the proposed conversion to state block grants of many currently federally funded programs.

Although legislation, mandates, laws, and the inclusion movement are intended to increase opportunities for students with mild disabilities in mainstream classes, generally, and in vocational education, specifically (Claxton, 1986; Stern & Gathercoal, 1986), present outcome data do not indicate that these intentions have been fully met. Rather, this review of literature suggests that a large number of students with learning dis-abilities continue to be unsuccessful at competing in or completing high school (U.S. Department of Education, 1994a; Wagner, 1989). Further, the most recent adult outcome data for levels of continuing education, employment, and independent living are also unsatisfactory (Sitlington & Frank, 1993; Wagner, 1991; Zigmond, 1990).

Certainly, interest is warranted regarding the number of students with learning disabilities who continue their education or training or are employed above entry level, as these are important indicators of successful transitions to adulthood. Passmore (1989) asserted that if individuals are unemployed, they have not successfully made the transition into adulthood; they are "a long way from maturity, responsibility, and admission to the citizenry" (p. 45). The outcome data have been and will continue to be affected by the appropriate placement of students with learning disabilities in vocational settings. However, the issues of teacher preparation and attitudes (in both vocational and special education) must be addressed in order to improve collaborative endeavors and, thus, improve students' rates of accessibility and success. Special educators must continue to defend the right of students with learning disabilities to be enrolled in all types of vocational education programs and safeguard the support systems provided under present federal and state legislation.

7. Transition Planning Assessment for Secondary-Level Students with Learning Disabilities

GARY M. CLARK

Transition planning and service delivery have traditionally been directed toward populations with severe disabilities; currently, some high school programs for students with moderate to severe disabilities are even labeled "transition" programs. By implication, this has led to the practice of making distinctions between these "transition programs" and other educational programs and services provided to all other secondary students with disabilities. That is, because most of these early programs were community-based employment programs, school-based and traditional academic programs for other disability groups were not perceived to be related to "transition." This is an unfortunate distinction because it has made the acceptance of the broader idea of transition programming (Halpern, 1985) more difficult. The Individuals with Disabilities Education Act of 1990 (IDEA) mandated that, at a minimum, the Individualized Education Program (IEP) team for *all* identified students who have reached the age of 16 must consider what each student's transition needs,

Reprinted, with changes, from "Transition planning assessment for secondary-level students with learning disabilities" by Gary M. Clark, *Journal of Learning Disabilities*, Vol. 29, 1996, pp. 79–92. Copyright © 1996 by PRO-ED, Inc.

preferences, and interests are in the areas of instruction, community experiences, employment, and other postschool goals.

The National Joint Committee on Learning Disabilities (NJCLD) included in its list of problems related to educating students with learning disabilities in general education classrooms the following statement: "Coordinated planning is lacking for students with learning disabilities as they make transitions from home to school to work, across levels of schooling, and among educational settings" (NJCLD, 1990, p. 70). The NJCLD position statement also provided a recommendation for action, proposing the establishment of "a system-wide plan for helping students with learning disabilities to make transitions from home to school to work and life in the community" (p. 72). A more recent NJCLD (1994) position paper specifically addressed the concern that many students with learning disabilities do not consider postsecondary education options because they are not encouraged, assisted, or prepared to do so. NJCLD's position makes it clear that providing transition plans and services is crucial in assisting youth with disabilities to prepare for adult life. These two position statements reflect a growing awareness of the need for adequate transition planning and services for students with learning disabilities (the categorical group most frequently associated with "mild" disabilities.) (See also chapter 7 by Dunn for further perspective on the importance of transition planning and service delivery to students with learning disabilities.)

From a policy point of view, the IDEA mandate to address transition planning for students with learning disabilities, even at the mild level, is an important new development in the field of special education. From a practical level, it requires school districts to change their IEP procedures for a wide range of students. Whereas in the past only a small number of students with disabilities were receiving any systematic transition planning, the numbers now affected are considerably higher, due to the IDEA mandate. They could increase even more. In addition to clarifying the categorical classifications to be included in transition planning at age 16, regulatory language in the IDEA strongly encourages extension of this process to students beginning at age 14. At least 10 states already have responded by specifying ages below 16 (most frequently, age 14) for implementing the IDEA transition services planning provisions. A strong lobby effort is in progress to amend the next reauthorization of the IDEA to move the mandate to age 14 (National Transition Network, personal communication, June 24, 1994; Council for Exceptional Children, 1994). Initiating formal transition planning earlier than age 16 is also recommended in position statements by the Division on Career Development and Transition of the Council for Exceptional Children (Clark, Carlson, Fisher, Cook, & D'Alonzo, 1991; Clark, Field, Patton, Brolin, & Sitlington, 1994).

The challenge of planning transition services for an exceptionally large number of students who have never before had such planning is enormous. Many states and local districts are revising IEP forms to be able to show legal compliance with the mandate. In some school districts, additional assessment procedures are being used or new ones developed to achieve recommended practices and full compliance. In spite of this, current practices lag behind IDEA mandates and innovative, recommended procedures.

Although schools have to organize programs and services to meet the needs of both individuals and groups of youth with disabilities, transition service provisions in the IDEA are clear that *individual* planning must drive the development of programs and services. The provisions of the IDEA and accompanying regulations prescribe individual planning for transition services via three components: *assessment, parent and student participation,* and *specific procedures to be followed in the development of the IEP.* All three of these components are discussed separately in this chapter, but the third is also addressed within the context of the other two components.

ASSESSMENT FOR TRANSITION PLANNING IN THE IEP

The IDEA, as an amendment to P.L. 94-142 (the Education for all Handicapped Children Act of 1975), continues the initial requirement that individual planning be based on *present level of performance.* For teachers and other school personnel who develop IEPs, there is the basic question, "Present level of performance of *what?*"

The professional literature related to the outcomes for individuals with disabilities once they leave school (i.e., adult outcomes) has focused on three general areas: *independent living* (residential and community living demands), *personal–social adjustment,* and *occupational adjustment* (Clark & Kolstoe, 1995; Halpern, 1985; Kokaska & Brolin, 1985). Dever (1988), Smith and Schloss (1988), Knowles (1990), Brolin (1993), and Cronin and Patton (1993) have elaborated on these three areas, streamlining the general adult outcome areas into critical life domains of adulthood. The consequence of this refinement is a specified array of life skills associated with the transition process that gives direction to both assessment and intervention for all students with disabilities. This array, or set of outcome areas, has particular implications for assessing students' present levels of performance for IEP planning. (For more information on this subject regarding students with learning disabilities, see the chapters in this book by Brinckerhoff, Cronin, Dowdy, and Sitlington.

One of the current problems with assessing present levels of performance in areas related to life skills and adult outcomes for the IEP is the narrow range of assessment areas institutionalized through testing practices in schools since 1978. For most teachers working directly with students with learning disabilities, "present level of performance" has been virtually restricted to academic and, in some cases, behavioral assessment data (McBride & Forgnone, 1985; Smith, 1990). Just as existing school instructional programs often drive individual planning and placement, existing school assessment practices emphasizing academic achievement drive IEP goals and objectives. The IDEA mandate for considering transition service needs for *every* student with a disability eligible for special services has the consequence of guiding schools into extending their academic assessment procedures to not only new ability and achievement performance outcomes areas (e.g., social skills, life skills, employability), but also types and levels of preferences and interests across all outcome areas.

Current practice in transition assessment includes a variety of approaches. Most state guidelines addressing assessment for transition planning under the new IDEA requirements suggest that assessment for transition services include tests, interviews, direct observation, and curriculum-based assessment. Using these approaches involves the use of both formal (standardized) and informal (nonstandardized) procedures. Hammill (1987) suggested that evidence of reliability and validity is a key to whether an assessment procedure is standardized or nonstandardized. He offered these helpful distinctions, conceptually and in terminology [emphasis is author's]:

> Techniques for which exhaustive evidence (e.g., multiple studies) is available that shows acceptable reliability and validity can fairly be called *highly standardized*. Techniques that have only minimal evidence (e.g., one or two studies showing acceptable reliability and validity) qualify for a *standardized* rating. Techniques for which no proof of reliability or validity is available, only nonsupportive evidence exists, or evidence is provided for only one of the two proofs must be considered *nonstandardized*. In general usage, *formal* is used as a synonym for "standardized" or "highly standardized," *informal* is used as a synonym for "nonstandardized." (pp. 29–30)

Using Hammill's terminology for distinguishing between standardized and nonstandardized instruments, the next two sections describe current practices in transition assessment.

Standardized Assessments

The following types of standardized assessment procedures or instruments are available commercially or through professional services:

- Learning styles inventories;

- Academic achievement tests;

- Intellectual functioning assessment;

- Adaptive behavior scales;

- Aptitude tests;

- Interest inventories;

- Personality scales;

- Quality of life scales;

- Social skills inventories;

- Prevocational/employability scales;

- Vocational skills assessments;

- Transition knowledge and skills inventories; and

- Medical laboratory procedures.

Some educators and agency personnel have used one or more of the types of assessment instruments from this list to determine students' present levels of performance and glean specific kinds of information that might help in IEP planning, in lieu of any specific transition assessment instruments.

   Achievement tests and learning styles inventories may yield data on reading and math abilities and preferences for learning conditions related to current instructional planning and postsecondary education or training decisions. Intelligence scales can provide some predictive validity for success in cognitive tasks and other demands of current instructional settings, as well as considerations for certain postsecondary education and occupational choices. Adaptive behavior scales can provide assessments of current daily living, communication, social, and independent living behaviors, and areas needing special planning or intervention. Personality assessment procedures may reflect some degree of adjustment in emotional and behavioral areas, highlight areas of strength or need that can be used in instructional or employment placement decisions, and indicate areas for guidance and counseling. Aptitude tests may provide relative areas of ability in domains associated with certain occupational skills for planning vocational or applied technology instruction in high school and for postsecondary education or training options. Interest assessments are designed to suggest current areas of interest, which opens up a variety of options for exploration and experience, both at school and in the community. Finally, medical laboratory procedures, although not a traditional educational assessment approach, can provide basic screening on health and physical status that may give new perspectives on students' energy levels or persisting health problems that have direct bearing on educational decisions and considerations for employment training and placement.

Among the published standardized assessment instruments available, only a few target the primary domains of transition planning, such as postsecondary education or training; employment; and life skills related to living arrangements, independent living, consumer skills, communication, personal–social skills, health, and self-determination. Adaptive behavior scales come the closest to focusing on overall transition skills and knowledge domains, but only one of the published adaptive behavior scales, the Weller-Strawser Scales of Adaptive Behavior for the Learning Disabled (Weller & Strawser, 1981), is designed especially for students with learning disabilities. Two examples of domain-referenced achievement tests that have been used in the area of postschool adjustment for well over a decade are the Social and Prevocational Information Battery (Halpern, Raffeld, Irvin, & Link, 1975; Halpern, Irvin, & Munkres, 1986) and Tests for Everyday Living (TEL; Halpern, Irvin, & Landman, 1979). These were designed primarily for students classified under the mild mental retardation category, and although they have not been widely used with students with learning disabilities, they have been used with low-functioning students classified as having learning disabilities. Each of these deserve mention here.

Social and Prevocational Information Battery–Revised (SPIB-R). The SPIB-R (Halpern et al., 1986) is designed to assess knowledge in five long-range-goal areas that are generally agreed to be important for the transition and community adjustment of adolescents and adults with mild mental retardation; those areas include Employability, Economic Self-Sufficiency, Family Living, Personal Habits, and Communication. The nine subtest areas relating to the five major goals areas include Banking, Budgeting, Purchasing Skills, Job Search Skills, Job-Related Behavior, Home Management, Health Care, Hygiene and Grooming, and Ability to Read Functional Signs. The battery was designed primarily for use with junior and senior high school students. The 277 items are true–false statements and are orally administered (except for a few picture items). The estimated time for administration is 20 to 30 minutes, with 20 minutes being the desirable limit.

Tests for Everyday Living. The TEL is an instrument for measuring achievement in seven life skill areas, including Purchasing Habits, Banking, Budgeting, Health Care, Home Management, Job Search Skills, and Job-Related Behavior. It was designed for all junior high school students and average- or low-functioning senior high school students. Students in remedial programs and those classified as having learning disabilities or learning handicaps (*not* students with mild or moderate mental retardation) at both junior and senior high school levels can be included in TEL assessment. The TEL is orally administered, except for 36 items in which reading skills are assessed. The test is intended to be diagnostic at the subtest level, permitting inferences to be made about individual strengths and weaknesses for program planning. There are 245 items in the TEL, and administration time is estimated at 20 to 30 minutes for each subtest. It is recommended that the administration be scheduled over several days.

New standardized instruments are required, to give teachers, school psychologists, and vocational assessment specialists more options. Six current examples of standardized assessment instruments designed specifically for transition planning are The Transition Behavior Scale (McCarney, 1989), the Life Centered Career Education Knowledge Battery (Brolin, 1992), the Quality of Life Questionnaire (Schalock & Keith, 1993), the Quality of School Life Questionnaire (Keith & Schalock, 1995), the Transition Planning Inventory (Clark & Patton, in press), and the Transition Competence Battery for Deaf Adolescents and Young Adults (Reiman & Bullis, 1993). Because of their direct applicability to students with learning disabilities, all but the last of these examples are described briefly below.

The Transition Behavior Scale (TBS). The TBS (McCarney, 1989) was designed to provide a measure of a student's readiness for transition to employment and independent living. It is a scale based on teachers' and employers' observations of behaviors that will be predictive of behavior in society in general and employment specifically. It can be used with students with a wide range of disabilities and severity thereof. The subscales of the TBS comprise the areas of Work Related Behaviors, Interpersonal Relations, and Social/Community Expectations. The scale has 62 items reflecting behaviors that are observed and rated by at least three persons (teachers and/or work supervisors) with primary observational opportunities. The rater is directed to rate each item on a 3-point scale: 0 equals *does not perform the behavior,* 1 equals *performs the behavior inconsistently,* and 2 equals *performs the behavior consistently.* The scale can be completed in approximately 15 minutes. Scoring is simple, and a raw score conversion table provides a percentile ranking for the student for comparison purposes with a national standardization sample. The percentile ranks provide a base of comparison for screening employment and community participation readiness, and aid in identifying areas of concern for transition-readiness decision making.

Life Centered Career Education (LCCE) Knowledge Battery. The LCCE Knowledge Battery (Brolin, 1992) is a curriculum-based instrument designed to assess the career education knowledge and skills of special education students, especially those with mild intellectual and severe learning disabilities in Grades 7 through 12. It is a standardized, criterion-referenced instrument consisting of 200 multiple-choice questions across each of the three domains of the LCCE model (Brolin, 1989) and the Life Centered Career Education Curriculum Program (Brolin, 1992). There are 10 questions for each of the first 20 of the 22 competencies of the LCCE model. The Battery is designed to be used in conjunction with the LCCE Performance Battery (see description in the section on nonstandardized transition assessments).

Quality of Life Questionnaire (QOL.Q). The QOL.Q (Schalock & Keith, 1993) was designed to assess quality of life as an outcome measure for persons with developmental disabilities, but the authors claim that it may be used with any population. Forty items are organized into subscale sections focusing on Satisfaction, Competence/Productivity, Empowerment/Independence, and Social Belonging/Community Integration. In addition to a total score, separate percentile scores are provided for each of the subscales. The scale is administered in an interview format, with questions directed to the individual and responses restricted to a 3-point-scale, forced-choice response format. Administration time is estimated at 20 minutes.

Quality of School Life Questionnaire (QSL.Q). The QSL.Q (Keith & Schalock, 1995) is complementary to the QOL.Q and grew out of the authors' work with the QOL.Q. The QSL.Q's focus on secondary and postsecondary students with disabilities is designed to assess the psychological and social indicators that represent subjective student reactions to and perceptions of life experiences while in school. The scale has 40 items measuring four factors: Satisfaction, Well Being, Social Belonging, and Empowerment/Control. The QSL.Q may be administered to students who have sufficient receptive and expressive language (natural or augmented) to understand and respond to the questions, through either an interview or a written questionnaire format. Administration time is estimated at 15 minutes. A total score can be obtained through hand scoring or through the QSL.Q scoring software. Percentile ranks can be estimated for hand-scored scales or are yielded automatically through the software scoring program. Norms are based on secondary and postsecondary student populations.

Transition Planning Inventory (TPI). The TPI is designed to provide school personnel with a systematic way not only to comply with the federal mandate for addressing transition service planning, but also to engage in the recommended practices in IEP planning for transition services found in many states' transition guidelines. The TPI is composed of four parts: a student form, a family form, a school-based personnel form, and a transition profile form. The student, the student's parents/guardians, and professionals at school participate in the assessment.

The TPI consists of 56 transition planning statements, organized according to the following planning areas: Employment, Further Education/Training, Daily Living, Living Arrangements, Leisure Activities, Community Participation, Health, Self-Determination, Communication, and Interpersonal Relationships. Each of the planning areas has one or more items related to knowledge, skills, or behaviors associated with successful adjustment in that area. The fundamental dimension evaluated in each TPI item is the level of agreement with statements reflecting present level of performance or current level of functioning that the student consistently displays in each planning area. A scale of 0 to 5 (0 equals *disagree*; 5 equals *agree*) provides the rater with a range of agreement over the extent to which the outcome represented in each item has been achieved and is consistently performed. In addition to the ratings of knowledge, skills, and behavior, the TPI student and parent forms request preferences and interests in likely postschool settings (employment, further education/training, and living arrangements). Further, the student form is divided into two parts, with Part 2 presenting 15 questions eliciting responses regarding interests and preferences on current and future activities. A similar component is provided for parents as an optional activity in the administration guide. Both of these sources of information supplement the data on present level of functioning, to help focus planning on the student's preferences and interests as well as his or her strengths and needs. The transition profile form provides a reference for summarizing the information obtained from all parties and for identifying the type of planning that needs to be undertaken (i.e., IEP goals or linkage activities).

Some formal/standardized assessments are inappropriate because of the developers' initial intent to assess behaviors of a particular population (e.g., individuals with mental retardation or deafness). Others may be inappropriate primarily due to the individuals' reading or language difficulties. Still others may be inappropriate because of cultural bias. Based on these major selection factors, some formal instruments/procedures may be inappropriate for any one student with learning disabilities. For this reason, rarely would any formal instrument or procedure be routinely administered to all students.

Informal Assessments

In addition to selected standardized assessment instruments, nonstandardized assessments can be used as designed or with appropriate adaptations with most students with learning disabilities. Keeping in mind the subjective nature of informal, nonstandardized procedures, the following types of assessment provide a variety of options in getting at useful information for planning. Table 7.1 presents sample items from each of the types of nonstandardized instruments or procedures mentioned:

- Situational or observational learning styles assessments;
- Curriculum-based assessment from courses;
- Observational reports from teachers, employers, and parents/ guardians;
- Situational assessments in home, community, and work settings;
- Environmental assessments (specific to student's placement options);
- Personal-future planning activities/procedures;
- Structured interviews with students;
- Structured interviews with parents/guardians/advocates/peers;
- Adaptive, behavioral, or functional skill inventories/checklists;
- Social histories;
- Rating scales of employability, independent living, and personal–social skills;
- Applied technology/vocational education prerequisite skills assessments; and
- General physical examinations.

Hundreds of informal assessment devices or procedures are currently in use with students with disabilities. Most of these are locally developed or are adapted versions of instruments and forms that teachers obtain through exchanges at inservice workshops and conferences. Included most frequently among informal assessments are curriculum-based assessments, short surveys, structured interviews, and checklists that relate to future goals, interests, values, preferences for activities and environments, and the like. Futures planning can be carried out through any one, or a combination, of a number of informal instruments or procedures. Such planning implies no more than a person-centered approach to working toward what is ahead.

Transforming data obtained from nonstandardized assessment instruments or procedures into a present-level-of-performance statement in an IEP is not as difficult as one might believe. The key issue in determining whether scores or data obtained from an assessment instrument

TABLE 7.1

Types of Nonstandardized Assessment Instruments or Procedures, with Sample Items and Information

Instrument/procedure	Sample items/information
Situational/observational learning styles assessment	Does student prefer to learn alone or in groups? Does student prefer visual or auditory input?
Curriculum-based assessment (course specific)	Name the three branches of the U.S. government. What does *toxic* mean?
Observational reports	M. C. has been absent 10 days in 6 weeks. P. M. has been turning in homework assignments regularly and on time in April. L. P. completed all tasks assigned every day this week.
Situational assessments (home, school, or community)	M. C. can perform multiple step tasks accurately in the kitchen (e.g., follows a recipe). P. M. cannot perform simple arithmetic operations beyond second-grade level. L. P. has a driver's license and drives to school.
Environmental assessments	M. C. is expected to prepare weekday evening meals for a family of five. P. M. is in a basic general math class with ninth-grade students this semester. L. P. lives 8 miles from town in an isolated hill country area; parents depend on her for family shopping.
Personal futures assessments	What is your dream in life? What is your greatest fear of the future?

Table continues

TABLE 7.1 (cont.)

Instrument/procedure	Sample items/information
Structured interviews with students	What do you like to do with your free time? What are three occupations that interest you?
Structured interviews with parents/guardians	What would you like to see M. C. doing after she leaves school next year? Where and with whom would you like P. M. to live when he leaves home?
Adaptive, behavioral, or functional skills assessments	Does M. C. manage her own money? Does P. M. use the bus to get to town? Can L. P. launder clothes independently?
Social histories	M. C. has shown consistent problems in interpersonal relationships with male peers. Since P. M.'s family moved and he went to live with his grandmother, he has run away from home six times.
Rating scales (employability, independent living, personal–social skills, etc.)	Follows directions without prompts. Relates well to co-workers. Cleans bathroom fixtures and floors.
Prerequisite skills assessments	Can perform linear measurements to 1/16th accuracy. Can multiply and divide fractions (with or without a calculator). Can demonstrate safety procedures on drill press, band saw, and jointer.
General physical examination	M. C.'s weight for her height indicates possible problems in nutritional intake. P. M.'s blood pressure, pulse rate, and shortness of breath after exercise need further evaluation.

are appropriate for use on an IEP is whether or not the instrument is valid. It is unfortunate that educators typically accept the published validity data from a standardized test manual as documentation of validity, when they are clearly only an indication of validity for a particular group of individuals, not necessarily for any one individual. Conversely, educators feel less confident in using a nonstandardized instrument that is designed specifically for a particular population but is intended to be used and interpreted with one individual at a time. If the persons using nonstandardized assessment instruments agree that the items have face validity for an individual student, and that the findings are reasonable for that student or support what is already known about him or her from observations or other data sources, then the results of the instrument may be affirmed as useful for planning and making decisions. It is important to include the student and his or her parents or guardians in this determination of face validity and appropriateness of results regarding present level of performance on the IEP. Documentation of such a determination should help to avoid a challenge of school assessment data at a later date.

Some nonstandardized instruments focusing on transition knowledge and skills are published and thus gain a wider user audience than those that are locally developed. Three examples of published instruments or procedures are the Enderle-Severson Transition Rating Scale (Enderle & Severson, 1991), the Life Centered Career Education Performance Battery (Brolin, 1992), and the McGill Action Planning System (Vandercook & York, 1989). Each of these is described below.

Enderle-Severson Transition Rating Scale (ESTR Scale). The ESTR Scale (Enderle & Severson, 1991) is a nonstandardized, criterion-referenced assessment device used to provide a statement of the transition needs of any student with a disability (ages 14 through 21). The subscales of the ESTR Scale are titled Jobs and Job Training, Recreation and Leisure, Home Living, Community Participation, and Post-Secondary Training and Learning Opportunities. There are 130 items on the assessment portion, plus 6 items related to specific actions that should be taken for most students with disabilities. The student's classroom teacher and a parent or primary caregiver individually rate each item on the scale as Yes ("learner performs this behavior independently and consistently") or No. The scale provides subscale scores and a total performance score. The "Framework for Transition Planning" on the back page of the scale is designed to apply the assessment results to the transition planning process.

LCCE Performance Battery. The LCCE Performance Battery is a nonstandardized, criterion-referenced instrument that accompanies the standardized LCCE Knowledge Battery. The Performance Battery is designed to assess critical life skills and includes 5 items each for 21 of the 22 LCCE competency areas. The response format includes a combination of open-ended questions on worksheets and actual performance activities related to life skills and adult demands. For example, a student may be asked to respond verbally to a problem or task, or to demonstrate skill through a hands-on task. Correct responses to four of the five items (80%) on 1 of the 21 competencies indicates mastery level for that competency area. The Performance Battery was developed to complement the LCCE Knowledge Battery, because knowledge itself is not always a valid predictor of a student's ability or inclination to perform required tasks.

McGill Action Planning System (M.A.P.S.).   The M.A.P.S. (Vandercook & York, 1989) is a published structured interview procedure for futures planning. Questions are systematically posed across a variety of life situations and environments to elicit information that can lead to specific planning statements for an individual. A parallel system is the Personal Futures Planning process based on the "circle of friends" concept of interdependence (Perske, 1988). Both of these systems are used primarily with students with severe or multiple disabilities, allowing parents or guardians, friends, and interested others to express their hopes, dreams, and fears about the future for the individual with a disability. Even so, the format is applicable to any disability group, and this type of assessment should not be discounted for students with learning disabilities.

Table 7.2 presents a summary of the current published standardized and nonstandardized transition assessment instruments, indicating target populations and special features of each of the instruments. An expanded list of commercially available tests and assessment procedures addressing nine critical transition planning areas is presented in the Appendix.

PARENT AND STUDENT PARTICIPATION

Ideal family participation in transition services planning involves the student and his or her parents, guardians, or advocates—individually and collaboratively. The IDEA specified no major change in the expectation for participation of parents/guardians/advocates for the IEP process as it relates to transition planning except in regard to specific notification when transition planning will be part of an IEP meeting. It did add a new dimension, though, with the statement that planned activities involving instruction "must be based on each student's needs, preferences, and interests" regarding long-range goals for instruction, community involve-

TABLE 7.2

Summary of Current Examples of Transition-Referenced Assessment Instruments

Instrument/ procedure name	Target group	Features
Social and Prevocational Information Battery–Revised (Halpern et al., 1986)	Adolescents and adults with mild mental retardation or low functioning students with learning disabilities.	1. Subscales include Banking, Budgeting and Purchasing Skills, Job Skills and Job-Related Behavior, Home Management, Health Care, Hygiene and Grooming, and Ability to Read Functional Words. 2. Orally administered except for items on functional signs. 3. Designed especially for secondary school students. 4. True-false item format. 5. 277 items in the battery. 6. 20–30 minutes' administration time.
Tests for Everyday Living (Halpern et al., 1979)	All junior high students and average to low functioning senior high school students in remedial programs, including those labeled as having learning disabilities or learning handicaps.	1. Subtests include Purchasing Habits, Banking, Budgeting, Health Care, Home Management, Job Search Skills, and Job-Related Behavior. 2. Orally administered except where reading skills are critical to an item. 3. 245 items across seven subtests. 4. Diagnostic at the subtest level. 5. 20–30 minutes estimated administration time per subtest.
Transition Behavior Scale (McCarney, 1989)	Any disability group; mild to severe levels of severity.	1. Subscales include Work-Related Behaviors, Interpersonal Relations, Social/Community Expectations. 2. Ratings are completed by at least three persons. 3. Items are rated on a 3-point scale. 4. Estimated completion time is 15 minutes. 5. Scores in percentile ranks are based on national standardization sample.

Table continues

TABLE 7.2 (cont.)

Instrument/ procedure name	Target group	Features
LCCE Knowledge Battery (Brolin, 1992)	Mild cognitive disabilities; moderate to severe learning disabilities; mild to moderate behavioral disorders; Grades 7–12.	1. Curriculum-based assessment related to LCCE Curriculum. 2. 200 multiple-choice items covering 20 of 22 LCCE competency areas. 3. Standardized on a national sample.
Quality of Life Questionnaire (Schalock & Keith, 1995)	Mild to severe cognitive disabilities; ages 18 and older.	1. Subscales include Satisfaction, Competence/Productivity, Empowerment/Independence, and Social Belonging/Community Integration. 2. Administered in interview format for most persons; alternative format is possible by obtaining two independent ratings and averaging. 3. Items are rated on a 3-point scale. 4. Administration time is estimated at 20 minutes. 5. Scores in percentile ranks are based on standardization sample.
Quality of Student Life Questionnaire (Keith & Schalock, 1995)	All disability populations, ages 14–25; mild through severe levels of disability.	1. Subscales include Satisfaction, Well-Being, Social Belonging, and Empowerment/Control. 2. Administered in interview format for most persons; alternative formats include a written format or obtaining two independent ratings and averaging. 3. Items are rated on a 3-point scale. 4. Administration time is estimated at 15 minutes. 5. Scores in percentile ranks are based on secondary and postsecondary standardization samples.
Transition Planning Inventory (Clark & Patton, 1995)	All disability populations, ages 14–25; mild through severe levels of disability.	1. Areas covered in the inventory include Employment, Further Education/Training, Daily Living, Living Arrangements, Leisure Activities, Community Participation, Health, Self-Determination, Communication, and Personal Relationships.

Table continues

TABLE 7.2 (cont.)

Instrument/ procedure name	Target group	Features
		2. 0–5 rating scale completed independently by student, parent/guardian, and a school representative.
		3. Administration may be self-administration, guided administration, or oral administration.
		4. 56 inventory items plus open-ended items on the student form (optional on parent form) related to preferences and interests.
		5. A profile sheet permits visual comparisons of the respondents' responses to each item.
		6. Planning notes form encourages transformation of relevant assessment data into IEP goals, objectives, and interagency linkages.
Enderle-Severson Transition Rating Scale (Enderle & Severson, 1991)	Any disability group; mild to severe levels of disability; ages 14–21.	1. The scale is an informal, criterion-referenced instrument.
		2. Subscales include Jobs and Job Training, Recreation and Leisure, Home Living, and Post-Secondary Training and Learning Opportunities.
		3. Scale is completed by the student's teacher and a parent or primary caregiver. Framework for transition planning.
LCCE Performance Battery (Brolin, 1992)	Mild cognitive disabilities; moderate to severe learning disabilities; mild to moderate behavioral disorders; Grades 7–12.	1. The battery is a nonstandardized, criterion-referenced instrument providing skill rather than knowledge assessment of critical life skills.
		2. Items are based on skills related to LCCE Curriculum.
		3. Estimated time for administration is 3–4 hours.

Table continues

TABLE 7.2 (cont.)

Instrument/procedure name	Target group	Features
Life Skills Inventory (Brigance, 1995a)	All disability populations, high school ages and adults; mild cognitive disabilities, with reading grade levels 2–8.	1. Subscales including Speaking and Listening, Functional Writing, Words on Common Signs and Warning Labels, Telephone Skills, Money and Finance, Food, Clothing, Health, Travel, and Transportation. 2. Administered individually or in groups; administration may be oral or written. 3. Criterion-referenced assessment, providing specific knowledge and skill assessments for life skill items paired with instructional objectives. 4. Learner Record Book provided to show color-coded record of performance and instructional objectives generated from the results. 5. Optional Program Record Book is available to track progress of a group or class; optional Rating Scales are available to evaluate behavior, attitudes, and other traits related to life skills and employability. 6. Companion assessment to Employability Skills Inventory (Brigance, 1995b).

ment, employment, and other postschool opportunities. Knowledge of a student's needs, preferences, and interests must come out of an assessment process that is focused on these issues. Parents, guardians, and advocates are needed to provide their perspective on the student's needs, preferences, and interests. It may also be important to know the parents', guardians', or advocates' own views of what they prefer for the student, especially when there is a discrepancy between their views and the student's or school's views.

All students with a disability over the age of 16 identified for special education now must be invited to the IEP planning meeting when it relates to transition service issues. Those states that require an Individualized Transition Plan (ITP) in addition to the IEP may or may not have this requirement for the ITP, but, in any case, the federal regulations must prevail as far as the IEP is concerned. This is an important provision, because the school not only has the responsibility of inviting the student, but also must include the student in the planning process in some fashion should the student choose not to attend. The regulations state that when a student chooses not to attend the IEP meeting, the school must "take other steps to ensure that the student's preferences and interests are considered" [34 CFR 300.344 (c)(2)]. The school's responsibility to provide evidence that the student's preferences and interests have been considered could be documented with an assessment procedure that addresses the critical areas of transition service needs required in the IDEA: instruction, community experiences, employment, and other postschool objectives.

USING TRANSITION ASSESSMENT IN DEVELOPING THE IEP

Although a variety of uses exist for the types of information that come out of a systematic transition needs assessment process, a key focus of this chapter is the role transition assessment data play in IEP planning. Transition goals and objectives, along with official linkages with nonschool agencies, should come directly from transition-referenced assessment. The data should have direct implications for instructional program decisions, including program design, program placement, curriculum planning, instructional procedures, and additional assessment requirements. If the concept of "present level of performance" is to be broadened to include transition knowledge and skills and any needs for linkage to postsecondary or adult agency services, it is apparent that assessment practices must extend beyond traditional academic-achievement assessment.

A transition-referenced assessment process actively engages both the parents and the students in the educational process in a way that academic achievement testing does not. The process of asking questions regarding real-life issues serves as a wake-up call to students and parents in a way that a psychoeducational achievement battery can never do. Both one's level of satisfaction with life and how satisfactorily one is meeting life's demands have a direct bearing on how one views the future. Students and parents who tend to approach life without any hope of changing what is happening to them (now or in the future) will see the school and the educational process in a very different way when they are included in the assessment, planning, and implementation of an IEP based on a transition/outcomes approach.

A systematic, comprehensive, transition-referenced assessment approach opens up all kinds of ideas for everyone in the IEP planning process. Some of these ideas require decision making, others only discussion and exploration. Without some sort of focus, it is difficult for a guidance counselor, secondary teacher of students with learning disabilities, or transition coordinator to help students or families explore possibilities, provide information, and make decisions. It is possible that many of the ideas that come out of the assessment process could have been addressed through existing programs and services, had those ideas been expressed previously. The nonstandardized transition assessment approach particularly lends itself to using assessment information for counseling and guidance concurrently with the assessment process. Teachers using certain surveys or checklists in the context of instruction can provide individual or group guidance on the basis of revealed information. Parents can follow up on ideas that were expressed at school, and teachers can do the same for ideas that were expressed at home. In other words, the role of counseling and guidance in transition services is not limited to school guidance counselors. Everyone in the assessment process can participate in exploring ideas that relate to developing an appropriate IEP.

An assessment process and IEP that are focused on little more than the completion of high school diploma requirements are likely to be highly internalized; that is, resources within the school are the logical foci of planning and the primary source of support. An assessment process and IEP that go beyond school achievement goals become more complex. It is particularly important that everyone using information from the transition assessment process have access to others outside the process for unique or complex concerns. It is also important to know when it is critical that a referral be made, rather than wasting time or compounding the problem by attempting to work in isolation or without assistance from referral sources. For example, a student might quite frankly share some information about her physical condition in the process of a physical strength, stamina, and coordination assessment. The piece of information shared may clearly be a medical issue that a school representative would find to be beyond his or her area of expertise and realize that a quick referral is needed. Other areas of concern that might come out of student or family input could include issues related to suicide; incest; child abuse; gang activity; fears; or barriers to full partici- pation at school or in the community, such as lack of clothing, food, hot water, and money for adequate child care. Assessment information may result in a determination that a referral is needed, but confidentiality and appropriate referral procedures must be addressed at the outset. If a student or family member requests confidentiality, then that must be honored. In other cases, general confidentiality and "need to know" criteria should be followed in any referral process or IEP linkages to nonschool agencies.

An important legal use for transition assessment information obtained in developing an IEP is the documentation that it provides. Clearly, documentation of assessment procedures for present level of per- formance for IEP planning, as well as evidence of student participation in the IEP planning process, is important. The data may also provide curcial documentation, in the event that a student's placement or pro- gram service delivery is challenged at a formal hearing or in litigation. Finally, the data may function as the documentation required for stu- dents to be able to access postsecondary education student-assistance services or vocational rehabilitation services.

RECOMMENDATIONS

Assessment for planning transition services for students with learn- ing disabilities need not be overwhelming or take on a life of its own. Assessment must be kept in perspective; it is a means to an end, and never an end in itself. However, because of the state of the field in assess- ment for transition planning, some initial time and effort in planning and implementation is necessary. Some suggestions for developing or expanding current transition planning assessment systems for students with learning disabilities may be in order. The following recommenda- tions might be considered.

1. Select assessment instruments and procedures on the basis of how to answer key questions in a student's individual transition planning: Who am I? What do I want in life, now and in the future? What are some of life's demands that I can meet now? What are the main barriers to getting what I want from school and my community? What are my options in the school and community for preparing me for what I want, now and in the future? The instruments reviewed in this article should provide a repertoire of basic transition assessment instruments, and informal, nonstandardized procedures should be developed for local use.

2. Make transition assessment ongoing. Assessment activities should start as early as possible, but no later than age 14, and continue through life. There may be specific times for intensive assessment activity, and there may be key points in a student's educational progress where certain types of assessment should be planned, but much of what is needed for week-to-week instructional planning is ongoing. If at any point a student is seen as "satisfactorily assessed" in any area (educational, vocational, or personal life skills), such that no more questions need to be asked for planning or instruction, then that student essentially has been declared a static, dehumanized object for the school to handle as it chooses.

3. Use multiple types and levels of assessment. No single assessment approach in transition planning is adequate. The variety of life demands on students for adjustment in school, at home, and in the community indicates the need for a variety of assessment approaches for planning how the students can best meet those demands. Standardized, nonstandardized, quantitative, qualitative, group, individual, educational, noneducational, professional, and nonprofessional approaches each have some value at certain points and for certain needs.

4. Make 3-year psychological reevaluations for all secondary students useful for their next likely placement or self-selected environment. One example of this is that any student at risk for dropping out at age 16 should be identified early enough that the reevaluation is relevant and useful for the agency or agencies most likely to need basic psychological data for eligibility determination. Students moving from middle or junior high schools into high schools who need reevaluations must receive assessments that relate to their preferences and interests for the near future as well as for long-range goals, so that accurate present-level-of-performance data become a basis for realistic and appropriate planning. Any student planning to go on to some type of postsecondary education or training may need some official documentation of the disability so that student assistance services are accessible. Careful selection of assessment instruments can facilitate students' access to other agencies.

5. Think of assessment procedures in terms of efficiency as well as effectiveness. A few accurate, powerful assessment procedures may be more efficient and effective than an extensive array of instruments, forms, and scores based on a "shotgun" approach. Batteries of tests or assessment procedures routinely administered to all students may be not only inappropriate but also inefficient. Assessments that cover a wide range of outcome areas are excellent for screening purposes, but whenever the results of such procedures are too general or not indicative of present level of performance, more specific choices of assessment must follow.

6. Organize assessment data for easy access in IEP planning and instructional programming. Good information that goes unrecorded and resides solely in the memory or inaccessible files of school personnel is not usable. Current recommended practices of portfolio assessment for students and families and well-organized student assessment folders at school are relevant in transition assessment. Some redesign of a school's forms or portfolio formats will be required, in most cases, to accommodate the new sources of transition assessment data.

7. Someone in the school needs to take primary responsibility for soliciting and coordinating various kinds of assessments and evaluations. This does not mean that person has to assume responsibility for doing all of the assessments; assessment is not the responsibility of any one person. School professionals, the student, the family, and all community resource persons are partners in the process of both planning which assessments are needed and collecting the data. See chapter 10 of this book for a description of the role the community transition council plays in community resource partnerships. The fact that transition planning for the IEP depends upon a variety of assessment data suggests that it may be necessary to have "area" assessment coordinators to share in the responsibility. The danger of this approach lies in the possibility that the student will be viewed from a fragmented perspective rather than as a whole person when the data are brought together for planning.

8. Develop a transition assessment approach that is not only culture/ language fair, but also culture/language enhanced. Transition assessment that meets the challenges of multicultural populations requires careful thought. The nature of cultural bias in traditional assessment approaches in psychoeducational assessment is evidence enough of that. There is a great risk of cultural bias in assessing nonacademic knowledge and skills, as well as preferences and interests, when the process is approached from a White, middle class orientation to life. Care must be taken, particularly with nonstandardized or locally developed assessment procedures, that questions are posed in culturally appropriate ways and at an appropriate language level. If and when formal assessments (both standardized and normed) are considered, selection of any instrument or procedure must be based on careful considerations of appropriateness of the instrument or procedure in the areas of content, cultural fairness, age appropriateness, language, and response requirements (e.g., sensory, motor, cognitive).

CONCLUSION

The need for workable transition assessment procedures for students with learning disabilities is urgent. Even as professionals become more sophisticated about assessment, planning, and program and service delivery, new questions arise about how to do each task better and meet the new federal mandates. Still, the IDEA mandate for IEP planning did *not* call for novel kinds of assessment and planning. Furthermore, newly developed transition assessment scales and inventories do not provide an assessment approach that is totally original for adolescent needs assessment. There is the need, however, to look at educational assessment and the boundaries of "present level of functioning" more openly. Fortunately, some existing instruments, procedures, and guidelines do exist that can be used immediately while we develop even better systems. The challenge will be to accomplish quality transition-referenced assessment in the context of all the other demands upon special educators for better outcomes with students with disabilities. The key to this challenge is determining the nature of "better outcomes." The way to do that is through sound assessment practices involving a variety of school personnel, with students and their families actively participating.

APPENDIX: COMMERCIALLY AVAILABLE TESTS/ASSESSMENT PROCEDURES

	Employment	Further Education/Training	Leisure Activities	Daily Living	Community Participation	Health	Self-Determination	Communication	Interpersonal Relationships
Achievement									
Adult Basic Learning Examination		X						X	
Brigance Inventory of Essential Skills		X						X	
Iowa Test of Basic Skills		X						X	
Peabody Individual Achievement Test		X						X	
Woodcock-Johnson Psycho-Educational Battery		X						X	
Adaptive Behavior									
AAMR Adaptive Behavior Scales	X			X	X			X	X
Adaptive Behavior Inventory	X	X		X	X			X	X
Normative Adaptive Behavior Checklist	X		X	X	X			X	X
Scales of Independent Behavior	X		X	X	X			X	X
Vineland Adaptive Behavior Scale	X			X	X			X	X
Street Survival Skills Questionnaire				X	X	X			
Aptitude									
APTICOM Program	X	X							
Armed Services Vocational Aptitude Battery	X	X							
Differential Aptitude Test	X	X							
General Aptitude Test Battery (GATB)	X	X							
JEVS Work Sample System	X								
McCarron-Dial Evaluation System	X								
MESA	X								
Micro-TOWER System	X								
Occupational Aptitude and Interest Scale-2	X	X							
Talent Assessment Program	X								
TOWER System	X								
Communication									
Communicative Abilities in Daily Living								X	
Woodcock Reading Mastery Test								X	
Individual Reading Placement Inventory								X	
Test of Written Language								X	
Functional Capacity									
Functional Assessment Profile	X			X			X	X	X
General Health Questionnaire						X			
Life Functioning Index	X	X		X				X	
Personal Capacities Questionnaire	X			X			X	X	X
Independent Living Behavior Checklist				X	X				
Learning Styles									
Learning Style Inventory	X							X	
Learning Styles and Strategies	X							X	
Manual Dexterity									
Crawford Small Parts Dexterity Test	X								
Minnesota Rate of Manipulation Test	X								
Pennsylvania Bi-Manual Worksample	X								
Purdue Pegboard	X								

Appendix continues

APPENDIX (cont.)

	Employment	Further Education/ Training	Leisure Activities	Daily Living	Community Participation	Health	Self-Determination	Communication	Interpersonal Relationships
Occupational Interest									
California Occupational Preference Survey	X								
Career Assessment Inventory	X								
Career Decision Maker	X								
Career Maturity Inventory	X								
Edwards Personal Preference Schedule	X								
Minnesota Importance Questionnaire	X								
Occupational Aptitude and Interest Scale	X								
Pictorial California Occupational Preference Survey	X								
Reading-Free Interest Inventory	X								
Self Directed Search	X								
Strong-Campbell Interest Inventory	X								
USES Interest Check List	X								
USES Interest Inventory	X								
Wisconsin Career Information System	X								
Personality/Social Skills									
Adult Personality Inventory									X
Analysis of Coping Style									X
Basic Personality Inventory									X
California Personality Inventory									X
Clinical Analysis Questionnaire									X
Differential Personality Questionnaire									X
Katz Adjustment Scale									X
Parent Adolescent Communication Scale									X
Personality Factor Questionnaire									X
Psychological Screening Inventory									X
Rosenberg Self-Esteem Scale									X
Tennessee Self-Concept Scale									X
Work Personality Profile	X								X
Work Values Inventory	X								X
Prevocational/Employability									
Brigance Employability Skills Inventory	X								
Job Readiness Scale	X								
Preliminary Diagnostic Questionnaire	X								
Social and Prevocational Information Battery	X			X	X	X			
Vocational Diagnosis and Assessment of Residual Employability	X								
Vocational Behavior Checklist	X								
Transition/Community Adjustment									
Brigance Life Skills Inventory				X	X	X		X	
Enderle-Severson Transition Scale	X	X	X	X	X				X
LCCE Knowledge and Performance Battery	X		X	X	X	X			X
Social and Prevocational Information Battery	X			X	X	X			
Tests for Everyday Living	X			X	X	X			
Transition Behavior Scale	X			X	X				X
Transition Planning Inventory	X	X	X	X	X	X	X	X	X
Quality of Life Questionnaire							X		X
Quality of Student Life Questionnaire							X		X

8. Making the Transition to Higher Education: Opportunities for Student Empowerment

Making a smooth transition from secondary to postsecondary settings is difficult for any student, but for students with learning disabilities (LD) these changes can be particularly dramatic (Aase & Price, 1987; Dalke & Franzene, 1988; Michaels, 1994; Trapani, 1990). Cowen (1993) pointed out that college-bound students with LD must go through the same process as their non–learning disabled peers, but, because of their learning disabilities, they may face additional challenges that need to be addressed. For example, many college-bound students with learning disabilities do not understand their individual disability, how it affects their learning, or how to describe it to others in plain language (Aune & Ness, 1991; Dalke & Schmitt, 1987; Goldhammer & Brinckerhoff, 1992). After years of academic struggle in high school, these students may view themselves as lacking any learning strengths or abilities, which further lowers their self-concept. Second, many college-able students with learning disabilities lack the content preparation necessary to succeed in college (Cowen, 1991; Dalke & Franzene, 1988; McGuire, Norlander, & Shaw, 1990) or

Reprinted, with changes, from "Making the transition to higher education: Opportunities for student empowerment," by Loring C. Brinckerhoff, *Journal of Learning Disabilities*, Vol. 29, 1996, pp. 118–136. Copyright © 1996 by PRO-ED, Inc.

have not been provided with learning strategies instruction that will permit them to generalize their skills across settings (Bursuck, 1991; Deshler & Schumaker, 1986). Without the prerequisite courses (e.g., mathematics, science, foreign language), high school students with learning disabilities may find that their postsecondary options are limited. Many of these students may need additional guidance on how to find a suitable college program—one with the range of LD support services that will be compatible with their interests, abilities, and perceived needs (Lipkin, 1993; Mangrum & Strichart, 1992; Michaels, Thaler, Zwerlein, Gioglio, & Apostoli, 1988a; Straughn, 1992). Finally, once students with LD have been admitted into college, they often need further assistance in how to *stay* in college so that they can graduate (Block, 1993; Brinckerhoff, Shaw, & McGuire, 1992; Vogel & Adelman, 1992).

Cowen (1993) observed that the "proliferation of services available in colleges and universities requires an extensive search, which requires knowledge of (1) how to read and evaluate the many guides available; (2) how to locate services in colleges not listed in the guides; and (3) how to evaluate the located services" (p. 40). This combination of factors underscores the need for systematic transition planning that should begin early in the student's high school career and continue into college. Effective transition planning must be a student-centered activity that reflects the developmental and educational needs of the student at different grades and times. It also requires the collaborative effort of parents/guardians, secondary personnel, and postsecondary personnel (National Joint Committee on Learning Disabilities, 1994).

Hartman (1993), executive director of the HEATH Resource Center, a national clearinghouse on postsecondary education for individuals with disabilities, suggested that transition planning should be viewed as a bridge "whose size, span, strength, beauty, efficiency, and direction depend on the individual who travels it" (p. 31). The intent of the present article is to examine this bridge and to focus on the central role that the student with LD plays in traversing the span from high school to higher education. Practical suggestions for service providers, teachers, and parents will be included as they relate to supporting students in this transition process.

DIFFERENCES BETWEEN HIGH SCHOOL AND COLLEGE

It is important that all members of the transition planning team consider the many inherent differences between high school and college settings when determining postsecondary options. According to Dalke and Schmitt (1987), as students with LD move from high school to college, they may be confronted with many more challenges than are their peers without learning disabilities. The inherent differences in the structure of these two settings are illustrated in Table 8.1 (Brinckerhoff, Shaw, & McGuire, 1993).

Two of the biggest differences between high school and college concern the amount of in-class time and opportunity for direct teacher contact. High school students are in class about 6 hours a day, and it is not unusual for them to have contact with their teacher five times a week. In comparison, college classes may meet only one to three times a week and thus the opportunities for direct teacher contact are much more limited. Dalke (1993) pointed out that classroom size may also be a variable: High school classes typically have 25 to 30 students, in comparison to college, where some classes may be as large as 200 or 300 students. Studying in high school is often synonymous with doing homework. Students in high school may spend a limited amount of time completing homework assignments; in contrast, many college students spend only 12 hours per week in class but invest 3 to 4 hours per day in studying. Brinckerhoff et al. (1993) noted that in college, studying may mean rewriting lecture notes, paraphrasing information from reading assignments, and integrating information gleaned from a variety of sources (e.g., texts, class lectures, library assignments). DuChossois and Michaels (1994) commented that for students with learning disabilities—who may take longer reading homework, taking notes on assigned work, and/or understanding important concepts in a given assignment—the time investment is often considerably more than for their nondisabled peers. Another contrasting point related to homework concerns the amount and frequency of direct teacher feedback that students receive on their work. In high school, homework is often assigned on a day-to-day basis and students are expected to turn in their homework weekly for feedback. In college, homework assignments are often long range and students are expected to work independently for a grade. Instead of receiving a grade at the end of each chapter or unit, college students may receive a grade only once a month or only during midterms and finals. In high school, students with LD may have been graded based on indicators such as effort or level of improvement; in college, these students may find that they are receiving significantly lower grades than in high school because grading has become less subjective and is based on their level of mastery of course material (Dalke, 1993). In addition, many college students find themselves competing for grades with high-achieving high school graduates, so grading is more competitive.

High school teachers are responsible for teaching a broad range of students and for teaching all students factual content. College professors often expect students to integrate information from a variety of sources, rather than "parroting" back isolated facts. Whereas it may be sufficient

TABLE 8.1
Differences Between High School and College Requirements

	High School	College
Class time	6 hours per day, 180 days Total: 1,086 hours	12 hours per week, 28 weeks Total: 336 hours
Class size	25–30 students.	Up to 300 students.
Study time	Whatever it takes to do your homework—1–2 hrs. per day.	Rule of thumb: 2 hours of study for 1 hr. of class—3–4 hrs. per day.
Tests	Weekly; at the end of a chapter; frequent quizzes.	2–4 per semester; at the end of four-chapter unit; at 8:00 a.m.; after Homecoming.
Grading	Passing grades guarantee you a seat. Performance evaluations may be subjective; based on level of effort or level of improvement.	Satisfactory academic standing requires grades of C or above; performance-based mastery of course content material.
Teaching	Teachers often take attendance. May regularly check notebooks and homework assignments. Teachers lecture from textbook and often use blackboard and worksheets. Teachers impart knowledge and facts.	Professors rarely take attendance. Seldom check homework or monitor daily work. Professors lecture nonstop and rarely teach you the textbook. Professors require library research. Professors challenge you to integrate information from a variety of sources.
Freedom	Structured time. Limits are set by parents, teachers, and other adults. High school buildings are monitored.	Managing time and personal freedom is greatest problem college students face. Self-reliance is the key. College campuses are often sprawling.

Note. Adapted from "Differences Between High School and College Requirements," by S. Shaw, L. Brinckerhoff, and J. McGuire, 1991, LDA Multidisciplinary Journal, 2, p. 22. Copyright 1991 by Learning Disabilities Association. Adapted by permission.

for high school students to memorize facts, college professors often require students to think analytically, as well as to synthesize abstract information (Shaw, Brinckerhoff, Kistler, & McGuire, 1991). Another related concern is that secondary teachers often provide external reinforcement of students' work without ever helping the students to develop the capacity to self-monitor their progress (DuChossois & Michaels, 1994). As a result, many students with learning disabilities exit high school without the ability to monitor their own work or predict academic outcomes.

Life and time demands in college are very different from those in high school. High school students find that their time is structured by limitations set by parents, teachers, and other adults. College environments require students to function independently by managing their time and organizing their days (and nights). Students are faced with the freedom to make their own decisions about scheduling time, choosing their classes and majors, and governing their social life (DuChossois & Michaels, 1994). In addition, most high schools are in one building, which can serve to control student access and make teacher supervision easier, versus college campuses, which may be a mile long and contain dozens of different buildings. Brinckerhoff et al. (1993) stressed that an increased level of personal freedom is one of the biggest adjustments that students with learning disabilities need to make as they enter college. Clearly, these dramatic differences between the demands of high school settings and those that characterize higher education create a challenging climate for students with learning disabilities.

A TIMETABLE FOR TRANSITION PLANNING

The National Joint Committee on Learning Disabilities (NJCLD; 1994) recently expressed its concern that "many students with learning disabilities do not consider postsecondary options (two and four-year colleges and vocational schools) because they are not encouraged, assisted or prepared to do so" (p. 98). The NJCLD further stated that many students with learning disabilities *should* select postsecondary education options, and, if transition plans are designed and implemented effectively, these students will be successful. For these objectives to be realized, transition planning requires young adults with learning disabilities to become actively involved in making decisions about their futures.

A review of recent data on secondary school outcomes indicates that students with LD are graduating from high school in record numbers each year (Henderson, 1992; U.S. Department of Education, 1994; Vogel & Adelman, 1992). Mangrum and Strichart (1992) indicated that studies now show that as many as two thirds of young adults diagnosed with learning disabilities want to extend their education beyond high school. More than half (52%) earn a high school diploma, and with the diploma often comes the perception that they are prepared for higher education. And, by and large, the secondary programs that are intended to shape these students and develop their skills for higher education have been successful (Scheiber & Talpers, 1987; Trapani, 1990). This is further evidenced by the fact that during the last decade, the number of college freshmen with learning disabilities has increased to over 35,000 students (Hartman, 1992).

The notion of transition planning is not new. Ideally, a transition planning team should comprise the student, parent(s), psychologist, guidance counselor, LD specialist, general education teachers, and, in the case of many high school seniors, a postsecondary LD service provider. Each team member has an important role to play in fostering student independence and decision making. However, many high school students frequently comment that they were not included in the decision-making process or that their parents "set everything up for them." Unfortunately, many well-meaning parents and high school personnel have protected these students from failure and stress by making transition decisions for them. Individualized transition planning should be viewed as a golden opportunity for students to shape their own academic destinies by learning about their disabilities, asking questions, presenting ideas, and advocating for themselves. This process should also be viewed as a critical juncture in students' lives for focusing attention on what it will take for them to achieve success and independence as adults (see Field, chapter 4 of this book; Haugh & McDonald, 1994). By developing a timetable for college planning that centers on the students, it will be possible to empower them in becoming active members of the transition planning team. Furthermore, now that all states are required by law to have a statement of a transition plan, it is incumbent upon service providers to carefully examine current practices regarding transition planning to ensure that these students will be prepared for the academic, vocational, and social expectations of life after high school. A timetable approach that begins in eighth grade and concludes with high school graduation allows students to gradually assume greater responsibility for their own learning outcomes and to view the postsecondary-planning process as a series of coordinated steps that involves input from a number of supporting players over a period of years.

One new, innovative approach developed to meet this objective is the Transition Planning Inventory (TPI; Clark & Patton, 1994). This instrument is designed for use with high school students with disabilities in planning their transition from school to adult life. The TPI is intended to "provide school personnel with a systematic way to address critical transition planning areas that are mandated by the Individuals with Disabilities Education Act (IDEA) and that are based on information regarding the student's needs, preferences and abilities" (Clark & Patton, 1994, p. 1). The form consists of three surveys, one to be completed by each student, the parent(s), and a school representative. For a more in-depth discussion of the TPI, readers are encouraged to consult Gary Clark's chapter, "Transition Planning Assessment for Secondary-Level Students with Learning Disabilities," which appears in this book.

Aune and Ness (1991) developed a comprehensive transition-related curriculum for high school students with learning disabilities that could supplement the Transition Planning Inventory. It includes units on enhancing students' understanding of learning disabilities, interpreting information from initial diagnostic reports into everyday language, understanding the Individualized Education Program (IEP), and actively planning for the future in vocational and postsecondary settings. An accompanying videotape presents realistic scenes that demonstrate and reinforce many of the self-advocacy skills taught in the curriculum. For a more in-depth discussion of curriculum issues, readers are encouraged to consult the chapters by Patricia Sitlington and Mary Cronin in this book.

Transition Programming Before High School

The transition from middle school to high school in itself appears to be a formidable challenge for many students with disabilities. Recent data from the U.S. Department of Education (1994) indicated that one quarter of all students with disabilities age 14 or older dropped out of high school before earning a degree. Of the 129,000 students with learning disabilities exiting high school in 1994, 48% did not receive a diploma (U.S. Department of Education, 1994). Zigmond and Thornton (1985) conducted a follow-up of graduates and dropouts with and without learning disabilities who attended an urban high school. The reported dropout rates for students with learning disabilities was 54.2%, whereas nondisabled peers were dropping out at rate of 32.8%. School records also indicated that most students left upon finishing ninth grade, which is the point at which transition planning for higher education should begin. Given this backdrop, it is apparent that transition planning should begin even earlier than current practice or legal requirements dictate under the Individuals with Disabilities Education Act. A handful of progressive states (e.g., New Jersey) have stipulated that all students with disabilities age 14 or older have an IEP with a transition component, which goes beyond the federal mandate of beginning transition planning at age 16. This revision is also in keeping with the recommendation made by the NJCLD (1994) that "student involvement in transition activities must be initiated as *early as possible* and no later than age 16" (p. 99). The following section will present a 5-year timetable for comprehensive transition planning that addresses the educational, vocational, and psychosocial needs of adolescents with learning disabilities as they move through middle school and high school toward graduation. High points from this discussion are presented in the Appendix.

Preparing for High School Success.   For students with learning disabilities to be successful in higher education, they first need to make the transition from middle school to high school. Guidance counselors, parents, special education teachers, and general education teachers need to encourage these students to take the most academically challenging program possible in the most integrated setting. Traditional resource room models that focus solely on academic remediation and content tutoring will not give these students the advantages they need when they move to content-driven coursework (Spector, Decker, & Shaw, 1991). DuChossois and Michaels (1994) found that many high school students with learning disabilities used their resource room as a glorified study hall. The resource room must not be "a place where students passively sit and hear reiterations of what has been presented in class. Rather, the emphasis should be placed on developing an understanding of the way the students learn and then teaching students how to learn better and more efficiently" (DuChossois & Michaels, 1994, p. 85). Aune (1991) interviewed high school students about what they were taught to do to compensate for their weaknesses; the most common response was, "Try harder." She also found that the repertoires of study strategies routinely used by high school students with learning disabilities were extremely limited; only 15% of the students reported that they had been taught any type of study strategy during the previous year.

During eighth grade, students should be taught a variety of skills that promote better study habits, time management, test preparation, and test taking. These students should also be encouraged to actively participate in their IEP meetings and to suggest goals for inclusion in that document. For some students with LD, it may be opportune to systematically explore vocational service options through the Division of Rehabilitation Services in addition to addressing educational services delivered through the special education system. Career exploration that includes vocational classes, field trips to work sites, and volunteer work experiences can help students identify preferences and interests in vocational areas. Furthermore, independent decision making and self-determination can be fostered by helping adolescents with learning disabilities learn how to set goals at school and home and on a job.

Transition Programming in the Freshman Year

Cowen (1993) carefully reviewed this critical juncture in students' education and development. She concluded that during the freshman year of high school, students for whom postsecondary education is appropriate should (a) develop a clear understanding of what learning disabilities are and are not, (b) develop a general understanding of the nature of their disability, (c) learn about their legal rights, (d) select courses that will prepare them academically for college, (e) explore career options and (f) develop greater independence. Each of these goals will be discussed as they relate to the transition planning process and the central role that the student with LD plays in reaching these goals.

   1. *Develop an understanding of learning disabilities.* The first step toward building future determination skills requires students to gain an understanding about the nature of what learning disabilities are and are not (Brinckerhoff, 1993b; Goldhammer & Brinckerhoff, 1992; Phillips, 1990). LD teachers should give students a general overview about learning disabilities and discuss basic definitional issues and common terminology (e.g., *ADHD, dyslexia*). They may need to clarify that learning disabilities are not the same as "learning problems" or "learning differences" but rather, by definition, are neurologically based, intrinsic to the individual, and present throughout the life span.

   2. *Develop an understanding of their own learning disability.* The second step to building greater self-advocacy skills is to help students develop a greater understanding of their own unique learning disability (Aune & Ness, 1991; Brinckerhoff, 1994; Wilson, 1994). Once students understand that a learning disability is not a reflection of limited intellectual ability and that it will not be outgrown, they may be more receptive to discussing their unique profile of strengths and limitations. Parents and LD teachers can be instrumental in helping students understand how their learning disabilities affect their lives, both academically and socially. Cowen (1993) believes that parents can be particularly helpful in assisting their child by identifying areas of cognitive strengths, athletic prowess, and creative talents (Cowen, 1993). Parents should also encourage their sons or daughters to participate in extracurricular activities that may further broaden horizons. They can help by communicating their confidence in their children's ability to be successful in high school and by actively encouraging them to reach for postsecondary options (NJCLD, 1994). Parents' primary role during the initial stages of the transition planning process involves encouraging their children to reach for realistic educational goals and helping them understand their profiles of strengths and weaknesses (Cordoni, 1987).

   LD specialists can further expand upon what the parent addresses at home by helping students understand the connection between their unique learning styles and academic performance. Aune (1991) pointed out that a student's understanding and acceptance of his or her strengths, weaknesses, and learning disability form the foundation for all other transition activities. One way of accomplishing this heightened awareness is to have students write a brief paragraph describing their strengths and weaknesses (Johnson, 1989). This writing sample can be included in a journal and used as a baseline by LD teachers when determining how much students have learned about their learning disability over time.

3. *Learn about their rights under the law.* Another related component of self-determination awareness that should be addressed by LD teachers involves teaching students about their legal rights under Section 504 and the Americans with Disabilities Act (Brinckerhoff & Eaton, 1991; Brinckerhoff et al., 1992; Scott, 1991). LD support staff should be prepared to discuss the ramifications of these laws in both high school and higher education settings. Emphasis should be placed on the fact that the law initially focused on physical access issues (e.g., ramps, accessible bathrooms) but more recently has expanded its scope to encompass programmatic access for individuals with hidden disabilities. The major components of the ADA should also be highlighted, with particular emphasis on accommodations that are appropriate for work, such as using tape-recorded materials or laptop computers with built-in spelling- and grammar-check functions (Kincaid, 1992). Many high school students with learning disabilities do not realize that they have a legal right to these accommodations and that academic adjustments are not "favors" to be granted by their general education teachers but requirements under the law. Many students with learning disabilities have not yet discovered that the academic adjustments provided in high school and college must also be offered as "reasonable accommodations" in the workplace under the ADA (Heyward, Lawton, & Associates, 1991).

4. *Select courses that will prepare students for college.* Guidance personnel need to be made aware that academic preparation begins with the selection of appropriate classes that will afford students with LD maximum opportunity for accessing higher educational opportunities (McGuire et al., 1990). Too often students with learning disabilities are counseled to take "modified," or simplified, courses, which allow academic credit toward graduation but provide only limited training for transition to postsecondary education or employment (Shaw et al., 1991). Whenever possible, waivers from mathematics or foreign language classes should be avoided in high school in lieu of course substitutions, because waivers may substantially limit a student's options when applying to college. Thus, parents as well as the students need to be informed about the implications a waiver can have for the college admissions process. If a waiver is granted in high school, it should be done only after the student has attempted a foreign language class with resource support and made a "good faith effort." Furthermore, the student's diagnostic testing should substantiate the need for the waiver based on a language-based learning disability with related processing deficits (Anderson & Brinckerhoff, 1989).

High school guidance personnel also need to be made aware that traditional resource room models that feature content and basic skills tutoring approaches may not provide these students with adequate preparation to succeed in college-preparatory courses (Decker, Spector, & Shaw, 1992). Subject matter tutoring may act as a short-term Band-Aid, but it does not provide strategic-learning and problem-solving skills that transfer across the curriculum (Shaw et al., 1991). Ideally, guidance personnel and high school LD support teachers should collaborate to be sure that students with learning disabilities are accessing study skills courses that have learning strategy instruction woven throughout (Bursuck, 1991; Decker et al., 1992; Ellis, 1990; Seidenberg, 1986).

For over a decade, researchers at the University of Kansas (e.g., Deshler, Schumaker, Lenz, & Ellis, 1984) have studied the benefits of a learning strategies approach, versus a more traditional content-focused approach, for teaching adolescents with LD. The research literature suggests that students with learning disabilities are either "strategy deficient" or unable to spontaneously tap previously learned strategies they need for a given task (Alley, Deshler, Clark, Schumaker, & Warner, 1983; Wade & Reynolds, 1989; Wang & Palincsar, 1989; Wong, 1987; Wong & Jones, 1992). The Strategic Intervention Model (SIM) developed at the University of Kansas Institute for Research in Learning Disabilities (KU-IRLD) includes a variety of strategies that have been specifically designed for these low-achieving students. The instruction systematically moves through an eight-stage process called the SIM Instructional Methodology, which begins with a heavy emphasis on an interactive process that is guided by the teacher (focusing on discussions of rationales for the use of the strategy, specification of strategy components, and explicit models by the teacher) and proceeds to an emphasis on student mediation of the learning process. If students are empowered with new strategic approaches to learning, they will be able to independently break down and prioritize assignments for themselves.

Block (1993) observed that students with learning disabilities often have inadequate organizational and study skills, as well as deficits in some combination of written language, reading, and mathematical skills. They may have difficulty locating and organizing the materials needed for study, allocating sufficient time for study, finding the right environment in which to study, making and adhering to schedules, or identifying the points they need to study. Seidenberg (1986) pointed out that many students with learning disabilities also exhibit skill deficits in reading-related study strategies (e.g., comprehension monitoring, summarizing, outlining, scanning). She maintained that these students can be supported in a regular academic curriculum by teaching them specific learning strategies or metacognitive skills. Explicit instruction in all these areas is critical if students are going to meet the demands of college (McGuire, Hall, &

Litt, 1991; Siperstein, 1988). Generalizable skills, such as outlining and note taking, memory techniques, test-taking strategies, and basic word-processing skills should be incorporated into the standard resource room curriculum. As a result of this kind of strategy-based training, high school students with learning disabilities can become more responsible learners (Bursuck & Jayanthi, 1993; Deshler et al., 1984).

Cowen (1993) stated that if students enter high school with basic competencies in reading and math (e.g., functional literacy skills at the fifth- or sixth-grade level), guidance counselors should encourage these student to take college preparatory courses. If they lack these basic skills, then deficits in reading or mathematics should be addressed early on in the student's high school career.

5. *Explore career options.* High school guidance counselors should encourage students to participate in a career exploration program. Biller (1985) stated that career exploration programs develop the following:

1. Awareness of the need to plan ahead and the relationship between present and future events;

2. Awareness of information necessary for career planning and knowledge of how and where to get it;

3. Understanding of how to make decisions;

4. Knowledge of general career-development information;

5. Knowledge of specific information about a variety of occupations and the organization of the world of work; and

6. Knowledge of specific information about clusters of occupations.

6. *Develop greater independence.* In addition to exploring possible career areas and occupational clusters, secondary students with learning disabilities need to actively work with their counselors and teachers to determine which skills are considered basic within the context of vocational preparation for employment. Michaels (1994) noted that many of the same skills described as important in postsecondary settings may also be critical in the world of work. He added that "preparation for transition and employment must consist of a delicate balance of capitalizing on strengths while simultaneously developing compensatory strategies for weaknesses" (p. 274). One of the best ways for students with LD to determine exactly what their strengths and weaknesses are and to evaluate their own level of independence is to secure a summer job. Maintaining the discipline of working a job will afford these students an opportunity to determine firsthand the viability of specific career clusters. For a more in-depth discussion of the importance of work experience at the secondary level for students with LD, readers are encouraged to consult Rebecca

Evers's chapter, "The Positive Force of Vocational Education: Transition Outcomes for Youth with Learning Disabilities," in this book.

Transition Programming in the Sophomore Year

By their sophomore year, students should be able to clarify the exact nature of their learning disabilities, as well as continue to develop and refine academic skills, explore career options, and further their independence (Cowen, 1993). One way to further a student's understanding of his or her learning disability is to help him or her understand the psychoeducational report. This can be a formidable challenge, as all too often the diagnostic report contains terminology that is too technical or vague for students to fully understand (Anderson, 1993; Anderson & Brinckerhoff, 1989). High school support staff need to interpret these diagnostic findings in a format that enables students to understand their unique profile of strengths and weaknesses and to identify the accommodations they need to compensate for their deficits. Students should be given an opportunity to meet with a school psychologist or LD specialist to discuss the psychoeducational evaluation and relate these findings to their self-perceptions and experiences. Anderson pointed out that analyzing diagnostic reports is frequently the most expedient method for determining appropriate academic adjustments and modifications. Consequently, students may need to be reminded that if accommodations are to be provided by their general education teachers, they should be rooted in the findings and recommendations contained in the diagnostic report (Anderson & Brinckerhoff, 1989). Important points contained in the report should be discussed, questions raised, and terminology clarified.

1. *College prep courses.* High school guidance counselors may need to remind students about the importance of continuing to take college preparatory classes. McGuire et al. (1990) held that "a retreat to lower-track classes at this point will limit the student's postsecondary options" (p. 72). Guidance personnel also need to be sure that the student is not scheduled in the resource room for assistance during the same time slot as essential college prep courses. If students do not select certain college prep courses, such as Algebra I or Chemistry, during their freshman or sophomore years in high school, they may find themselves woefully underprepared for the rigors of a college curriculum. Furthermore, many college admissions officers carefully consider the *quality* of the high school courses the student elected. As important as general education classes might be, college-bound students should be advised to avoid more than one or two such classes (e.g., "Nutrition Today" or "Basic Math 99") each semester. Although it may look impressive on a high school transcript that a student with LD has earned all As, these basic classes, or electives,

do little to excite college admissions personnel, who routinely recalculate high school GPAs based on solid course work. It is better for a student with LD to take a mainstreamed college prep class and earn a C+ than to enroll in a noncollege course and earn a grade of A.

It is often better to advise college-bound students with learning disabilities to take more difficult classes with the support of the LD teacher than to allow them to forgo the opportunity to challenge themselves. High school students with LD should also be advised to steer away from advanced placement or honors classes if those courses will either demand a disproportionate amount of their study time or pull their overall high school GPA down. However, if the student with LD can earn a solid grade of B or above in one of these accelerated classes, this could help to support his or her application to a competitive college by further indicating that the student is "otherwise qualified" despite the learning disability. The high school transcript should be reviewed carefully at this midpoint in the student's career to be sure it reflects the quality of course work necessary for entrance to college. If it does not meet those standards, then the program of study should be upgraded accordingly.

2. *Planning.* Effective transition planning and program implementation are achieved through collaborative effort, involving the student, family, school, community agencies, employers, and adult service providers (Haugh & McDonald, 1994). One of the key roles often assumed by LD teachers is the planning and coordination of the transition planning team (NJCLD, 1994). The transition team leader assigned to the student's case must be sensitive to cultural differences and the values of the student and family when he or she recommends resources and collaborates with other high school staff. The transition team leader also needs to be sure that the student does not become a passive bystander in the process of carving out transition goals in the IEP or the Individual Transition Plan (ITP). The IEP document becomes the blueprint for service delivery and for transition planning. In keeping with the Individuals with Disabilities Education Act (IDEA), which mandates that students become active voices in transition planning at age 16, students should be at the center of this process, with the LD teacher serving as the team coordinator in conjunction with school personnel and the parent(s). Ideally, student input about secondary and postsecondary goals, curriculum options, and the level of support services needed to meet these goals should be solicited by teachers in advance of the meeting. During the planning meeting, students should be encouraged to express concerns, show preferences, and give opinions based on personal experience. They may also need to learn how to express their thoughts at the meeting in a way that makes others listen to them and respect their views (West et al., 1992).

Students should be encouraged by LD specialists or school psychologists to develop transition planning goals that include trying out accommodations or technological aids, such as taped textbooks, laptop computers, or extended time on exams, while they are still in the structured setting of high school. LD teachers need to assure high school students that it is to their advantage to use these accommodations in their general education and college prep classes, rather than trying to "tough it out" without benefiting from academic adjustments. During the sophomore year, LD teachers and guidance personnel should be sure that students with learning disabilities are aware of the range of accommodations that are available to them for the PSATs, so that when they take the Scholastic Assessment Test I (SAT) or Admissions College Test (ACT) in their junior year, they will have already experimented with a variety of testing accommodations.

3. *Learning-strategies instruction.* If a high school student is lacking basic skills, then the remediation of these skills should be addressed as soon as possible. If students have mastered basic remedial skills, then it may be appropriate to teach them a variety of learning strategies. The LD specialist and the student should work together in selecting a repertoire of learning strategies for the student to master that will promote academic success (Dalke, 1991). These skills may be taught in a resource room setting or as an integral part of a study skills course. Bursuck and Jayanthi (1993) pointed out that a learning strategies approach is "much more comprehensive than most study skills programs, in that in addition to learning how to perform particular skills, students also learn why and when to use these skills as well as how to monitor their implementation" (p. 179). Spector et al. (1991) noted that when learning strategies, organization, and time management skills are integrated into the resource room curriculum, students become more responsible learners, thus limiting the role of school personnel to one of progress monitoring. Without such skills, students with learning disabilities are often ill-prepared for the transition to postsecondary education and employment.

4. *Fostering self-determination.* Individuals with learning disabilities must be empowered with skills to advocate for themselves. Ideally, parents, high school teachers, and guidance personnel should prepare students with learning disabilities for adulthood by teaching them self-determination skills. This training would focus on helping students to set goals for themselves and then to actively develop and implement a plan to attain those goals (Wilson, 1994). In addition, young adults need to be able to monitor their efforts at reaching their goals and "to modify the task-attack strategy and time lines for goal attainment based upon feedback from a variety of sources" (Wilson, 1994, p. 180). The skills that are designed to enhance self-advocacy often involve assertive communication, understanding oneself as a learner, and utilizing self-monitoring techniques. Unfortunately, the research literature suggests that despite their importance, self-advocacy skills are seldom directly taught in high school

(Aune & Ness, 1991; Dalke & Franzene, 1988; Ryan & Price, 1992; Wilson, 1994). Students with learning disabilities need to develop a talent for realistic self-appraisal and risk taking (NJCLD, 1994); by being knowledgeable about themselves and skilled in knowing when and where to self-advocate, these students can obtain personal independence and meet success in both their educational and their career goals (Brinckerhoff, 1993b; Goldhammer & Brinckerhoff, 1992). One intervention approach that has been particularly successful with students who have difficulties with social interactions is to encourage them to participate in a support group (Block, 1993; Johnson, 1989; Price, 1988). Support groups can give students an opportunity to openly discuss their personal frustrations with school, teachers, parents, and their friends in a supportive environment. A trained group leader or facilitator can assist these adolescents in refining an array of social interaction skills, such as maintaining eye contact, using the appropriate voice or tone, using good body posture, and good listening (Johnson, 1989; Price, 1993). For an in-depth discussion of the role that self-advocacy plays in promoting independence and fostering self-esteem in adolescents, readers are encouraged to consult Sharon Field's chapter, "Self-Determination Instructional Strategies for Youth with Learning Disabilities," in this book.

  5. *Career exploration.* Compared to their nondisabled peers, individuals with learning disabilities are often more focused on the present, due to the disability itself, which is often characterized by problems with abstract thought and an inability to perceive the "big picture." As a result, many high school students with LD have particular problems with making long-range vocational or educational plans (Michaels et al., 1988a; Wehman, 1992). They may not choose to actively explore the range of options available to them after high school because they are more focused on the present. Given that postsecondary planning takes years of forethought, this lack of direction often places these students at a disadvantage. Consequently, young adults with learning disabilities may need assistance from parents, teachers, and guidance personnel in order to develop their understanding of

- the world of work,
- the differences between the work and school environment,
- individual strengths and weaknesses,
- ways to maximize strengths and minimize weaknesses,
- ways to incorporate interests and strengths into career plans, and
- setting short- and long-term goals. (Michaels et al., 1988a, p. 50)

Students should also continue career exploration through participation in extracurricular activities, hobbies, and a variety of work experiences (Cowen, 1993). Identified interests, aptitudes, values, and opportunities provide a basis for tentative occupational decisions. Evaluating interests in these experiences contributes to career maturity. For students with LD, the learning disability itself may be an important influence in the choice of a major or career. Self-administered, self-scoring instruments, such as The Self Directed Search (Holland, 1971), can be provided to the student for a cursory assessment of interests as they relate to various occupational fields. SIGI PLUS (Educational Testing Service, 1991), an interactive computerized interest and career inventory, affords the student an opportunity to participate in a more detailed exploration of likes, dislikes, values, and goals in relation to potential majors and careers. Students may need to be cautioned not to make hasty career decisions based on an area of weakness or on what they think their parents want them to do.

Michaels et al. (1988a) stated that "separating parents' wishes and desires from realities and abilities is one issue that must be confronted by students" (p. 72). He further acknowledged that the transition from high school to college often marks the beginning of the student's adult life. The attendant changes are difficult for both the student and the parents. DuChossois and Michaels (1994) suggested that, to address these transition concerns, secondary special education teachers implement a six-step strategy to prepare students with learning disabilities for the demands of the postsecondary environment. This strategy focuses on (a) reviewing college catalogs, (b) reviewing sample college textbooks, (c) reviewing college course syllabi, (d) interviewing college students with learning disabilities, (e) providing direct instruction in accessing student support services, and (f) building transitional skill training into the curriculum. Ideally, all these long-term planning skills would be incorporated directly into the student's IEP.

Transition Programming in the Junior Year

The junior year is perhaps the most critical year for high school students as they lay the final groundwork for their postsecondary experience. During this time, planning should focus on matching the student's interests and abilities with the most appropriate postsecondary setting. Patton and Polloway (1992) pointed out that a wide range of educational and vocational opportunities are now available to young adults with learning disabilities. Guidance personnel can be especially helpful by describing the diverse range of 2- and 4-year options available to students after graduation based on the counselors' own personal visits to these institutions. The educational alternatives available after high school include 4-year colleges and universities, junior and community colleges, vocational or technical schools, 13th-year (postgraduate) programs, home study, and adult education. College-bound students should begin this process by developing a tentative list of 2- or 4-year colleges, vocational technical schools, or universities that are of interest to them (McGuire & Shaw, 1986a).

1. *Exploring postsecondary options.* Guidance personnel need to keep in mind that a variety of postsecondary options are now available to students with learning disabilities. An increasing number of high school students with LD realize that to be better prepared for adult life and the world of work, additional training is necessary after graduation. Some students with learning disabilities may elect to pursue careers in technical areas that deemphasize reading and writing skills and capitalize on hands-on activities. For those students, vocational training might be the most appropriate option for reaching their goals (Michaels et al., 1988a). For other students, a technical college curriculum that specifically emphasizes mathematics, science, or engineering while requiring less verbal ability may be a more appropriate choice. Some students may meet more success in college settings that feature a co-op curriculum that focuses on both course work and work experience, rather than at an institution with a more traditional, liberal arts curriculum.

The attraction of community colleges is very strong for many students with learning disabilities who would like to attempt some college work but simultaneously maintain the support of friends and the familiar routines of living at home. Because community colleges have open admissions policies; smaller class ratios; comparatively low tuition fees; academic and personal counseling; and a wide range of vocational, remedial, and developmental courses, they are often a logical and advantageous first step for students with more severe learning disabilities. In fact, community colleges serve a larger proportion of students with learning disabilities than any other segment of postsecondary education (Barnett, 1993). As a result, many community colleges have developed effective, creative disability support practices and programs that help these individuals reach their fullest potential (Bursuck, Rose, Cowen, & Yahaya, 1989).

Students need to be shown how to use college resource guides or directories and the latest computer-guided software available to assist them in the college search process. Colleges can be sorted based on their location, size, major offerings, campus environment, cost, financial aid, campus housing, and other personally valued factors (Cowen, 1993; DuChossois & Stein, 1992; McGuire & Shaw, 1986b). Students with learning disabilities should pay careful attention to admissions criteria that often vary widely from one institution to another. Generally speaking, information should be collected regarding minimum entry requirements based on high school class rank, grade-point average, prerequisite course work, and SAT or ACT scores. In addition to these factors, students with learning disabilities who are able to meet the minimum standards for admission may want to consider the academic qualifications of the average student for a given institution. He or she may want to eliminate colleges that seem to be too competitive or that do not provide an array of generic student support services (Cowen, 1991; McGuire & Shaw, 1986b).

2. *Evaluating LD support services.* The most recent edition of *Peterson's Colleges with Programs for Students with Learning Disabilities* (Mangrum & Strichart, 1995) listed nearly 1,000 institutions with services for students with learning disabilities in the United States. "As students became better prepared, as their aspirations were raised by supportive parents and teachers, and as colleges and universities come to understand the strengths and potential that such students add to campus life, the number of such programs multiplied" (Hartman, 1992, p. vi). Once students have developed a tentative list of 15 to 20 colleges that seem appropriate, they should seek more detailed information regarding admissions and specific information on the range of LD support services available on campus. By perusing college directories that are specifically targeted to students with learning disabilities, students are better able to determine the type and range of services they need. The student and his or her counselor should work closely together as they try to distinguish between comprehensive LD programs and those with limited support services (HEATH Resource Center, 1993; Kravets & Wax, 1991; Lipkin, 1993; Straughn, 1992). One word of caution: Each listing should be verified with a follow-up phone call to the designated LD contact person, as program staff and resources frequently change and directory information is not always accurate (McGuire & Shaw, 1986b).

Depending on the postsecondary setting, students with learning disabilities are often assisted in their pursuit of a postsecondary education through offices that are described as either providers of *services* or providers of a *program* (Brinckerhoff et al., 1993; Lipkin, 1993). High school students need to understand the difference between a comprehensive LD program and a support services model. An LD program is often characterized as having one person who spearheads the efforts to develop the program; that individual typically has expertise in the area of learning disabilities (Vogel, 1982). Mangrum and Strichart (1988) identified the following as components of postsecondary programs for students with learning disabilities: diagnostic testing, individual education programs, academic and program advising, basic skills remediation, subject area tutoring, specialized courses, auxiliary aids and services, and counseling. Although not every component will be offered on every campus, the critical aspects of LD programs are individualization, a basis in diagnostic data, and coordination by a professional with training in learning disabilities (Brinckerhoff et al., 1993).

In contrast, support services at the postsecondary level are defined as those generic activities that are carried out to ensure equal educational opportunity for any student with a disability. Brinckerhoff (1993a) outlined a variety of "minimal resources" (p. 55) that will ensure adequate support services in a climate of fiscal austerity. Basic LD services typically include the minimal requirements mandated under Section 504, such as access to taped textbooks, tape recorders, assistance in arranging testing accommodations, readers, note takers, and provisions for arranging course substitutions. The operative word in a service approach is *generic*, meaning that the services are inclusive of and available to all students with disabilities (Brinckerhoff et al., 1993).

Members of the student's transitional planning team should refer to the continuum of postsecondary LD support services (see Figure 8.1) as they anticipate how much support will be necessary in college. The model includes five points on a service continuum: (a) no services available, (b) decentralized and limited services, (c) loosely coordinated services, (d) centrally coordinated services, and (e) data-based services. The points on the continuum refer to the level of support available to students at the postsecondary level. DuChossois and Michaels (1994) aptly pointed out that for a student with LD, the effort involved in finding the right school is further complicated by "the requirement to find appropriate support services suited to the student's individual learning needs" (p. 102). This time-consuming process of college selection and "comparison shopping" for the best level of LD support services should be included as a student-generated goal in the Individual Transition Plan.

3. *SAT and ACT preparation.* Every year, about 2 million high schoolers take SAT exams and almost as many take the ACTs (Rubenstone & Dalby, 1994). During the fall of their junior year and even during the later part of their sophomore year (if requested), students can take the Preliminary Scholastic Assessment Test (PSAT) in order to prepare for the new SAT I: Reasoning Tests. The "A" in SAT now stands for "Assessment," not "Aptitude," a change designed to reflect increased emphasis on skills learned in school rather than innate abilities (Rubenstone & Dalby, 1994). As in the past, the SAT I focuses on verbal and mathematical skills. The SAT II: Subject Tests (formerly "Achievement Test") are two subject-specific examinations that include English, foreign language, history, and natural sciences. The scoring system has also been recalibrated on a "re-centered scale" that will increase national test score averages.

Guidance counselors should assist students in registering for the PSAT or for the PLAN, which is a warm-up exam for the ACT. Guidance personnel and special education teachers should encourage students to take these tests with accommodations, such as tape-recorded versions, large block answer sheets, extended time, or use of a private room. The

1	2	3	4	5
No Services Available	**Decentralized and Limited Services**	**Loosely Coordinated Services**	**Centrally Coordinated Services**	**Data-Based Services**
• Meets minimal requirements under Section 504	• No formal contact person • Limited services • Few established policies • Students dependent on sympathetic faculty	• Contact person available • Generic support services available • Peer tutors available to help at-risk students • Students referred to other on-campus resources • Services available only during the academic year	• Full-time learning disability coordinator • Services often housed in disability student services office • Accommodations provided for testing and coursework • Established policies on admissions and service delivery • Strong emphasis on student self-advocacy • Peer support groups • Specially trained tutors may be available • Student required to provide documentation of learning disability • Services available throughout the year	• Full-time learning disability director • Learning disability assistant coordinator • Full range of accommodations provided • Development of Individualized Semester Plans • Tutoring available from trained staff and graduate-level interns • Data-based contact records and service use profiles generated for annual report

Figure 8.1.   Continuum of postsecondary LD support services. *Note.* From *Resource Guide of Support Services for Students with Learning Disabilities in Connecticut Colleges and Universities,* by J. M. McGuire and S. F. Shaw (Eds.), 1989, Storrs: University of Connecticut. Copyright 1989 by University of Connecticut. Adapted with permission.

school psychologist or the private diagnostician who wrote the student's report should be contacted to provide written verification regarding the need for alternative testing arrangements. In December, the results of the PSAT should be reviewed carefully to determine individual areas of strength and weakness. The results of this test can be helpful in determining future courses the student should select in order to prepare for college (Cowen, 1993). If students do not do well on their first attempt, then a special course in test preparation or a workshop on test anxiety might be warranted. Students should make preliminary arrangements with their guidance counselors for alternative testing accommodations for the SATs before the first of January. Preparation for the SAT I should begin by utilizing the sample test booklet and reviewing the new computerized format. Students should also be informed that if they seek alternative testing accommodations, their scores will be stamped "Nonstandardized Administration" when they are sent to the institution. Some students may be concerned that this intentional flagging of their scores will result in adverse treatment by a prospective college. Therefore, guidance counselors should be aware of which postsecondary institutions are not receptive to reviewing applicants with disabilities and which institutions do not require SATs or ACTs at all.

4. *The personal transition file.* The academic program for the junior year should be selected with considerable thought, given that college admissions officers look very carefully for any changes or trends in the educational rigors in the program of study. Depending on students' postsecondary goals, they should be advised that if they elect to take only two or three college-prep classes per semester, they may not look like they are prepared for a competitive college curriculum that typically consists of four or five courses. Guidance counselors should address these issues early on to be sure that the student understands the ramifications of his or her choices.

Vogel (1993) recommended that students become actively involved in developing their own "personal transition file." The parent(s) should help their child collect and maintain material for this ongoing personal file that includes school and medical records, IEPs, resumes, and samples of academic work (NJCLD, 1994). The file should also include the most recent psychoeducational evaluation that includes a statement regarding the diagnosis of a learning disability and the nature of the disability. Vogel recommended that in addition to high school transcripts and ACT or SAT I scores, students include nonconfidential letters of recommendation, and even a brief autobiography, along with other significant writing that highlights special talents or abilities. Students with learning disabilities need to be advised to bring their transition file to the campus interview so they can highlight their high school academic and extracurricular records as well as talk about their learning disabilities. The Highland

Park High School (Illinois) Special Education Department has developed a "College Interview Preparation Form" (Rolfe, 1989), which students complete before their campus visit. This summary sheet can be used as an advance organizer for structuring the college interview, as an ice-breaker during the interview, and as a powerful way of showcasing the student's credentials and self-advocacy abilities.

The College Interview Preparation Form is an excellent example of how LD specialists and guidance staff can work together to help students become central players on the transition planning team. Ideally, this collaborative effort would be expanded to include a postsecondary LD support person who could help high school personnel and students anticipate postsecondary expectations (Aune, 1991; Dalke & Franzene, 1988; Bursuck & Rose, 1992). Such ongoing communication between high school and postsecondary service providers can help to alleviate a number of common problems evidenced in the transition process, including chronic difficulties in obtaining student records for the purpose of assessing student eligibility for services; lack of communication regarding the number of students who plan to attend community college after completing their senior year; new college students with disabilities registering for courses that are too difficult for them; and lack of, or inconsistency in, methods used by high schools to inform their students with disabilities about postsecondary education options and vocational rehabilitative services. Bursuck and Rose (1992) noted that each of these problems regarding the inefficiency of the transition process is particularly evident from feeder high schools to community colleges.

5. *Narrowing postsecondary options.* During the spring of their junior year, students should finalize all arrangements for the ACT or SAT I, write preselected colleges for application materials and information regarding their LD services, and seek out college admissions representatives who visit local high schools during "LD College Nights." Meetings with regional representatives from 2- and 4-year colleges on high school college nights provide students and their parents an opportunity to discuss admissions requirements, curricular and recreational options, and the range of disability services available on campus. For many students with learning disabilities, these discussions with campus representatives will be a real eye-opener as they realize that very few community colleges and even fewer 4-year institutions offer the comprehensive array of special education services that are available in most high schools (Rose & Bursuck, 1989). After gathering preliminary information about a particular college or course of study, students should narrow their choices by making a phone call to the director or coordinator of LD support services to arrange for a personal interview. Typically, it is the parent who makes these arrangements, but this is one more instance where students should be given the opportunity to make their own arrangements.

The campus visit and interview is especially important for students with LD who might look marginal on paper but whose true potential and abilities come across in an interview. Students should be prepared by organizing their personal portfolios prior to the interview, and by generating a list of questions regarding the admissions process, the college's curricular offerings, and specific learning disability support services. Given that college may be a $100,000 investment, students and parents should take the time to visit the campus together and to meet with LD support staff directly. The campus interview typically involves both the student and the parents. However, parents need to be reminded not to overpower the interviewer with their input regarding their child. Postsecondary service providers may prefer to interview the student alone, without benefit of parent prompting, in order to get an accurate reading of a student's level of motivation, social skills, and understanding of his or her disability. Prospective students should be encouraged to arrange to meet other college students with LD who have used the support services on campus and to sit in on a class so they can develop a realistic view of college life. The foreshadowing of the college experience through another peer can be very powerful.

After visiting the campus, the student and his or her parents should evaluate the overall campus environment across a variety of academic, social, and recreational domains. Specifically, they should evaluate the social and learning climate of that postsecondary setting, its geographic location, and the availability of housing and financial aid, if desired. Cowen (1993) stated that "the most important comparisons will be their comfort level with the service coordinator and staff and the comprehensiveness of the needed services" (p. 49). Students may want to personalize their approach to the college search by writing a thank-you note to the individual who interviewed them during their campus visit. This brief note should come from the student, not the parent, if it is to have any positive impression on the admissions officer. Prospective attendees of community colleges or vocational–technical education programs should pay particular attention to how they will manage the academic rigors and social changes within a particular degree or certification program (Sitlington, 1986). They should also explore what they will need to do in order to be prepared for transfer to a 4-year setting or for employment. Based on these firsthand comparisons of a range of postsecondary options, the student and parents will be better prepared to decide which programs or services are best.

If students are interested in a more formal approach to preparing for the transition to higher education, they may want to consider a campus-based orientation program. One such program, "A Taste of College" at Boston University, is specifically designed for high school juniors and seniors with learning disabilities. This 5-day program at the end of

June affords students a chance to meet with professors, attend college lectures, learn self-advocacy skills, and live in a dormitory. Specialty workshops on time management, active textbook reading, note-taking skills, and test preparation are part of the program. By learning firsthand, and in advance, which skills are necessary for college, these students are better prepared for postsecondary experiences on *any* campus (Brinckerhoff, 1994).

Regardless of the approach taken, students should work at developing a list of questions that will be helpful in sorting out college options. In recent years, numerous step-by-step transition planning guides have been produced to guide high school students with learning disabilities and their parents through the decision-making process (Cowen, 1990; DuChossois & Stein, 1992; Kuperstein & Kessler, 1991; McGuire & Shaw, 1986a; Rose & Bursuck, 1992; Vogel, 1993). Two of these guides— *Choosing the Right College* (DuChossois & Stein, 1992) and *Postsecondary Decision-making for Students with Learning Disabilities* (Vogel, 1993)—are commercially available and are specifically designed to help students with learning disabilities organize their college search. Both guides include a checklist for evaluating LD support services, and appendices with a variety of resource materials and information on state and national resources. One advantage of the *The Postsecondary Decision-making for Students with Learning Disabilities* manual is that the student booklet includes a series of program objectives that could be incorporated directly into the IEP. Ideally, these objectives would be completed during the junior year of high school. Also available are a companion teacher's guide and a set of overhead transparencies that can be used by LD specialists or guidance counselors to teach students about the college-search process. One advantage of *Choosing the Right College* is that it includes a school/self-assessment chart that students fill in as they compare their unique needs with the services available in different postsecondary settings. The manual also contains a two-page listing of "Tips for College-bound Students with Learning Disabilities," which will be invaluable to students and parents as they prepare for the college search.

Another resource that should be useful to parents, students, and professionals is the HEATH Resource Center in Washington, DC. Their toll-free line (1-800-54-HEATH) provides callers with up-to-date information and publication materials on disability issues in higher education.

Transition Programming in the Senior Year

The senior year often commences with students filling out applications and writing college essays. Students with learning disabilities should be encouraged to use a common admission application form that can be used with a variety of colleges. The Common Application is a standard format that can be photocopied and is used by more than 120 colleges nationwide, all of whom have agreed to honor it (Rubenstone & Dalby, 1994). In this way, time can be saved, and students can focus on developing one or two well-thought-out essays that can be submitted with their applications. Another time-saving approach is to hook up with the CollegeLink program. This service allows applicants to complete a single application on their personal computer that can be forwarded to about 500 institutional subscribers for a fee. Students bring their diskettes to their guidance counselors, who then forwards all transcripts and recommendations to up to eight member colleges (Rubenstone & Dalby, 1994).

Students should be advised to fill out applications neatly, in ink or, preferably, on a typewriter. For the essay, they should write about a topic that is exciting rather than something that "sounds intellectual" or is too routine (Kuperstein & Kessler, 1991). A student's learning disability can be a good topic, if it is handled in a creative and self-affirming manner. Applicants should also be advised not to send more information than is requested and to avoid exaggerating their achievements—a thick file does not necessarily impress the admissions staff. A student who provides a brief historical overview of his learning disability and then focuses on just one or two events that changed his life may come across better on paper than, for example, a student with dyslexia who attempts to tell her life story in two pages. A lengthy list of extracurricular activities that have been pursued casually, deluging admissions officers with letters from "connected" people, and "sending a life preserver in the school's colors with a plea to rescue you from the wait list will not help" (Day, 1994, p. 54). Admissions officers have tremendous integrity, and such ploys are frowned upon.

Students would be well advised to choose their references very carefully. For example, a letter of recommendation from a general education teacher in a college prep class who feels comfortable writing that despite the learning disability, this student is college-able is likely to get more attention than a routine letter from a guidance counselor who hardly knows the student. Letters from special education teachers can shed valuable light on a student's prospects for success in college, if they realistically highlight the student's abilities and address his or her level of motivation to succeed in school. If the student chooses to self-identify as having a learning disability in the admissions process, then a letter from the LD resource room teacher will be appropriate if it substantiates the student's potential and level of motivation toward college-prep course work. For example, a letter from a supervisor at McDonald's who can speak from daily experience with the candidate carries more weight than one from a famous U.S. senator who went to school with the applicant's father (Day, 1994). Letters of recommendation from family, friends, clergy, and elementary school teachers carry little weight in the admissions process. Finally, students should ask their guidance counselors to review all application forms for completeness 2 or 3 weeks prior to the application deadline.

By the beginning of their senior year, it may be appropriate for students to narrow their career exploration process to a preferred area of study at the postsecondary level. Job shadowing and internship experiences should be provided to allow students to test their hypotheses about career choices and to determine if and how their learning disabilities might interfere with performance (Dowdy & McCue, 1994; Michaels, Thaler, Zwerlein, Gioglio, & Apostoli, 1988b; Sitlington & Frank, 1990). The student, parents, teacher, and guidance counselor should work together to establish a tentative career goal and to determine areas of college study that are consistent with that goal (Cowen, 1993; Wehman, 1992). In some instances, it may be appropriate to refer a student to a Department of Rehabilitative Services (DRS) counselor for an initial in-take interview to determine eligibility and establish a need for services. Once an individual is determined to be eligible for services, a DRS counselor will be assigned to a student in order to gather as much information as possible about the his or her work history, education and training, abilities and interests, rehabilitation needs, and possible career goals (Dowdy & McCue, 1994). If finances are a consideration, students should be encouraged to ask their local vocational rehabilitation counselor if they qualify for financial assistance. The DRS can assist with college tuition if students demonstrate that their college program is the most cost-effective method for them to reach their vocational goal as specified in their Individual Written Rehabilitation Plan (IWRP). For a more complete discussion of this topic, readers are encouraged to consult Carol Dowdy's chapter, "Vocational Rehabilitation and Special Education: Partners in Transition for Individuals with Learning Disabilities," in this book.

Given the costs of attending college, parents often need to be reminded to file financial aid forms early. The good news is that federal and state government educational institutions and private agencies are committed to making higher education accessible to students, regardless of need. According to the College Scholarship Service, more than 5 million students were awarded almost $28 billion in aid for the 1993–1994 school year (Rubenstone & Dalby, 1994). Students with learning disabilities may have some additional expenses that need to be factored into the financial aid request. For example, some colleges may charge an additional fee for specialized LD tutorial support, students may need to buy adaptive equipment for their computer, or they may need to purchase a four-track tape recorder for textbook reading. All these expenses should be anticipated so that the financial aid package will be adequate for the upcoming year.

Letters of acceptance generally begin to arrive in mid-March. However, many colleges routinely hold the final acceptance notice until they have an additional quarter of high school grades. Students should not be alarmed, as this process is often standard at more competitive institutions. However, if a student has not heard within 4 to 6 weeks of the date that admissions decisions typically are made, the student, *not* the parent, should phone and check on the status of his or her application. It is possible that documentation is still missing or transcript grades were inadvertently not sent. If a student receives several letters of acceptance, then he or she is in the pleasant position of having to rank-order college choices. If the student is unsure about which college to accept, then a follow-up phone call or a second visit may be appropriate (Kuperstein & Kessler, 1991; Lipkin, 1993). After carefully deciding what college to attend, based on the above considerations, the student should write a brief acceptance letter and mail in the deposit with the housing request early.

Sometimes parents are unrealistic about their child's potential for college success. DuChossois and Michaels (1994) commented that parents may have difficulty accepting the compromise of a local community college rather than the "big name" school that they had originally envisioned for their child. Families must sometimes confront feelings of disappointment if the student is not qualified to attend a school at the academic level they would prefer or at the level of the student's peers. If a student with a LD is denied admission, then the student and the family need to be reminded of the following:

> Not getting into college doesn't mean that your child is not bright, or is incapable of academic success or even unworthy of higher education. What it does mean is that the colleges selected may be very competitive, or that space was limited, or that the college believes your child is not ready right now. (Rubenstone & Dalby, 1994, p. 156)

In such instances, it might be appropriate to consider a postgraduate year, specialized LD preparatory school, community college with strong academic supports, or time off. Of these options, the most popular alternative is community college, as it can afford such students an opportunity to mature socially, to improve their academic skills, and to select college-prep courses that can be transferred to a more competitive postsecondary setting after a year or two.

FINAL THOUGHTS

Secondary education must be a process of moving students with learning disabilities from a state of dependency to independence

(DuChossois & Michaels, 1994). Secondary school personnel can help to prepare students with learning disabilities for the challenges of higher education by beginning to replicate some of the demands of postsecondary education while the student is still in high school. Postsecondary LD service providers can help by collaborating with their secondary-level colleagues and by realistically foreshadowing the higher education experience for applicants with disabilities. Parents can assist their sons or daughters by validating their dreams and nurturing their social development and academic growth. However, the key ingredient to success in higher education, and, ultimately, in the world of work, lies within the students themselves: They are the ones who need to master the critical study skills, learning strategies, and daily living and vocational skills that will enable them to journey through life with dignity and independence.

APPENDIX

A Timetable for Transition Planning for Students with Learning Disabilities

Grade 8

- Seek opportunities for full involvement in the general education program.
- Consult LD teachers, as needed, on how to become independent learners.
- Actively participate in the IEP meeting and suggest IEP goals that focus on effective study skills, time-management, and test-prep and test-taking strategies.
- Keep a calendar for activities and homework assignments.
- Begin to identify preferences and interests in vocational areas.
- Explore career areas through vocational classes, field trips to work sites, and volunteer work.
- Develop appropriate social skills and interpersonal communication skills.
- Be afforded opportunities that will foster self-determination and independence through increased responsibility at home and in school.
- Develop money management skills and assist in meal preparation, shopping duties, and caring for clothing.
- Learn about high school expectations and offerings.
- Expand academic interests through electives and extracurricular activities.

Grade 9

- Continue to practice Grade 8 goals.
- Demonstrate independence by writing some of their own IEP goals.
- Select classes with parent input that will prepare them academically for college or vocational/technical school (e.g., word processing, public speaking, study skills).
- Enroll in remediation courses, if necessary.
- Develop and use social skills.
- Seek classroom teachers and learning environments that are supportive.
- Learn what learning disabilities are and are not.
- Develop an understanding of the nature of their disabilities and learning styles.
- Learn about their civil rights and the responsibilities of high schools and colleges under Section 504 and the Americans with Disabilities Act.
- Explore career options with guidance counselor or teachers.
- Consider working a part-time summer job or in a volunteer position.

Grade 10

- Continue to practice Grade 8 and 9 goals.
- Self-advocate with parents, teachers, and peers.
- Provide input on who should participate in planning team.
- Become a co-leader of the transition planning team at the IEP meeting.
- Clarify the exact nature of their LD by reviewing psychoeducational report with LD specialist or school psychologist.
- Try out accommodations and auxiliary aids that LD teachers deem appropriate (e.g., taped textbooks, note takers, laptop computers, extra time on exams).

- Know how, when, and where to discuss and request needed accommodations.
- Arrange with counselor to take the PSATs/PLAN with accommodations.
- Gain a realistic assessment of potential for college or vocational technical school.
- Avoid temptation of "retreating" to lower track classes if college bound. Select solid college-prep classes.
- Be aware of peer advisement regarding which classes to take or avoid.
- Be wary of course waivers and carefully consider the implications of these choices.
- Use LD support and accommodations in math or foreign language classes, rather than seeking a waiver, if possible.
- Balance class schedules by not taking too many difficult classes in the same semester, or classes that play into an area of weakness.
- Participate in extracurricular events and community activities.
- Meet with guidance counselor to discuss PSAT scores. Discuss strategies for improvement.
- Register for SAT II tests, if appropriate.
- Learn about technological aids, such as talking calculators, four-track tape recorders, voice synthesizers, word prediction software, optical scanners, and hand-held spell checkers.
- Know how to access information from a large library.
- Arrange with counselor to explore career options and interests through a computer-guided career search.
- Apply for a summer job or volunteer position.

Grade 11
- Continue to practice Grade 8, 9, and 10 goals.
- Review IEP and ITP for any changes or modifications for upcoming year.
- Present a positive self-image by stressing strengths, while still understanding the influence of the learning disability.
- Advocate for a complete psychoeducational evaluation to be conducted by the beginning of 12th grade as a goal in the ITP.
- Consult several LD college guides and meet with a college advisor to discuss realistic options.
- Use college computer searches in helping to further define college choices.
- Explore advantages and disadvantages, given the learning disability, of community colleges, vocational–technical schools, and four-year colleges.
- Match vocational interests and academic abilities with appropriate postsecondary or vocational options.
- Arrange for PSATs with accommodations in mid-October. Apply for a social security number.
- Start with a list of 15 to 20 colleges and request general information about the institution and specific information about the LD services offered.
- Review results of PSATs with counselor and plan for SATs based on results.
- Meet with local Department of Rehabilitation Services (DRS) counselor to determine eligibility for services. If eligible, ask counselor for assistance in the areas of vocational assessment, job placement, and/or postsecondary education/training.

- Begin career exploration within a high school LD support group.
- Seek LD role models in school through a peer-mentor program.
- Narrow college listing to 10 preliminary choices based on competitiveness, location, curriculum, costs, level of LD support, etc.
- Finalize arrangements for the SATs or ACTs with necessary accommodations.
- Request any additional information needed from the college (e.g., applications to LD program, specific fee information, financial aid forms, etc.).
- Discuss with parents, counselor, general education teachers, and LD teachers the anticipated level of LD support needed in a postsecondary setting.
- Take SAT I and II or ACT with testing accommodations.
- Attend LD college nights at local area high schools. Ask college representatives your own questions.
- Develop a Personal Transition File with parent and teacher assistance. Contents should include current diagnostic testing, IEPs, grades, letters of recommendation, etc.
- Be sure LD psychoeducational evaluation is up-to-date and is comprehensive enough for college planning.
- Narrow postsecondary options down to five or six schools that range in competitiveness and levels of LD support.
- Prepare a College Interview Preparation Form to use during campus interviews.
- Arrange in advance for campus visits and interviews. Consider sitting in on a class, or arrange to meet college students with learning disabilities who can share their experiences.
- Meet with the designated LD services coordinator to determine the level of support offered and to assess the nature of the services offered (e.g., remedial, compensatory, learning strategies, etc.).
- Stop by the campus student assistance center to determine availability of services.
- Follow up with a personal thank-you note after the campus visit.
- Consider a private LD preparatory school or a "13th-year" program, if postsecondary education does not seem to be a viable option.
- Consider enrolling in a summer orientation program specifically for students with learning disabilities, such as "A Taste of College." Contact HEATH Resource Center at 1-800-54-HEATH for more information.
- Apply for a summer job or volunteer position.

Grade 12
- Continue to practice Grade 8, 9, 10, and 11 goals.
- Update IEP and ITP and follow up on a quarterly basis.
- Retake SATs or ACT to improve scores.
- Confirm postsecondary choices and options with guidance counselor and parents.
- Select several colleges that are "safe bets" for admission, several reasonable reaches, and one or two "long shots."
- Note all application deadlines. Finish application process carefully.
- Write a personal cover letter describing disability to accompany application, if desired.

- Use a common application form to several colleges, to minimize paperwork.
- Be alert to early application deadlines for some LD college programs.
- Submit completed applications to counselors at least 3 weeks in advance of deadlines.
- Role-play the college interview with guidance counselors or special education teachers.
- Carefully select persons to write letters of recommendation; recognize that such letters may include comments about the learning disability. Keep a personal copy in Personal Transition File.
- Keep a list of names, phone numbers, and addresses of postsecondary contact persons and copies of the application in the Personal Transition File.
- Arrange to have high school midyear grade reports sent to colleges.
- Tap into Department of Rehabilitation Services. If eligible for job guidance, consider enrolling in internships, or job-shadowing experiences that permit hands-on skill building.
- Discuss options for financial support after high school with DRS counselor.
- Pick up all necessary financial aid forms from guidance counselor. Remember that males who are 18 years old must register for the draft to be eligible for federal aid funds.
- Formulate a realistic career plan.
- Wait for the news from colleges. . . . If the news is good, then
  1. Rank-order postsecondary choices based upon ability to compete successfully and the provision of support services to meet unique learning needs.
  2. Notify all schools of your decision.
  3. Pay housing deposit by May 1st, if appropriate.
  4. Arrange to have final high school transcript sent to the college.
  5. Hold an exit interview with guidance counselor and LD teachers.
  6. Carefully consider course load, depending on the competitiveness of the college, the level of difficulty of the courses, and the time needed to work with LD support staff.
- Wait for the news from colleges. . . . If the news is *not* good, then
  1. Appeal the admissions decision, especially if some new LD-relevant data were not considered.
  2. Pursue a variety of alternatives, including applying to a less competitive college with a rolling admissions policy, enrolling in a postgraduate year at an LD preparatory school, or enrolling in a community college with academic support services.
  3. Consider taking a college course for credit over the summer at a community college, or in conjunction with a special summer orientation program, such as the Summer Transition Program.

---

9. Vocational Rehabilitation and Special Education: Partners in Transition for Individuals with Learning Disabilities

CAROL A. DOWDY

Transition plans for individuals with learning disabilities (LD) have only recently been developed by public education in collaboration with adult service agencies such as vocational rehabilitation (VR). This is in part because many educators have had the narrow view of learning disabilities as being primarily academic deficiencies. Individualized Education Programs (IEPs) developed at the high school level have generally focused on remediating academics and services in existing high school academic curricula. Some IEPs include components that address social skills, study skills, and learning strategies; however, skills addressing independent living, career exploration, employment seeking, or job maintenance are seldom included (Michaels, 1994).

In addition, special educators and vocational rehabilitation counselors are often caught off guard by the hidden limitations of learning disabilities. Certain limitations (outside of classroom failure) are not as

Reprinted, with changes, from "Vocational rehabilitation and special education: Partners in transition for individuals with learning disabilities," by Carol A. Dowdy, *Journal of Learning Disabilities*, Vol. 29, 1996, pp. 137–147. Copyright © 1996 by PRO-ED, Inc.

obvious for students with learning disabilities as they are for students with mental retardation or physical disabilities. Often, teachers who regularly work with VR counselors in IEP development for students with other disabilities will not include a VR counselor on the IEP team for their students with learning disabilities. As a result, the majority of young adults with learning disabilities have had to depend on families or deal with their independent living and employment challenges alone, without sufficient support and intervention from special educators or VR personnel (Dowdy, Carter, & Smith, 1990).

Although state and federal VR programs have helped individuals with disabilities achieve employment since 1920, in 1981 these services were made available specifically to individuals with learning disabilities. Since that time the federal Rehabilitation Services Administration (RSA) has grappled with many of the same identification and service delivery issues that have plagued the field of special education in its attempts to serve this population. RSA has made significant efforts to adopt a definition (Rehabilitation Services Administration, 1985), clarify diagnostic criteria (American Psychiatric Association, 1994), establish policy to guide counselors in documenting eligibility and determining the existence of a severe disability (Rehabilitation Services Administration, 1990), and develop and expand appropriate rehabilitation services for individuals with learning disabilities (Dowdy & Smith, 1994; Dowdy, Smith, & Nowell, 1992). One of the biggest challenges has been to train RSA personnel to work effectively with individuals with learning disabilities and their families and to collaborate with public schools to develop effective Individual Transition Plans (ITPs).

To meet the needs of individuals with learning disabilities, VR and public school personnel must collaborate. The most significant roadblocks to collaboration between these two programs have been the differences in professional jargon and practices, and the academic emphasis of special education versus the employment-outcome emphasis of vocational rehabilitation. However, recent amendments to the legislation governing these two agencies include mandates that should lead to more frequent and successful collaboration efforts in the area of transition.

The mandates for special education transition planning and service delivery included in the Individuals with Disabilities Education Act of 1990 (IDEA) were reviewed in the first chapter of this book. The purpose of this chapter is to provide an overview of the VR process that is often applied to meet the transition needs of individuals with learning disabilities as mandated by the 1992 Amendments to the Vocational Rehabilitation Act of 1973. Information will be included on the purpose and principles of VR, the requirements for determining eligibility for individuals with learning disabilities, and the impact of the mandate on serving individuals with the most severe disabilities first. VR guidelines for assessment of individuals with learning disabilities, and the range of services available, will also be reviewed. Specific recommendations will be made to help families and students with learning disabilities, VR counselors, and special educators become more effective partners in the transition process.

VOCATIONAL REHABILITATION

VR is a state and federal program whose purpose is to empower individuals with disabilities to achieve gainful employment consistent with their strengths, resources, priorities, concerns, abilities, and capabilities. This is a partnership program, with the federal government providing leadership, technical assistance, monitoring, and 78% matching funds to the states. RSA, a component of the Office of Special Education and Rehabilitative Services, U.S. Department of Education, is the federal agency responsible for the VR program. Each state has a VR agency that is responsible for, and provides direct assistance to, individuals with disabilities under an approved state plan that provides basic assurances that the program will be administered in a manner that is consistent with federal statutory, regulatory, and policy requirements. The provision of services is usually accomplished through local VR offices.

A referral can be made to VR by the individual with a disability or anyone familiar with him or her. Typically, a VR counselor is assigned to the individual and an initial interview is held to gather information; this is the beginning of an assessment process to determine eligibility. The process includes gathering as much information as possible about the individual's work history, education and training, strengths, interests, VR needs, and possible employment goals, with emphasis placed on the use of existing information (Dowdy & McCue, 1994). When eligibility has been determined, the counselor, with the individual and/or the individual's representative, develops an individualized written rehabilitation program (IWRP).

According to the 1992 Amendments to the Vocational Rehabilitation Act, each IWRP shall (a) be designed to achieve the employment objective consistent with the individual's unique strengths, resources, priorities, concerns, abilities, and capabilities; (b) include long-term goals based on the assessment and on the individual's vocational rehabilitation needs, including his or her career interests and the extent to which those long-term goals shall be accomplished in integrated settings; (c) include the intermediate rehabilitation objectives related to attainment of the long-term goals; (d) include a statement of the specific VR services to be provided and the projected dates of services; (e) include a statement of rehabilitation technology services to be provided, if appropriate; (f) include a statement of specific on-the-job and related personal assistance services to be provided, if appropriate; (g) include indication of the need for postemployment services; (h) include a description of how services will be provided or arranged through cooperative agreements with other service providers; and (i) include the evaluation procedures and evaluative criteria for determining if the goals and objectives have been met.

The IWRP must also include a statement from the individual describing how he or she was involved in choosing among the goals, objectives, services, and service providers. The IWRP must be signed by the individual or the individual's representative, and they must be provided a copy of the IWRP. Each IWRP must be reviewed at least annually, and any changes must involve full participation of all parties.

The discussion above provides special educators with a general overview of the rehabilitation process. This knowledge is critical if they are to be effective partners in transition planning and to educate students with learning disabilities to actively participate in the transition process. The following is a detailed discussion of the transition process relevant to VR for individuals with learning disabilities: purpose and principles, assessment, eligibility, and available services.

Purpose and Principles

The governing legislation for RSA is the Rehabilitation Act of 1973 as amended through the 1992 and 1993 Amendments. The purpose of the Act is to

1. Assist States in operating a coordinated, comprehensive, effective, accountable VR program designed to assess, plan, develop and implement VR services for individuals with disabilities considering their strengths, resources, priorities, concerns, abilities, and capabilities in order for these individuals to prepare for and engage in gainful employment [Section 100(a)(2)].

2. Empower individuals with disabilities to maximize employment, economic self-sufficiency, independence, and inclusion and integration into society through comprehensive, state of the art vocational rehabilitation programs, independent living centers, research, training, demonstration projects, and the guarantee of equal opportunity; and,

3. Ensure that the Federal Government plays a leadership role in promoting the meaningful and gainful employment and independent living of individuals with disabilities, especially individuals with severe disabilities. [Section 2 (b)(1)(2)]

The programs and activities carried out under the auspices of the Act should be consistent with the following principles:

- Individuals with disabilities, including individuals with the most severe disabilities, are generally presumed to be capable of engaging in gainful employment and to benefit from VR services to enhance their ability to become gainfully employed;

- Opportunities for employment must be provided in integrated settings;

- Individuals with disabilities must be active participants in their own rehabilitation programs, including making meaningful and informed choices in the selection of personal vocational goals and the VR services they receive;

- Families or other natural supports can play a significant role in the VR process;

- Individuals with disabilities and their advocates are full partners in the VR program and must be involved in a meaningful manner and on a regular basis in policy development and implementation. [Section 100(a)(2)]

The Act also states that programs funded under the Act must demonstrate

- Respect for individual dignity, personal responsibility, self-determination, and pursuit of meaningful careers, based on informed choice of individuals with disabilities;

- Respect for privacy, rights, and equal access of the individual;

- Inclusion, integration, and full participation of the individual;

- Support for family involvement, if desired or needed; and,

- Support for individual and systematic advocacy and community involvement. [Section 2(b)(1)(2)]

The policies stated in the 1992 Amendments to the Act stress collaboration with community agencies, and the Act specifically refers to special education services offered through IDEA. The relationship between the two agencies is significant. Both agencies are now required to collaborate on behalf of individuals with disabilities. There is no age criterion in the VR programs; however, usually, as a matter of practice, the age is 16. Since the 1992 Amendments to the Act adopted the definition of "transition services" used in IDEA, both VR counselors and school personnel must agree on the coordinated set of activities needed for a successful transition. Both agencies are required to develop a coordinated program based on the individual's preferences or choices, needs, and interests.

In addition, the 1992 Amendments to the Act specify the establishment of agreements between agencies and the development of working groups that

1. Identify procedures, policies, and practices that facilitate coordination in areas of definition, referral procedures, eligibility determination, and assessment;

2. Identify resources and fiscal responsibilities for each agency;

3. Ensure coordination and cooperation through development of meaningful agreements. [101(a)(11)(C)(ii)]

To meet the mandate of the law, representatives from adult agencies need to discuss services and procedures for collaboration. This interagency collaboration serves to improve communication and ultimately provide individuals with learning disabilities better access to adult services. Table 9.1 provides a comparison of the special education and VR policies regarding a definition of LD and eligibility and diagnosis of individuals with learning disabilities. A more thorough discussion of the VR policies is found in subsequent sections.

The 1992 Amendments also call for a comprehensive system of personnel development to be planned in coordination with the personnel development specified under IDEA. Another catalyst for interagency collaboration is the mandate in the 1992 Amendments for the provision of joint staff training, such as special education personnel training, regarding the availability and benefits of VR services, and the eligibility standards. The purpose of this training is to increase the opportunity for individuals being served by other agencies to receive VR services. Specific information regarding eligibility for VR, assessment techniques, and the range of services will assist teachers in making appropriate referrals to VR and in following their students through a successful VR process.

Determination of Eligibility

In the educational system, the identification of a learning disability automatically makes a child eligible for services, because special education is an entitlement program. In the VR system, diagnosis of a learning disability does not automatically entitle one for services (Abbott, 1987).

According to the 1992 Amendments to the Act, to be eligible for assistance from VR, an individual must

1. Have a physical or mental impairment that results in a substantial impediment to employment;

TABLE 9.1

Comparison of Special Education and Vocational Rehabilitation Policies on Definition, Eligibility, and Diagnosis for Learning Disabilities

Special education	Vocational rehabilitation
Definition	
Specific Learning Disability means a disorder in one or more of the basic psychological processes involved in using language, spoken or written, which may manifest itself in an imperfect ability to listen, think, read, write, spell, or to do mathematical calculations. The term includes such terms as perceptual handicaps, brain injury, minimal brain dysfunction, dyslexia, and developmental aphasia. The term does not include children who have learning problems which are primarily the result of visual, hearing, or motor handicaps; mental retardation; emotional disturbance; or environmental, cultural, or economic disadvantages. (Federal Register, December 29, 1977).	The target population (SLD, Federal code 632) will be defined as follows: "A specific learning disability is a disorder in one or more of the central nervous system processes involved in perceiving, understanding, and/or using concepts through verbal (spoken or written) language or nonverbal means. This disorder manifests itself with a deficit in one or more of the following areas: attention, reasoning, processing, memory, communications, social competence and emotional maturity." (Recommended by Policy Directive, March 5, 1985, U.S. Department of Education, Rehabilitation Services Administration)
Diagnosis[a]	

A. The child does not achieve commensurate with his/her age and ability level when provided appropriate learning experiences.
 	
B. A severe discrepancy exists between achievement and intellectual ability in:
1. oral expression
2. listening comprehension
3. written expression
4. basic reading skills
5. reading comprehension
6. mathematical calculation
7. mathematical reasoning
	School records may be used to document the disability; new diagnosis generally derived from one of the following classifications in DSM-IV (1994).
	
	I. Specific Developmental Disorders
	  A. Learning Disorders
	    Reading
	    Math
	    Written Expression
	  B. Communication Disorders
	    Phonological
	    Expressive
	    Mixed Receptive-Expressive
	  C. Motor Skills Disorder

Table continues

TABLE 9.1 (cont.)

Special education	Vocational rehabilitation
	Diagnosis[a] (cont.)
	II. Attention Deficit and Disruptive Behavior Disorders
	Attention-Deficit/Hyperactivity Disorder
	III. Organic Mental Disorder
	Cognitive Disorder
	Not otherwise specified
Eligibility	
If a student meets the identification criteria, placement and services are automatically available.	Individuals must
	1. have a physical or mental impairment that is a substantial impediment to employment;
	2. be able to benefit from VR services in terms of an employment outcome; and
	3. require services to prepare for, enter, engage in, or retain employment
	In some states individuals must be coded severely disabled.[b]

[a]*Federal Register*, December 29, 1977. [b]In states in which resources are not sufficient to serve all eligible individuals, the state must invoke an order of selection in providing services, with priority given to individuals with the most severe disabilities.

2. Be able to benefit from vocational rehabilitation services in terms of employment; and,

3. Require vocational rehabilitation services to prepare for, enter, engage in, or retain gainful employment. [Section 102 (a)(1)]

The determination of eligibility is made by a VR counselor after reviewing existing data. If existing data are not sufficient or current, the VR counselor can obtain additional assessments to generate the information needed to make an eligibility determination. Counselors are required to use determination of a disability made by other agencies, including the education agency, provided those determinations are consistent with the requirements of the Act. Sources of such information include school records; medical and developmental histories; psychological and neuropsychological testing; interviews with parents and others, such as teachers and past employers; vocational evaluations; and situational assessments (McCue, 1994).

The counselor must determine eligibility within a reasonable period of time, but no longer than 60 days after the individual applies for services. The 1992 Amendments to the Act require that individuals be presumed to be able to benefit from VR services in terms of employment unless the state VR agency can demonstrate by clear and convincing evidence, through a period of extended evaluation, that the individuals are incapable of benefiting. Prior to the 1992 Amendments, acceptance for VR services was lower for individuals with learning disabilities than it was for other groups with disabilities (Berkeley Planning Associates, 1989; Smith, 1992). However, the changes in the rules for eligibility justification have resulted in increased acceptance rates. In the first 6 months of 1995, 75.7% of all referrals were determined eligible. Individuals' rights are protected, both by due-process procedures related to a fair hearing by an impartial hearing officer and by the Client Assistance Program located in each VR state agency.

A careful study of the RSA definition of specific learning disability (SLD) reveals the functional limitations that need to be explored for eligibility determination. The definition of SLD used to determine eligibility was recommended to the states in a policy directive issued in 1985. That definition stated the following:

> A specific learning disability is a disorder in one or more of the central nervous system processes involved in perceiving, understanding, and/or using concepts through verbal (spoken or written) language or nonverbal means. This disorder manifests itself with a deficit in one or more of the following areas: Attention, reasoning, processing, memory, communication, reading, writing, spelling, calculation, coordination, social competence, and emotional maturity. (Rehabilitation Services Administration, 1985, p. 1)

Historically, counselors have been cautious in determining individuals with SLD to be eligible for VR because of their generally average intellectual abilities, their lack of physical limitations, and the idea that an academic disability does not always limit an individual in terms of employment. For example, some counselors reason that if an individual had a math disability, he or she could obtain a job not requiring math; or an individual with a reading or writing disability could obtain employment not requiring reading or writing. Using this line of reasoning, counselors could determine that VR services would not be needed and thus eligibility could not be justified.

It is important for counselors to understand that a specific learning disability is much more than intellectual ability accompanied by academic deficits. The range of deficits referred to in the definition—in attention, memory, reasoning, coordination, social competence, and emotional maturity—must be explored fully in the assessment process. Because this comprehensive scope of assessment is often not necessary to determine eligibility in the school setting, additional assessment is often required. The Rating Scale of Functional Limitations (Dowdy, 1994) is one device that has been used nationally to document the range of behaviors manifested by individuals with learning disabilities. This instrument was designed to evaluate the aforementioned areas noted in the LD definition. Executive function was added, due to the importance of this area in independent living and employment. Each area contains specific behaviors that are characteristic of individuals with SLD. The instrument can be used to screen for further testing in specific areas, to identify functional limitations, to support decisions related to eligibility and severe disability, and to assist in designing an IWRP (Dowdy, 1992). These skill areas were also used to structure the *Guide to Vocational Impact and Intervention for Specific Learning Disabilities* (Dowdy, 1994).

The 1992 Amendments to the Act place emphasis on serving individuals with severe disabilities. Those states in which all eligible individuals cannot be served must initiate an order of selection that provides services first to those individuals determined to be "the most severely disabled." The criteria for the "most severely disabled" must be established by each state and must be based on the statutory definition of the term *severe disability*. According to the 1992 Amendments to the Act, an individual with a severe disability is defined as an individual

1. Who has a severe physical or mental impairment which seriously limits one or more functional capacities such as communication, self-care, mobility, self-direction, interpersonal skills, work tolerance, or work skills in terms of employment outcome;

2. Whose vocational rehabilitation is expected to require multiple vocational rehabilitation services over an extended period of time;

3. Who has one or more physical disabilities resulting from such conditions as . . . a specific learning disability. [Section 7(15)(A)]

Because this definition of severe disability is more readily applied to persons with mental retardation or a physical disability, counselors have had difficulty applying the criteria to persons with SLD, a hidden disability. Data from RSA indicate that, whereas 68.5% of all individuals in the VR system are classified as severely disabled, only 52% of individuals with specific learning disabilities are so classified (Mars, 1995). In 1990, RSA appointed a task force to study this and other issues related to application of VR services to individuals with SLD. As a result, RSA issued a program assistance circular to the states that stressed the importance of a comprehensive assessment to identify the limitations of SLD and its impact on individuals' functional capacities and the work environment (Rehabilitation Services Administration, 1990).

Assessment Guidelines

The 1992 Amendments specify that the assessment process must be comprehensive enough to determine eligibility (which includes a diagnosis to identify VR needs) to identify the need for rehabilitation technology services, and to develop the individualized written rehabilitation program. The Amendments also stress using the existing data available from other providers (such as education personnel) to the maximum extent possible. Data available from individuals with disabilities and their families are also considered critical to the assessment process.

As noted in the eligibility section above, the first consideration in determining eligibility is the presence of a physical or mental impairment that poses a substantial impediment to employment. The RSA definition of learning disabilities that was recommended to the states does not include a specific categorization system. The 1992 Amendments to the Act require that the determination of the existence of the impairment be made by "qualified personnel"; however, because most states require that the disability be diagnosed by a physician or psychologist knowledgeable in the identification of SLD, it has been generally inferred that the individual must meet the criteria for diagnosis established in the *Diagnostic and Statistical Manual of Mental Disorders IV* (DSM-IV; American Psychiatric Association, 1994) or the *International Classification of Diseases–9th Revision* (ICD-9; U.S. Department of Health and Human Services, 1980). Table 9.2 provides a list of the DSM-IV categories used most frequently to diagnose a learning disability in the VR system. (For further study of a diagnosis of LD for VR purposes, refer to McCue [1994].)

The purpose of the comprehensive assessment in VR goes beyond establishing a diagnosis. It is also important to determine the individual's

TABLE 9.2
DSM-IV Diagnostic Options for Learning Disability

Specific developmental disorders
    Learning disorders
        315.00 Reading disorder
        315.10 Mathematics disorder
        315.20 Disorder of written expression
        315.90 Learning disorder, not otherwise specified
    Communication disorders
        315.39 Phonological disorder
        315.31 Expressive language disorder
        315.31 Mixed receptive-expressive language disorder
        307.90 Communication disorder, not otherwise specified
    Motor skills disorder
        315.40 Developmental coordination disorder
Attention deficit and disruptive behavior disorders
        314.01 Attention-deficit/hyperactivity disorder
        314.90 Attention-deficit/hyperactivity disorder, not otherwise specified
Organic mental disorders
        294.90 Cognitive disorder, not otherwise specified

Note. From *Functional Assessment of Individuals with Cognitive Disabilities: A Desk Reference for Rehabilitation* by M. McCue, S. L. Chase, C. A. Dowdy, M. Pramuka, J. Petrick, S. Aitken, & P. Fabry, 1994, Pittsburgh, PA: Center for Applied Neuropsychological Associates. Copyright 1994 by Michael McCue. Reprinted by permission.

unique strengths, resources, priorities, interests, and needs, including his or her need for supported employment. To determine eligibility, a counselor must have documentation of the impact of the learning disability; therefore, all areas suspected of posing a vocational limitation must be explored. Because of the heterogeneous nature of learning disabilities, this may include attention, memory, reasoning, communication, reading, writing, spelling, calculation, coordination, social competence, and emotional maturity (Dowdy & McCue, 1994). Table 9.3 illustrates the impact on daily living activities and employment that nonacademic characteristics of specific learning disabilities can exert. This functional information must be obtained from the assessment process to justify eligibility and to determine vocational goals and objectives, and the nature and scope of vocational rehabilitation services. Areas of assessment include interest, interpersonal skills, personality, intelligence and related functional capacities, education achievements, work experience, vocational attitudes, personal and social adjustments, and employment opportunities. Medical, psychiatric, and psychological reports, along with other information, such as cultural, recreational, and environmental details, that is pertinent to the employment and rehabilitation needs of the individual, are also included.

TABLE 9.3
Vocational Impact of Specific Behavioral Deficits in the Cognitive Domain

Cognitive domain	Vocational impact of deficits
Executive functioning	Disorganized or unfocused job search strategies Confusion over how to register for classes Excessive time and distress when grocery shopping Unable to determine vocational goals Chronic tardiness or missed deadlines Unable to schedule own time or projects effectively Unaware of how supervisors assess their work Often surprised by and unprepared for problems on the job Unrealistic expectations Slow to catch on to office procedural changes Poor follow-through on direction and assignments
Attention	Loses track of current task Frequently observed to be off task Unable to sit through a lecture at school Difficulty in proofreading Excessive socialization Distracted by outside noise
Language and communication	Difficulty with telephone use, misunderstands messages Poor or very slow report writing Does not catch on to "hints" from others Talks too slowly for others Confuses other staff when attempting to explain or teach job tasks Frequently misinterprets supervisor memos
Sensory perceptual skills	May get lost easily Unable to learn how to read blueprints Requires repetition/simplification of messages Incorrect recording of telephone messages Unable to recognize differences between similar work materials Problems assembling items from a diagram
Motor skills	Clumsiness or slowness handling equipment Frequent accident/injury on the job Messy work samples due to poor dexterity Slow or inaccurate typing, data entry, or handwriting Problems with mobility or lifting
Social/emotional skills	History of conflict with supervisors or co-workers Unable to "connect" with customers or deal with complaints Problems accepting constructive feedback Highly distressed or agitated over everyday work demands Perceived as cold or unhelpful by retail customers Shares personal-life details with clients or co-workers

Note. From *Functional Assessment of Individuals with Cognitive Disabilities: A Desk Reference for Rehabilitation* by M. McCue, S. L. Chase, C. A. Dowdy, M. Pramuka, J. Petrick, S. Aitken, & P. Fabry, 1994, Pittsburgh, PA: Center for Applied Neuropsychological Associates. Copyright 1994 by Michael McCue. Reprinted by permission.

The 1992 Amendments to the Act also specify the use of situational assessments, which can provide a more realistic appraisal of work behavior or the services needed to develop the desired occupational skills. In situational assessment, an individual is placed in a job setting, either simulated or real, and asked to perform part or all of a job. The evaluator looks for work attitudes, work habits, work tolerance, and social and behavior patterns that are either consistent or inconsistent with job performance. Modifications or accommodations that may facilitate job success can also be explored during a situational assessment. Other types of assessment techniques include a clinical interview, developmental history, review of school history, behavioral observation of the individual in a variety of settings, and norm-referenced tests (McCue et al., 1994).

Services

One of the mandates of the 1992 Amendments is interagency cooperation and utilization of services and facilities of any state assistance programs, veterans' programs, or other programs for individuals with disabilities. Agencies that can be accessed by the VR counselor on behalf of an individual include community mental health agencies, manpower programs, public employment offices, and the Social Security Administration. IDEA and the Carl H. Perkins Vocational and Applied Technology Education Act also are important resources in making services available to individuals with learning disabilities.

Vocational rehabilitation services available under the Act include any services or goods necessary to prepare an individual with a disability for employment. Services that are appropriate for an individual with a learning disability include but are not limited to the following:

1. Assessment for determining eligibility or vocational rehabilitation needs, including assessment of rehabilitation technology needs if appropriate;

2. Counseling and work related placement services, including assistance with job search, placement, retention, and any follow-up or follow-along needed to assist in maintaining, regaining, or advancing in employment;

3. Vocational and other training services including personal and vocational adjustment, books, or other training materials. Training in higher education institutions cannot be paid for unless maximum efforts have been made to obtain grant assistance from other sources;

4. Physical and mental restorative services such as corrective surgery, eye glasses, and diagnosis and treatment for mental and emotional disorders;

5. Occupational licenses, equipment, tools, and basic stocks and supplies;

6. Transportation needed to participate in any vocational service;

7. Technological aids and devices; and,

8. Supported employment services. [Section 103 (a)]

Individuals with learning disabilities can benefit from any of the services listed above; however, their vocational rehabilitation needs extend beyond traditional services (Berkeley Planning Associates, 1989). During the assessment process, these individuals often need assistance in understanding their abilities and limitations and in identifying the obstacles they may encounter in pursuing training or employment objectives. Some individuals will underestimate their abilities, while others overestimate theirs. Often they need a functional assessment that actually places the individual in a job situation within a career interest area; the experience should be followed with a counseling session in which the individual reflects on the job demands and his or her own interest in and ability to do the job. These supported, experiential learning opportunities enable the individuals to participate more effectively in making appropriate career decisions.

Individuals with learning disabilities also need assistance with identifying and requesting reasonable accommodations and modifications. As part of the self-discovery process, it is important to accept one's strengths and limitations and to be able to identify the impact that these limitations may have in a school or work environment. When the impact is determined, reasonable accommodations can be generated to circumvent the problem or reduce the impact.

Many of these services should begin during the middle school and high school years and can be provided very effectively in collaboration with the special education or vocational education personnel (Dowdy & McCue, 1994). It is especially important for individuals to be trained to function as self-advocates in obtaining these modifications. This need for self-advocacy skills will continue across the life span.

FACILITATING THE COLLABORATION PROCESS

In order for students with learning disabilities to have a better opportunity for a successful transition from school to work, VR professionals and public school personnel must work closely as a team. For school personnel, this could include educating students and their families about VR services, preparing students to make informed choices, educating VR counselors about learning disabilities, and preparing special educators to enhance the high school curriculum so that a focus on employment considerations is achieved.

Preparing Students

Students with learning disabilities and their parents often think of VR as a program for persons with mental retardation or physical disabilities. They may not even relate to the term *disability* at all. Students may have been assigned to classes called "resource rooms," "study skills classes," or "learning labs" to lessen the stigma of being placed in special education. Often, these students and their parents have not been educated as to the lifelong implications of learning disabilities. Students and families often believe that if the student can just pass the high school exit exam and graduate, everything will be all right. As a result, time and resources specified on the IEP focus on the present challenges of high school and provide limited attention to life after high school (Smith, Finn, & Dowdy, 1993). Often it is just assumed that students with learning disabilities can get a job or go to college without continuing special accommodations or assistance from an adult agency (Michaels, 1994).

When students with learning disabilities and their parents do apply for VR services, they are often offended by the VR counselor's reference to disabilities. Blunt terms and predictions regarding future employment opportunities may make the parents feel that the VR counselor does not understand their child's capabilities. Frequently, first encounters between students with learning disabilities and their parents and VR personnel result in negative feelings about VR services (Michaels & Dowdy, 1995). On their part, the counselors may feel that the parents are unrealistic, and the students uninterested or unmotivated. One way to help alleviate this problem is to educate students regarding their specific capacities or strengths and disabilities, and provide training in self-advocacy skills.

Gerber and Ginsberg (1990) studied the profiles of highly successful individuals with learning disabilities and found that the variables that contributed to success included the quest to gain control of one's life, a desire to succeed, individual persistence, and goal orientation. The VR program encourages these behaviors as important prerequisites for successful VR intervention. A major theme of the 1992 Amendments is the assurance of the individual's involvement in all phases of the VR process and his or her informed choice of goals, services, and service providers.

However, the opportunity for choice is seldom available to special education students in the development of their high school curriculum or their IEP. Michaels (1994) called special education students the "innocent victims" (p. 14) of the IEP process. He also noted that parents and educators rarely share the results of individualized testing with students with learning disabilities. Most leave high school with the knowledge, stemming from a lifetime of failure, that they have learning problems, but they cannot describe their limitations and strengths or describe the accommodations or modifications they need to succeed in inclusive settings. Many high school students with learning disabilities feel disempowered, without any sense of ownership for the direction of their lives. They have been conditioned to look outside themselves when decisions need to be made or when problems arise in their daily lives, and they do the same when vocational choices are presented (Pramuka, 1994).

The ability to participate in self-determination or self-advocacy activities is not available upon command. It is a process that must be developed purposefully. These skills begin with understanding one's disability. Van Reusen, Bos, Schumaker, and Deshler (1995) defined self-advocacy as "the ability of an individual to effectively communicate, convey, negotiate, or assert one's own interest, desires, needs, and rights. It assumes the ability to make informed decisions. It also means taking responsibility for those decisions" (p. 6). They added that providing students with opportunities to make decisions about what they learn can help prepare them to become full participants in a democratic society.

Pramuka (1994) proposed six goals of empowerment for self-advocacy:

1. Students must know themselves well. They should be able to discuss their strengths and limitations and be able to describe areas of life they approach differently because of their disability;

2. Students should be competent in gathering and managing information;

3. Students should view professionals and their families as "consultants" as they make their own life choices;

4. Students must be able to effectively communicate their goals;

5. Students should develop metacognitive skills to compensate for their limitations in planning, organizing, goal setting, and self-monitoring; and,

6. Students must be able to generalize knowledge and skills from the school environment to the work environment.

For more information in this important area, refer to Wilson (1994) and Field (chapter 4 of this book).

Preparing VR Counselors

Because learning disabilities are new to the VR field, counselors may need additional training regarding the wide range of behaviors that are characteristic of a learning disability and the impact of the disability, particularly with respect to employment considerations. The academic levels that teachers most frequently use to describe the limitations of a student with a learning disability are not as important to the VR counselor as are the individual's functional capacities in terms of specific characteristics, such as memory, attention, social skills, emotional maturity, persistence, reasoning, and coordination, that may affect his or her work. Teachers must learn to describe their students' capacities—what they can do—as well as their limitations.

When describing students to VR counselors, teachers need to emphasize a student's ability to function in the workplace without accommodations or modifications. Teachers often describe students as "able to follow directions"; but in the school setting, students are provided written and oral directions and even given a demonstration as part of the directions. A teacher may note that a student "finishes work," but not note that the work is finished only after extended time is given, or the assignment is reduced. A teacher may describe a student as "motivated and persistent," when actually the students' motivation is the result of parents' making sure homework is completed and relevant questions are asked and answered.

Teachers must remember that VR counselors are looking for individuals with disabilities who need VR services because of impairments that pose substantial limitations to employment. Thus, the teacher must balance functional-capacity information with information that also describes behaviors that interfere with successful functioning, as well as information on the need for appropriate accommodations, modifications, or services.

Another problem is communicating that a student's learning disability might include characteristics that may interfere with meeting deadlines or following through with assignments, such as poor organization and time management. These behaviors should be considered as functional limitations—a manifestation of the learning disability; unfortunately they frequently are interpreted as lack of motivation or lack of cooperation. The hidden nature of a specific learning disability is often an impediment because of others' inaccurate perceptions. This can be helped if the student has a good understanding of his or her disability and its impact on daily requirements, and the ability to be a self-advocate to improve communication. For these skills to evolve, the high school curriculum must address these and other functional abilities. It is important to train special educators to make these changes in the curriculum.

Preparing Special Educators

Significant changes in the high school special education curriculum are being encouraged as a result of the 1990 Amendments to the IDEA mandating the provision of transition services. The new transition curriculum must produce outcome-oriented results in the areas of postsecondary education, vocational training, integrated employment, continuing adult services, independent living, and/or community participation. The curriculum should be developed by a group of individuals, generally called a transition team, who discuss students' needs and determine the availability of existing services in related agencies.

Although guidelines for curriculum change can be found in the literature, a transition curriculum has not been implemented on a large scale for students with learning disabilities. Typical curricula for students with learning disabilities have had less of a transition orientation than do those for students with other disabilities. Many learning disability teachers are asked to teach content classes, such as government or English, for students at risk for failure in general education content classes. In resource rooms, learning disability teachers spend a lot of time tutoring students who are struggling to pass in general classrooms. Teachers may team teach with a general educator in an inclusive classroom, focusing on the modification of academic demands to enable students to succeed. Teachers may not have a schedule that permits a transition class, or they may not be trained to develop or implement components of a successful transition program. The logistics of developing and implementing a transition curriculum may be overwhelming, but it must be done.

A study by Michaels (1994) suggested that parents, VR counselors, and special educators differ significantly in their perception of the importance of various components of the special education curriculum and the current availability of each. His study did suggest that the domains agreed upon as necessary for successful adult living include academic skills, vocational skills, and life skills (a combination of social and independent living skills). Michaels suggested that the specifics of the transition curricula in each school district be developed cooperatively through a needs assessment, with input from employers and postsecondary service providers, the receivers of the special education graduates, community representatives, general and special educators and administrators, related service personnel, and, most important, the parents and the students themselves.

After the needs assessment, the transition team must determine the transition activities to be made available and the person or agency responsible for each. If any designated agency or individual fails to participate, the transition team must reconvene to determine how those services/activities will be provided. This team approach to transition planning can provide teachers the necessary support for making these important changes.

SUMMARY AND RECOMMENDATIONS

VR services can be a significant resource for individuals with learning disabilities and their families. To date, persons with learning disabilities have not taken full advantage of this adult service agency, for a variety of reasons. If special education and vocational rehabilitation personnel will work cooperatively, they can empower individuals with learning disabilities to succeed in full participation in work and community living.

The following is a summary of key points for special educators and vocational rehabilitation counselors to use in collaborating in the transition process.

1. Teachers and VR counselors should be educated about the transition process, including the transition services available in the district.

2. VR counselors should provide an inservice for teachers on the VR system of eligibility and service provision.

3. VR counselors should visit the classroom and meet with the students informally to discuss VR services. Involve parents, if possible.

4. The counselor should become involved with each student as early as possible. Some states will begin to work with students as early as age 15; others activate students only during their senior year.

5. Assessment data should be made easily accessible to counselors; they particularly need data on functional limitations and strengths.

6. Use at least part of each student's time in the resource class for transition activities. Find ways to infuse transition activities into content classes.

7. The VR counselor should participate in teaching a few of the transition classes, with a particular focus on the job market and career alternatives that do not require a traditional college education.

8. Discuss the value of nonacademic experiences and their relationship to exploration of personal interests, awareness of strengths and limitations, and general knowledge of the working world. Include discussions of part-time work, internships/apprenticeships, volunteer work opportunities, and community service activities.

9. Have students discuss disabilities and the legal rights of individuals with disabilities guaranteed by IDEA, Section 504 of the Rehabilitation Act, and the Americans with Disabilities Act.

10. Discuss learning disabilities with the students. Each student should be able to describe his or her own strengths and limitations that may affect postsecondary education and employment success.

11. Model and require appropriate employment behavior in the classroom, such as timely arrival and completion of assignments, assign-

ments requiring group decision-making, brief oral and written summaries of activities, development of agendas, and so forth.

12. Prepare students for the VR interview by developing personal portfolios that include medical reports, academic achievement, work history, interest/career inventories, transcripts, psychological/social work reports, transition IEPs, and accommodations or modifications that have been used successfully.

13. Have students describe their own needs in terms of modifications or accommodations. Provide opportunities for students to use self-advocacy strategies and practice self-determination.

14. Invite students to participate in the IEP process. Consider the VR counselors' preference in scheduling (e.g., always on the same day, several close together, spaced apart).

15. Encourage students to try part-time employment to enhance their work history.

16. Maintain regular contact with team members regarding students' progress and the transition services available.

AUTHOR'S NOTE

I would like to acknowledge the technical assistance of Jerry Abbott, policy analyst for the Office of Program Operations, Rehabilitation Service Administration, U.S. Department of Education, Washington, DC, in the preparation of this chapter.

10. Community Transition Teams as the Foundation for Transition Services for Youth with Learning Disabilities

GINGER BLALOCK

Individuals with learning disabilities represent a diverse group; yet the educational system has tended to treat them as a homogeneous group in many facets of their instructional programs. This narrow perspective is particularly evident in the scarcity of transition services expected for, and demanded by, adolescents with learning disabilities. The range of transition services required by this population reaches beyond what schools alone can provide. For example, students with learning disabilities may need support in planning to attend a postsecondary institution, in determining a career direction, in preparing to live independently, in establishing social support networks, or in establishing transportation options outcomes that require cooperation and support from many sources in addition to schools. The Individuals with Disabilities Education Act (IDEA) provides the power to address the transition support needs of persons with learning disabilities by requiring consideration of transition services for *every* student in special education. Youth and young adults with learning disabilities can take charge of their destinies with prepara-

Reprinted, with changes, from "Community transition teams as the foundation for transition services for youth with learning disabilities," by Ginger Blalock, *Journal of Learning Disabilities,* Vol. 29, 1996, pp. 148–159. Copyright © 1996 by PRO-ED, Inc.

tion in self-determination and self-advocacy (see Field, chapter 4 of this book).

WHY COMMUNITY TEAMS ARE NEEDED

Communities across the United States have found that the establishment or improvement of transition programs for youth with learning disabilities involves numerous supporting players (Stodden & Leake, 1994). Educators play an essential role in preparing students for future educational and work demands, but they have neither the time nor the ability to accomplish those outcomes alone.

Representation by parents and students with learning disabilities is critical as the team explores transition and its meaning across our educational, rehabilitation, and social service systems. Students are finally recognized as core team members; they have the most at stake in transition programs and must communicate their goals, interests, and preferred instructional activities. Family members serve as the lifeline of support throughout the students' lives and provide essential information about each student's (and their own) functioning, dreams, and interests; however, parents of students with learning disabilities may be reluctant to get involved with transition-related activities for a variety of reasons (e.g., prior focus of the transition initiative was primarily on students with severe disabilities), or they may be unaware of the need for action.

Other critical partners include employers, who can provide real-life training and employment opportunities along with feedback about meaningful curricular directions. In addition, adult agency personnel need early notice of referrals in order to prepare budgets and to respond to consumer needs after school completion; they often already share strong linkages with the private sector and other adult systems. Postsecondary educators offer advanced training and educational opportunities, as well as support, referral, and job placement services, to young adults from widely diverse backgrounds. Other useful partners include tribal or religious leaders, directors of recreation programs, scout leaders, entertainment/sports organizers, mental health personnel, county extension agents, or community center staff, among many others.

When the range of representatives described above work as a team in planning and implementing a service program in a given community, a comprehensive continuum of transition options is developed and maintained in meaningful ways. The team members can work together to identify the community's goals regarding transition services, to build on the community's existing strengths, and to respond to targeted needs specific to that locale. Due to their close knowledge of and connectedness to the community, the team of representatives identified above can ensure that a broad, long-range perspective takes into account the educational, economic, cultural, and social factors relevant to that community. Halpern, Benz, and Lindstrom (1992) labeled this feature of community transition team activities as "uniform procedures yielding individualized outcomes" (p. 113). Such individual tailoring to each community's particular goals and activities is central to each team's success; a single model imposed on an array of locales simply does not work (Blalock, Hessmiller, Webb, & Schlee, 1995).

Encouragement to use representative transition teams exists within our laws, such as the Individuals with Disabilities Education Act (IDEA) and the Reauthorization of the Rehabilitation Act, through their emphases on interagency linkages and coordinated activities that bring all key parties into joint action (IDEA, Sec. 602(a)(20) and 602(a)(19)). Most statewide change projects and model demonstration projects have discovered that systems change requires a systemic, multilevel approach, of which community-level activities are the cornerstone. A good example of such collaborative, outcome-oriented activity is the creation of Tech Prep programs involving school and postsecondary institution staff, employers, family members, and students within a community. (Consult Evers, chapter 6 of this book, about the potential exclusion of students with learning disabilities from such programs.)

Federal initiatives in the 1980s that were designed to promote transition services for youth with disabilities may not have adequately emphasized the notion that change must occur from the bottom up, that is, that postschool opportunities will remain extremely limited without a representative, active group of community "leaders" creating valuable career development opportunities. Rusch, Kohler, and Hughes (1992) analyzed all prior research and model development projects sponsored by the Office of Special Education and Rehabilitative Services (OSERS), U.S. Department of Education. They found that few employment-focused or education-focused projects were aimed at the community level. This gap has occurred in spite of substantial recognition that change *must* happen at the community level if the change is to be long-lasting and meaningful (Rusch, DeStefano, Chadsey-Rusch, Phelps, & Szymanski, 1992).

In fact, a more recent trend of community involvement and input into transition programs has emerged. Halloran (1995) reported that the multidistrict outreach projects funded by OSERS between 1991 and 1995 had to demonstrate coordination with relevant agencies, organizations, and state systems transition projects. Several of the funded projects specifically addressed community interagency transition teams, including the Collaborative Transition Teams Outreach Project, led by Sharpton at the University of New Orleans; Project ACTT (Arizona Community Transition Teams), directed by Love and McLaughlin at the Arizona Department of Education; the Transition Model for Secondary Students with Moderate and Severe Disabilities, led by Alberto of Georgia State University; and the Culturally Relevant Community-Based Curricula, directed by Field of Wayne State University (Halloran, 1995).

This chapter proposes that team formation and team activities are critical for real change in transition programs and occur most meaningfully at the local level. The efforts of community transition teams can dramatically enhance the secondary preparation and postschool options for *all* youth, including those with learning disabilities; reference is made, where pertinent, to components that particularly relate to learning disabilities. The levels and memberships that make up teams will be described as a "menu" of options from which communities can select. Descriptions of team activities and a few projects' outcomes will follow. Finally, challenges faced by community transition teams will be described, to suggest critical directions for ongoing and future efforts.

TRANSITION TEAMS

Team Levels

Legislation (such as IDEA) typically depicts teams at either the student level (for individualized transition planning) or, at the other end of the spectrum, the state level (pursuing interagency collaboration). However, in reality, more than two levels exist: individualized transition planning, school-based, community, regional, and state levels. The teams vary significantly by location and purpose, which subsequently drives their membership and activities. All teams should be multidisciplinary in nature, with members sharing a common aim. This section briefly presents an overview of the levels and their broad functions; Table 10.1 depicts the five levels, their major functions, and their possible memberships.

1. *Individualized transition planning (ITP)* committees help a single student at a time to identify, plan for, and achieve his or her future goals in education, work, and life. This first level is student focused and is sometimes referred to as an Individualized Education Program (IEP) team in many locations; the Iowa Transition Initiative (1993) refers to this group as a "multidisciplinary team." The same committee should then translate the outcome-oriented planning into goals and objectives for the IEP. ITP teams should meet at least annually for each student, if not more frequently, to ensure that the long-range goals initially identified remain the most appropriate guideposts for educational interventions. Otherwise, the ITP runs the risk of "tracking" students in misguided directions.

TABLE 10.1
Levels and Membership of Transition Teams Serving Youth

Team	Primary function	Usually present	Present as appropriate
Individualized Transition Planning Committee	Design, implement, and evaluate a single student's transition plan	Student Parents/guardians Transition coordinator Special education teacher/chair General education teacher/chair Counselor or administrator	Juvenile Probation Officer Social Services Representative Postsecondary Special Services Staff Vocational Rehabilitation Counselor Adult Agency Staff
School-based Transition Committee	Develop and/or monitor schoolwide practices related to transition (assessment, curriculum, delivery options)	Teachers or dept. heads (general, special, vocational, bilingual ed) Transition coordinator Work-study/COOP/DECA coordinator Parents or consumers	Administrators Counselors or Social Workers School Board Members Related Services Personnel Students or Former Students
Community Transition Team	Create partnerships to influence improved secondary and adult services, programs, and life choices	Students or consumers Parents/guardians School administrators Special education teacher/chair Transition coordinator Advocacy agency representatives School board members Juvenile corrections staff Others	Adult Vocational Program Staff Vocational Rehabilitation Counselor Department of Labor Counselor or Staff Chamber of Commerce Representative Employers/Trade Organization Reps Postsecondary Special Services Staff Tribal Representatives Social Security Administration Rep.
Regional Transition Team	Same as Community Transition Team's	Same membership as Community Transition Team, drawing upon several communities at once; could be county-wide or based upon other regional divisions. Often, several communities share the same vocational rehabilitation counselor, Department of Labor Center staff, and employers	

Table continues

TABLE 10.1 (cont.)

Team	Primary function	Usually present	Present as appropriate
State-level Transition Team[a]	Develop the state-level infra-structure needed for communities to develop and improve services	Students or consumers Family members University faculty members Vocational rehabilitation staff Department of labor personnel Practitioners (all relevant areas) Social security administration Social services representative Advocacy organization members Tribal representatives	Statewide systems change project staff Mental health system representative Postsecondary education representatives State department of education transition coordinators (special education, vocational education, etc.) Corrections system representative(s) Developmental disabilities system representative Employers Others

[a]All or most members listed in both columns would be likely to participate.

2. *School-based transition committees* typically work on making curricular changes, developing individualized transition planning tools and procedures, integrating vocational assessment into transition planning, or developing instructional delivery options. These groups may already exist in the form of building-based curriculum committees, student support teams, or other entities, or they may evolve specifically to address transition education.

3. *Community and regional transition teams* are similar in purpose; therefore, a state would tend to focus on one or the other level, rather than both. These groups identify common goals and develop action plans, problem-solve how to make interagency collaboration happen, create community training and employment opportunities for students, and seek additional sources of support (financial, governmental policy, etc.), as needed, to carry out their area's plans. For example, Iowa's systems change project has involved transition advisory boards that are associated with 15 area education agencies, the state's regional intermediate units. The transition advisory boards help develop and systematize transition procedures across the state and work closely with individual communities to support them in accomplishing their transition goals (P. Sitlington, personal communication, September 15, 1994).

4. *The state-level transition team* (sometimes called a "transition advisory council") primarily opens doors for interagency collaboration at the state level that is intended to enhance cooperation at the local level. State-level interagency teams serve as vehicles for developing model transition programs or identifying transition goals and procedures, for training school and agency personnel, and for maintaining communication among geographic areas.

The specific purposes of each team level vary significantly, but all serve to enhance transition options and programming for individual students. The designs also differ, regardless of level. For example, Palace and Whitmore (1988) examined collaborative transition planning systems in 24 school districts of Los Angeles County that served many students with learning disabilities, as well as other types of exceptionalities. Eighteen districts said they had district-level transition teams (and two more were soon to have them), consisting most often of students, parents, regional center staff, Department of Rehabilitation staff, special educators, "other" personnel, and staff from regional occupational programs (ROPs). These district-level teams were unusual in that they operated as individualized transition planning groups, meeting once or twice annually for each student. Broader interagency planning teams were identified in only 10 districts; those teams met once or twice annually, with one district meeting four times per year. For an area the size of Los Angeles County, these collaborative interagency teams may have operated like community or regional teams, making policy changes and offering new opportunities for students.

For the remainder of this chapter, the level of teaming discussed will be the community transition team. Although the individual-level team is essential for ensuring appropriate programming for each student with learning disabilities, these students are likely to face minimal opportunities to prepare for, and move successfully toward, adulthood without the efforts of the community-level teams. The value of these teams was highlighted by Minnesota's transition coordinator, Sandra Thompson, who stated, "Our biggest system change agent is at the community level" (LaRue, 1994, p. 14). Minnesota Statute 120.17, Subdivision 16, actually requires local communities to form community transition interagency committees (Bates, Bronkema, Ames, & Hess, 1992). Their mandated functions are to

> (a) identify current services, (b) facilitate the development of multiagency teams, (c) develop a community plan for service improvement, (d) recommend changes for improving transition services, (e) exchange information to spotlight needs, and (f) prepare a yearly summary of community transition activities. (Bates et al., 1992, p. 118)

Team Membership

In order for community transition teams to perform the above functions in ways that mesh closely with local circumstances, the membership of each team must represent the inhabitants of the area as much as possible. The issue of representative membership encompasses diversity in ethnicity, culture, socioeconomic level, discipline or occupation, gender, age, and disability. Halpern et al. (1992) defined members of community transition teams as "the full array of people who are concerned about secondary special education and transition programs in their communities" (p. 113). They delineated membership according to four groups: (a) people with disabilities and their families; (b) school personnel; (c) adult agency personnel; and (d) general citizens, such as employers.

Often, the memberships of the various team levels look similar and have overlapping compositions (see Table 10.1). What vary across the team levels are not necessarily the types of agencies or constituents but, rather, the specific positions or job titles held by staff representing those agencies. For example, access to a local vocational rehabilitation counselor is critical at the individual and community levels, but an area director for the rehabilitation agency would be needed at the regional level, and a state agency coordinator would participate in the state-level transition committee. *Individuals* with learning disabilities have the greatest investment in what is accomplished by the various teams, relative to other team members, and therefore should be represented at every level. After that, the particular level of the team and individual students' needs should drive the membership.

All five levels should involve *school personnel* (generally, both special educators and vocational educators as well as counselors or administrators) and *family members*. Typical participants in individualized, community, regional, and statewide teams include adult agency personnel (vocational rehabilitation, community vocational, or residential service providers); social services representatives (e.g., social security, mental health); corrections staff (probation officers, correctional educators); postsecondary educators (special services staff, trades department heads); and employers. In contrast, school-based teams typically consist of school personnel and students or parents, who jointly address school-based priorities.

Ensuring the representativeness and effectiveness of members is challenging. For instance, the National Council on Disability (1989) found that parents were not actively involved in their children's transitions from school to adult life and had difficulties accessing appropriate adult services and postsecondary programs. The council also reported that partnerships between the business community and schools aimed at enhancing job opportunities for students with disabilities were insufficient. As a result of these problems, strategies have emerged to support greater community participation. Stodden and Leake (1994) described local transition teams whose initial task was to identify the roles and responsibilities of persons needed to carry out team-directed activities. Team members then invited any interested persons (external to the team) to provide input (Smith & Edelen-Smith, 1993). Other strategies to encourage team participation have included offering common meeting sites for teams, tuition stipends and university credit, administrative support, and even minigrants to teams for implementing their action plans (Smith & Edelen-Smith, 1993).

Lindsey and Blalock (1993) found that facilitating ownership of the transition process and outcomes among cross-disciplinary participants (family members, school staff, and employers) was an effective incentive. Early decision making and goal setting by consensus ensured that all parties contributed and became a foundation for their involvement. Blalock et al. (1995) encouraged local facilitators and team members to meet preliminarily with families and employers in community centers, restaurants, or tribal chapter houses, just to explain the concept of transition and its importance to local youth with learning disabilities. Thus, citizens could make more informed decisions about whether or not to join the community team.

Different projects have had varying results regarding promoting a single leadership position for the teams versus more shared or diffused roles. Stodden and Leake (1994) reported that transition specialists were too frequently add-on personnel who were removed from the total school system and who therefore were not extremely effective. Lindsey and Blalock (1993) found that a regional transition specialist provided the critical support that district and community personnel needed to get organized and keep the momentum going. However, once the specialist was gone, the momentum died significantly in some sites. Halpern et al. (1992) reported favorable results when staff from the state education agency served as "change facilitators," providing essential technical assistance, networking, and other support as requested, as well as the promise of long-term support due to their positions.

GOALS AND FUNCTIONS

The primary aim of community transition teams is to enhance, develop, and support effective transition programs and services for students. According to Benz, Lindstrom, Halpern, and Rothstrom (1991), "the essence of the Community Transition Team Model is to provide structured support for local control" (p. 2). Essential elements of model transition projects include planning within the local community context; active involvement of students and family members; sharing of school and community resources, such as vocational rehabilitation; school–business connections; and collaboration between vocational and special education (Wehman, 1990). All of these elements directly relate to the community team activities and outcomes that are described below. Examples from diverse transition projects will illustrate the myriad ways in which teams can achieve their goals within their particular contexts.

Team Development

The tasks at hand for community transition teams are related to group formation, management, and evaluation, all in order to effectively pursue an agreed-upon plan. This plan is designed to empower the group to accomplish specified local outcomes for youth and young adults. The initial stage must be team formation and team building, which includes identifying initial members, selecting a team leader, establishing rapport among members, and agreeing upon a goal (not necessarily in that order). When considering youth with learning disabilities, identification of a shared transition purpose will likely center on training and employment opportunities, postsecondary education options, and appropriate secondary curricula.

Benz et al. (1991) and others have illustrated the phases and tasks of the community transition team. Several manuals are now available to guide teams in their formation, meetings facilitation, and effective task management (Benz et al., 1991; Carl, n.d.-b; McAlonan, 1992; Vermont Department of Education, n.d.). Figure 10.1 represents a composite of these in its outline of community team functions.

Community Needs Assessments

Student and program needs must be the cornerstone of any assessment process, and they can be determined at several levels and in several ways. Common methods involve individual and district-wide student outcomes data from follow-up studies, evaluation of program quality via comparison to standards, surveys of school personnel and local citizens, team-generated strengths and needs related to transition, and local labor-market analyses.

The short-term and long-range outcomes of students with learning disabilities must be regularly identified through follow-up studies in order to better guide programming decisions and curricular options for this group. Most communities find that their youth with learning disabilities share outcomes similar to those shown in national trends: 61% graduation rate, 35% dropout rate, 16.7% participation in postsecondary training, and 9% attendance at community or 4-year colleges (Wagner, 1989). Unemployment is certainly an issue after high school: Only 70% to 75%

- Team Development

- Community Needs Assessment

- Action Plans

- Education, Training and Employment Opportunities

- Staff Training and Technical Assistance

- Interagency Collaboration and Shared Resources

- Monitoring and Evaluating Team Progress

Figure 10.1. The major functions of community transition teams.

of individuals with learning disabilities typically are employed in full- or part-time competitive jobs 1 or more years after school. Underemployment and its subsequent correlates of dependence on others, lowered job status, and low income are of particular concern for this population (Okolo & Sitlington, 1988; Sitlington, Frank, & Carson, 1990).

Needs can also be meaningfully examined in the context of program standards or criteria, particularly when they are generated from the field. Benz and Halpern (1986, 1987) and Halpern and Benz (1987) used practitioners' input to identify five major categories of concern about secondary special education programs: (a) curriculum and instruction, (b) coordination and mainstreaming, (c) transition services, (d) documentation of student outcomes, and (e) need for adult services (Halpern et al., 1992). These standards are very useful assessment criteria for any teacher, parent, student, or administrator taking a look at current secondary special education and transition services at the individual, building, or community level.

Blalock et al. (1995) found that several districts identified community needs assessment as a priority for long-range planning; training or technical assistance in the development of instruments to match their local situations was subsequently provided. Coombe (1993) advocated carefully designed needs assessments involving school personnel and community members, as a strategy for establishing program goals—similar to an IEP approach, but with a broader scope. Subsequent sharing of the results with respondents and other constituents was recommended to facilitate prioritization of goals and development of action groups or committees. In this manner, special education supervisors could design transition-to-work programs for youth with disabilities that fit local circumstances and thus offered the best chances for success.

Akridge (1992) created an ambitious community event called a "jobs rally" to help communities respond better to the needs of their citizens with disabilities. He outlined a four-step community needs assessment and gave a rationale for community-level interventions. Individual participants could conduct self-assessments related to working, and the team would then assess the levels and types of community resources that could support the employment of persons with disabilities. The Department of Labor Bureau of Economic Research and Statewide Occupational Information Coordinating Committee has been particularly helpful in some states by providing examples of their labor-market analysis tools, as well as lists and mailing labels of large and small employers in the area.

Action Plans

All projects involving community or regional transition teams have incorporated development of action plans that are set within the community context. Stodden and Leake (1994) described the evolution of school improvement teams, which initially targeted high school transition services. Their project's activities were based on a three-phase collaborative process applicable to any group. Phase 1 involved collaborative team building, Phase 2 was "Infusing Transition Values and Practices," and Phase 3 was "Action Planning." This latter step was defined as "Specifying activities, responsibilities, and timelines for infusing innovations to improve post-school outcomes" (p. 72).

Community team model projects have found that action planning must be embedded in an agreed-upon philosophical framework. Halpern et al. (1992) infused four guiding principles: (a) local control of implementation, (b) an evolutionary perspective on change, (c) a focusing of change efforts on program capacity (simultaneous person-centered planning within the IEP with intervention-centered planning), and (d) networking to connect the teams' efforts. Smith and Edelen-Smith (1993) reported that teams worked first to generate by consensus a precise vision, or mission statement, for their schools (requiring a minimum of 2 months, or 16 hours of meetings). Then teams were given the freedom to act as they needed to achieve their identified goals. Targeting continuous program improvement as an ideal ("how good your program can be") was inherent within both of these models. Utah's community transition councils have pursued a similar format for action planning (G. Clark, personal communication, September 15, 1994).

After the creation of mission statements, teams have defined and developed numerous options for achieving the identified mission (Smith & Edelen-Smith, 1993). Identifying objectives, tasks, timelines, intended outcomes, resources, and responsible parties; developing an annual calendar and annual budget; and solidifying relationships are critical steps (Halpern et al., 1992). Subcommittees worked on each planned objective, while the entire team met monthly or bimonthly to monitor, coordinate, and revise activities. Stodden and Leake (1994) allowed team members the autonomy to identify their own vision or direction, thereby enhancing their commitment to team and student success.

Education, Training, and Employment Opportunities

Defur and Reiff (1994) delineated a continuum of transition service options essential for diverse students with learning disabilities, grounded within individualized transition planning tied to the IEP and conducted by a team. In many cases, identification of such programmatic needs, and the authority to create new programs, can come only from a broader community team not bound by typical school district constraints. Blalock et al. (1995) found that administrators and school board members would listen to business leaders who stressed curricular directions; these curricular areas typically have included social skills, reasoning abilities, work-related behaviors (such as a work ethic, taking initiative, and dependability), and basic academic skills (at the bottom of the list). Employers also can offer their own worksites for training or employment, or can effectively recruit their colleagues to support students' training or hiring needs.

Postschool employment is more likely if (a) comprehensive vocational training is a primary component of the high school program and (b) students have a job secured at graduation (National Council on Disability, 1989). Every site will approach postschool employment differently. For example, one team promoted collaboration between a special educator and a business education instructor (both team members) that led to creation of the "snack attack": Special education students carried out the midmorning school-based snack business, while business education students developed its plan (e.g., purchasing, packaging, marketing, distribution, and inventory management). In addition to the valuable, multilevel skills that students acquired, the profits allowed them to rent a nearby apartment for independent living skill development, to donate gifts to the school and a battered women's program, and to attend and present at the Oregon Vocational Association Conference (Halpern et al., 1992).

Staff Training and Technical Assistance

Smith and Edelen-Smith (1993) found that program restructuring required that stakeholders: (a) gain internal direction toward outcomes-oriented action plans; (b) better understand the relationship of secondary special education programs to future adult situations; and (c) creatively engage all other key parties, including students, in building appropriate IEPs/ITPs. To support these directions, in-state "experts" have proved to be very effective providers of long-term training and technical assistance; in addition, their efforts have generated statewide networks of professionals engaged in transition-related activities who now rely on each other for support and information.

In one system, university faculty were assigned to each school team from the start, providing technical or research information on vocational-related best practices or best outcomes. The state education agency also assisted in this respect, helping to clarify federal and state regulations. Examples of inservice presentations included the Carl Perkins Act Reauthorization of 1990 (leading to vocational educators' joining the team) and a full-day training by employers on "What Work-Related Behaviors, Knowledge, and Skills Are Present in the IDEAL Employee" (Smith & Edelen-Smith, 1993). In another case, transition project staff and district or agency personnel from around the state provided the requested support, matching identified topics with individuals' expertise (Lindsey & Blalock, 1993). The most commonly requested topics have included developing functional curricula, functional assessment, vocational education/ special education collaboration, parent involvement in transition, community needs assessments, and employer networking (Blalock et al., 1995).

Change facilitators are essential in situations in which, historically, one or two persons have had to grasp the full complexity of the problem, lead and assist in implementing the planned procedures, and evaluate the outcomes of the change process. In Oregon, staff from the state education agency performed these functions (Halpern et al., 1992), whereas staff of Utah's statewide systems change project (the STUDY Project) filled the same role (G. Clark, personal communication, September 15, 1994).

Carl (n.d.-b) outlined four critical steps toward skill development that regional transition team members must take in order to accomplish their aims. The steps include an overview of team building, building powerful mission statements, understanding the group process, and setting strategic priorities through cooperative processing. Networking skills have also been identified as essential (Carl, n.d.-a).

Several manuals currently exist to guide community transition teams through the evolution that must occur if they are to make a difference. Colorado's *Transition Manual* (McAlonan, 1992) serves as a rich resource regarding the procedural steps and tools that can facilitate the team's work and steer reluctant participants through the change process. Minnesota's interagency planning manual provides community transition interagency committees with information on getting started, assessing community needs, group process strategies, and community action planning (Minnesota Department of Education, 1990). The Iowa Transition Initiative (1993) generated a team-building training package consisting of four modules (Carl, n.d.-a) and a networking training unit with five modules (Carl, n.d.-b), as well as other documents that support the statewide transition model. New Mexico's technical assistance document on transition outlines the composition, goals, and activities of community transition teams (Blalock et al., 1994). Utah's Community Transition Council manual also was recently developed (G. Clark, personal communication, September 15, 1994). The Oregon Community Transition Team Model (CTTM) has produced precise materials to support replication by other states or districts, including a team leader's manual (Halpern, Lindstrom, Benz, & Nelson, 1991), a needs assessment instrument (Halpern, Lindstrom, Benz, & Rothstrom, 1991), and a facilitator's manual (Benz et al., 1991). Finally, Vermont's Transition Systems Change Project has also created a capacity-building manual (Vermont Department of Education, n.d.).

Interagency Collaboration and Shared Resources

Various projects have involved outside support to teams, typically at the request of the teams themselves. Stodden and Leake (1994) demonstrated that two factors are essential for far-reaching success of the team process: externally supplied support and facilitation to teams, and team members' perceptions that their individual needs are being met. Stodden and Leake's project provided four levels of support and facilitation: (a) guidance in conducting the teaming process until members felt they could do it themselves, (b) information on best practices in transition, (c) help in problem solving and overcoming local barriers, and (d) training of team members in carrying out their roles and responsibilities.

Federal initiatives and legislation related to transition are now heavily influencing "agencies that typically function independently to establish ways to function interdependently" (DeFur & Reiff, 1994, p. 102); this is similar to the way that early childhood interagency councils have operated over the past 15 years. In the case of students with learning disabilities, the expertise offered by professional organizations, such as the Council for Learning Disabilities, the Division for Learning Disabilities of the Council for Exceptional Children, the Learning Disabilities Association, and the Orton Dyslexia Society, can greatly improve transition services. In addition, some communities find that the creation of a local interagency agreement provides such advantages as continuity in the face of staff turnover, justification for staff time spent on transition services tasks, and agreed-upon procedures for shared and transferred responsibilities. Other locales find the process unnecessary and cumbersome. Many states find that concurrent development of agreements at state and local levels greatly enhances the impact of those joint guidelines.

Monitoring and Evaluating Team Progress

Formal strategies for assessing the actual impact and outcomes of community transition teams are essential for ensuring that their directions are appropriate. Smith and Edelen-Smith (1993) described five components, identified by Hawaiian teams, all of which were intertwined with evaluation of their impact. The final activity was infusion of formative and summative evaluation procedures into teaming efforts, so that those results could then inform evaluations of adult outcomes. Halpern et al. (1992) completed a structured year-end report that reviewed their accomplishments and addressed plans for the coming year. In addition, project staff created a "transition team management information system" to help with processing needs assessment data, annual plan development, processing year-end reports, and networking. Colorado's *Transition*

Manual includes "Team Effectiveness Scales" (McAlonan, 1992), which analyze team functioning.

Follow-up and follow-along data on students are also required to provide feedback at several levels, including that of the broader team. By investigating the adult adjustment of students with learning disabilities, as Sitlington and Frank (1993) recently did in their study of school dropouts with LD, schools can share the findings with students, parents, business people, and adult providers as ammunition for participation and change.

OUTCOMES

Halpern et al. (1992) listed numerous accomplishments of the network of transition teams in Oregon. The more visible outcomes included the creation of new instructional programs; the less direct results involved better communication and collaboration among local service providers and increased student self-esteem and self-worth. Nevada, Kansas, and Arizona were listed as additional sites where the CTTM model has been explored (Halpern et al., 1992).

Stodden and Leake (1994) reported a snowball effect for teaming efforts aimed at integrating transition into the school system core. Additional members and schools were inspired by the activities of the self-managed teams. Stodden and Leake reported that 6 original teams sponsored by the University of Hawaii University Affiliated Program (UAP) have now increased to 19 (out of 24 public high schools in the state). In addition, interagency transition planning committees formed in each of the state's seven school districts are also using the collaborative teaming process.

The University of Hawaii UAP has provided technical assistance to three or more other states seeking to adopt and demonstrate the teaming process. Their research on the impact of transition teams on the lives of exceptional students is currently under way (Stodden & Leake, 1994). In addition, they anecdotally report that participants in the teaming process felt empowered and inspired by collaborating to create a desired future for students. Other outcomes were decreased feelings of isolation on the part of the teachers, and opportunities to work on projects in which they deeply believed. Stodden and Leake urged all parties interested in truly integrating transition into a system's core to take part, if possible, in broader restructuring endeavors. The current debate surrounding inclusion of students with disabilities in general education programs is an example of broader efforts that tie closely with transition programs. A major effort was made to recruit parents, who now have a stake in each of the 11 teams (Smith & Edelen-Smith, 1993).

A recent survey of New Mexico's districts indicated that only 35% of respondents were members of an interagency community transition team (CIRCLE of Life Transition Project, 1994). Formal procedural links between the schools and vocational rehabilitation were still not in place in many communities. Findings indicated a need for interagency agreement at both state and local levels, cross-training between agencies, and incorporation of a formal system of transition for students into the operating manuals of both agencies. Adult service providers offered many suggestions for improving the delivery of transition services—for example, they noted that high school preparation and interagency planning are inconsistent (CIRCLE Project, 1994).

All of the models for establishing community transition teams for systemic improvement demonstrated significant utility in enhancing local transition services and programs for students with learning disabilities and other types of disabilities. Once again, "staying close to the knitting," or focusing on individual students within a specific locale, led concerned citizens to create real change. In addition, the local teams' overall impact provided invaluable frames of reference for state-level efforts and university research. Partnerships that emerged among state agencies, higher education, and local communities proved to be strong mechanisms for creating long-term, meaningful change for students in yet more communities across participating states. Dissemination to new states is occurring rapidly and offers hope for significant reform in education's response to transition needs in the future.

CHALLENGES FOR COMMUNITY TEAMS

Several major challenges face community transition team members as they work together to improve transition outcomes for youth with learning disabilities. Some of these demands are addressed in this section, along with recommendations that can serve as guideposts for future efforts.

Generic Barriers to Transition

Many needs assessments have identified transportation as a barrier to transition goals in most communities (Rusch et al., 1992). Rusch et al. also listed other factors as possible inhibitors or facilitators of transition outcomes, such as access to generic social services; media or local perceptions about individuals with disabilities; economic climate; employment trends; and cultural, religious, and institutional customs. Data on these aspects affecting employment, residential, and social outcomes of persons with learning disabilities must be gathered and analyzed by the community transition team if effective planning is to occur.

Rural and Multicultural Issues

Team members are often required to address rural challenges related to transition (i.e., deficiencies in available work, adequate resources, transportation, volunteer support, and personnel to assist with placements, Helge, 1984). In addition, a local community's ethnic and language variables often dictate the need for representative "voices" to assist in problem solving. Blalock et al. (1995) sought advice from area experts experienced at providing consultation-based interventions at rural, culturally diverse sites, and they generated some of the basic principles that guided project activities. These principles fell into five categories: (a) making "bad" assumptions (e.g., do not assume that an expression of interest means one has the time to do something; do not assume that the school or the administrator truly represents the community's viewpoint); (b) making initial contacts; (c) promoting ongoing activities; (d) following through on tasks; and (e) determining basic issues to address with each site (e.g., readiness for change; careful identification of issues, strengths and needs; guaranteeing input from all participants). The initial interview questions used to evaluate readiness for change and to identify training and support needs (see Figure 10.2) were adapted from Bracey's (1991) checklist of readiness for educational change. Greater insights regarding the effects of cultural, linguistic, geographic, socioeconomic, and other variables on community team outcomes are needed.

Major Educational Reform Initiatives

The challenge faced by community transition teams related to recent reform initiatives is to ensure that students with learning disabilities are not left behind (see Bassett & Smith, chapter 11 of this book). The excellence-in-education-reform/school restructuring initiative virtually ignores special education students at the national level, promotes academic excellence only, and fails to consider the crucial need for alternative programs for large numbers of students. The inclusion movement certainly targets millions of students with learning disabilities in the United States, promoting their placement in general settings with support services as needed; however, the excitement over this model's potential

District:_____   Date(s):_____
Contact Person:_____   Interviewer:_____
   ****

How many residents in community?_____
How many students in school?_____

Roughly, what is the ethnic makeup?
Is your transition team representative of ethnic makeup?
If not, is it possible to be more inclusive?

Are you likely to be the person to take the lead in this transition training process?
If not, who?

How is your district involving parents?
Would a translator help participation for parents?

What is working very well in your overall special education program and where does it break down?

Can you describe the general curriculum to which special education students are exposed?
What are the functional components, if any?

Are the team members you've listed solid enough in terms of energy, power to make decisions, and representation of your community?

What do you see as the greatest barriers to (developing/improving) your transition process?

Would people in your district see this as coming from the top down, or the bottom up?
How about people in your community?
How well does the school know the community? (jobs, cultural values, attitudes)

Is your superintendent supportive?
What exists in your district to encourage teachers to make changes?

Are there any other details about your situation that would help us in our decision-making?

Figure 10.2. As part of the New Mexico Transition Specialist Training Project, districts that wanted to receive support to improve their transition programs were asked a series of questions. These questions preliminarily assess the district's readiness for educational change and pinpoint areas needing support.

has also inadvertently eliminated planning for alternative programs, or threatens to do so, in many schools. Finally, the School to Work Opportunities Act mandates work-based learning, school-based learning, and connecting activities embodied in such exemplary components as applied academics, concurrent enrollment in both high school and postsecondary education, and seamless transitions between high school and 2-year and 4-year colleges, as well as to employment (Lyon, 1994). Access to those mainstream options is not automatic for persons with learning disabilities; it, too, must be bargained for by local teams who are committed to providing such experiences for students.

Efforts that create more opportunities for *all* students (but also protect and address the needs of students with learning disabilities) offer greater chances for sustained success. The broader local community (e.g., employers, families) likely will be much more supportive of creating change if many students will benefit, not just those with certain disabilities. Community transition teams have the potential to serve as a powerful integration vehicle for youth and young adults with learning disabilities and other exceptionalities. Electing to expand transition services and options for all the young citizens of a community can allow teams to establish a sound, long-term system of connectedness. The plans and activities of teams choosing such a direction should be carefully studied for their direct implications for educational practice and for the outcomes of individuals with learning disabilities.

The Need for a Collaborative Ethic

Outside forces too often attempt to make major changes in school and adult systems from the top down, without including those individuals most affected by changes in the system design and other decisions (Stodden & Leake, 1994). Broadening the membership of the community transition team has appeared to foster its subsequent development of innovative solutions. Lindsey and Blalock (1993) discovered that multilevel participation and multilevel decision making were critical in developing transition services in one rural area. Partner status was granted to a wide range of players, including parents, students, administrators, teachers, and employers. As a result, that particular team developed a collaborative ethic that, according to Phillips and McCullough (1990), "empowers professionals to assist each other in solving problems" (p. 295) through joint responsibility for problems, joint accountability for resolution, and an underlying belief in the merits of such collaborative work. The local team evolved from other elements as well: administrative support (administrators were team members, and the team reported monthly to the school board in one district); participant ownership in the outcome goals and the process (generated by members' part in developing both); format feasibility (i.e., planning activities and outcomes that were realistic and meaningful); and staff development (Phillips & McCullough, 1990).

Shift to an Outcomes Orientation

Asking schools (and sometimes those outside the schools) to shift their thinking to focus on the future requires a monumental change in perspective by these groups. Many teachers are solidly grounded in the curricular expectations for their particular grades and content areas, and in a year-to-year focus. They may not feel a need to look further ahead, or grasp the potential of concrete, short-term objectives that can lead to desired postschool outcomes. Administrators may also be very comfortable with their current roles (or overwhelmed by their current demands) and feel no urgency to change the status quo. Stodden and Leake (1994) cited these and other barriers to restructuring as they called for transformation of the core of the education system itself in order for students in transition to truly gain support. They suggested that schools, like other organizations, tend to continue in their traditional directions unless forced to change by external agents. The collaborative interdisciplinary teams' experiences taught them that the process of spurring transition through teaming was most common in locales where people had expressed an interest in change and a commitment to pursue it (Smith & Edelen-Smith, 1993).

Lack of Legislative Support

The fact that all of the identified projects have been externally funded highlights an underlying problem. Only in the state of Minnesota has legislation supported the development of community transition teams, as well as of a state office designated to oversee the work of those teams. State and local institutional support will be necessary for long-range activity of this nature.

Limited Scope of Transition Teams

The existing community transition team systems have, of necessity, focused on either (a) students with moderate and severe disabilities or (b) a broad range of special education students. Findings about youth with learning disabilities and their specific relationships to community transition team activities are sorely lacking in the literature. Perhaps as more states implement community or regional transition teams, more focused data will become available. Proliferation of community teams would also highlight the need to learn more about many aspects of team functioning. For instance, controversy surrounds the direction that team leadership should take (i.e., single leader vs. shared leadership).

The model and pilot projects driven by state and federal grants have provided very valuable information about community transition team development, task achievement, and (to a limited extent) outcomes. Several common elements of community teams' activities have been identified in prior sections. However, transition projects that incorporate community teams remain fairly small in number; many more communities and states need to explore the most beneficial mechanisms for improving transition programs at the local level. At this juncture in the evolution of school-to-adulthood support, community transition teams appear to be a viable mechanism for improving local services for youth with learning and other disabilities.

11. Transition in an Era of Reform

DIANE S. BASSETT AND TOM E. C. SMITH

Transition services for students with learning disabilities are just beginning to be recognized as essential to the students' success in post–high school environments. Traditionally, students with more severe disabilities have been provided transition services and life skills coursework as a matter of course, whereas students with learning disabilities have been seen as possessing adequate skills to seek employment and training, live independently, and seek meaningful relationships without the benefit of such supports. We now know that a lack of transition support for individuals with learning disabilities may be just as problematic as it is for their more severely disabled peers (Haring, Lovett, & Smith, 1990). As noted in previous chapters in this book, students with learning disabilities tend to be unemployed and underemployed more frequently than their non-disabled peers. They tend to live at home with parents for longer periods of time, and to express greater frustration with isolation and lack of relationships in their lives. Although many students realize what they need to do in order to pursue their goals, they lack the confidence, the executive functioning skills, and the supports to be able to achieve them. For these individuals, transition services would both supply the necessary supports and help students identify their goals and the specific actions needed to accomplish them.

Reprinted, with changes, from "Transition in an era of reform," by Diane S. Bassett and Tom E. C. Smith, *Journal of Learning Disabilities,* Vol. 29, 1996, pp. 161–166. Copyright © 1996 by PRO-ED, Inc.

Students with learning disabilities may not qualify for many of the supports offered by adult service agencies. For example, in many states, the Division of Vocational Rehabilitation operates under an "Order of Selection" that precludes offering services to any individuals whose disabilities are not considered severe. Many individuals with learning disabilities do not fit the criteria set forth through the Order of Selection. Likewise, other agencies (Social Security, community-center boards for individuals with developmental disabilities, etc.) do not have resources to extend to individuals with learning disabilities. An unfortunate Catch-22 is created: Students with learning disabilities are entitled to services under the mandates of the Individuals with Disabilities Education Act (IDEA), but entitlement to adult service agencies upon exiting from school may be nonexistent. It is critical, therefore, that school personnel work hard to ensure the appropriate delivery of transition services to students with learning disabilities while the latter are still in secondary school. School personnel helping to plan for a student's future may well be his or her last formal support.

Transition services for students with disabilities offer what many believe to be the ultimate challenge of our school system—looking beyond school to the outcomes necessary for successful adult living (Wehman, Moon, Everson, Wood, & Barcus, 1988). However, current educational reform issues (in higher education, public education, and state and federal legislation) tend to emphasize increased attention to academics, rather than to the eventual transition to adulthood and citizenship (Smith, Finn, & Dowdy, 1993). Many of the new initiatives included in the Contract with America criticize and seek to rescind the enactment of Goals 2000, portions of IDEA, equity sections of the Elementary and Secondary Education Act, and the job training and vocational education legislation set forth by previous congressional sessions. It is imperative that we become familiar with the reform agenda set forth in general education and in state and federal governments. Effective transition planning for students with learning disabilities can be accomplished in our schools, but only if we are aware of the possibilities inherent in reform initiatives for students with disabilities and utilize them accordingly.

ROLE OF EDUCATIONAL REFORM

Public education in the United States has been at a crossroads for nearly a decade (Smith, 1990). The reform movement that began in the 1980s and was highlighted by the Nation at Risk Report seems to be a never-ending process of recommendations, task forces, and goals set by different levels of government. The result is a continuous *system of change* that affects schools differently every year. This system of change is being both articulated and implemented by universities, administrators, and public schools at a frenetic pace.

All reform efforts relate in part to Goals 2000, which was recently signed into law by President Clinton and will be enacted over the next several years. The passage of Goals 2000, which is an extension of former President Bush's Education Summit of Governors held in 1989, has opened some doors for students with learning disabilities while inadvertently closing others. Educators need to be aware of these systemic changes and use them for the benefits of students with learning disabilities in the transition process.

The Inclusion Movement

Inclusion of students with disabilities has been the emphasis in special education since the implementation of P.L. 94-142 in the late 1970s. The early efforts in inclusion, referred to as *mainstreaming*, were partly the result of efficacy studies that reported limited success of students placed in self-contained, segregated classrooms (see Smith, Price, & Marsh, 1986, for a discussion). This encouraged schools to move from serving students in self-contained classes to using a combination of resource rooms and general education classrooms. Too often, early efforts of mainstreaming students with disabilities focused on physical placement in general education classes, and not on other classroom interactions that are now considered part of inclusion.

Current efforts to include students with disabilities in general education settings have gone well beyond these early mainstreaming attempts. In fact, the term *inclusion* takes on significantly greater breadth today in its interpretation than mainstreaming did 15 years ago. Inclusion can range in meaning from integrating all students with disabilities, regardless of the severity of their disability, in general education classrooms all day every day, to a more moderate interpretation that promotes the placement of all students with their chronological-age peers in general education classrooms as much as possible, with whatever supports are needed. The intent is to provide those supports in the general education setting whenever possible; however, some services may be provided in other settings.

Current inclusion efforts focus more on substantive inclusion as opposed to physical inclusion. The intent is not only to physically place students in general education settings, but also to promote social interactions between students with disabilities and their nondisabled peers. This substantive inclusion requires a great deal more effort than simple physical placement. Regardless of the nature of inclusion for individual children, whether it is more substantive or physical, transition planning must address the individualized placement needs of students across academic, social, vocational, and life skill domains.

The inclusion movement has resulted in fewer changes in programs for students with learning disabilities than for students with other types of disabilities. This is because most students with learning disabilities were served, at least for a large part of the school day, in general education settings even before the current movement advocated more inclusion. This lessened impact of inclusion on students with learning disabilities may have an adverse effect on their getting appropriate transition services. As noted earlier, students with learning disabilities have often been perceived as needing no transition services. This attitude, along with the likelihood that students with learning disabilities will be easier than some other students to include in general classrooms full time, may result in a tendency to continue to overlook their transition needs. As the inclusion movement results in more and more students with severe disabilities being placed in general education programs, more attention will likely be paid to providing appropriate services to that group than to students with learning disabilities. Therefore, an unintended outcome of the inclusion movement could be less attention to the successful transition of students with learning disabilities.

Teacher Education Programs

Teacher education programs are struggling to reinvent teaching, both as a response to the demand for more academically trained professionals and to train leaders who can help change teaching through emerging site-based management practices. The Carnegie Task Force document *A Nation Prepared: Teachers for the 21st Century* (Carnegie Forum on Education and the Economy, 1986) proposed to employ a professional practice model for teachers, similar to the mentoring model used in medicine and law. In this model, new teachers would not be expected to face the same professional challenges as seasoned veterans but would instead develop their practice based on professional partnerships of collegial learning and sharing. The Task Force also seeks the establishment of a National Board for Professional Teaching Standards to evaluate educators and provide a ladder of professional development.

In addition to the Carnegie Task Force, the Holmes Group, comprising deans from colleges of education around the country, developed a blueprint for change. Their document speaks in global terms of the changes that must occur in preservice teacher training programs: broad liberal arts curricula, literature of education, the subject matter of teaching, and reflective practical experience (Murray, 1986). The Holmes Report urges intellectual soundness, commitment to education, entry standards for teachers, diversity, and university/school partnerships.

Still another report that targets school reform was prepared by the Renaissance Group (1989), a consortium of eight teachers' colleges. Their document, titled *Teachers for a New World*, advocates for teachers to be trained to meet a pluralistic society by establishing outcome expectations, providing rigorous learning expectations, and facilitating extensive field experiences.

Unfortunately, these various reports have been decried as rhetoric, overly simplistic and naive, without solid bases for responding to the realities of the teaching profession. The result has been that little change has been affected by these professional efforts at reform. Rather, the changes that have occurred are due for the most part to political action.

For special educators interested in transition efforts, educational reform under the Carnegie, Holmes, and Renaissance reports becomes moot. There is nothing in any of the documents that considers students' transition or life-span learning needs. Vocational and life skills education are not even mentioned. Education is still talked of only in academic terms as it occurs in traditional settings, namely, school classrooms. Further, although most special educators require graduate coursework to train or retool, educational reform does not address this lifelong learning process. An excellent example is the training needed by teachers of students with learning disabilities in the area of transition. Training in this area is critical for all special education staff, including teachers of students with learning disabilities who may still be teaching only remedial academic work in pull-out or self-contained settings. Although some students with learning disabilities benefit from such intervention strategies, others require a more comprehensive program that will better prepare them for their transition from school to postschool environments.

Efforts at education reform, including teacher education reform, have been massive; however, for the most part special educators have not been included. As a result, professionals in special education must find other ways to actively participate in these dialogues. This can occur through professional organizations at the state and national levels, individual activism on college campuses, and teachers' groups in local schools. Without special educators' participation, new initiatives, such as transition for students with learning disabilities, will not move forward successfully, and students will not be afforded opportunities that should be available.

Special Education Reform

In addition to general education reform, including reform in teacher education, significant efforts have come from within special education to reform programs and services for students with disabilities. Although there have been numerous initiatives, the vast majority of changes in special education have focused on students with disabilities in inclusive settings. As we have noted, these settings are primarily in students' neighborhood schools and are connected to the concept of *supports* needed to ensure compliance with IEP mandates.

Both *Winners All*, a document produced by the National Association of State Boards of Education (NASBE, 1992), and *Leading and Managing for Performance*, produced by the National Association of State Directors of Special Education (NASDSE, 1993), discuss the need for a strong policy regarding the inclusion of students with disabilities with their nondisabled peers in general education settings. The NASDSE document goes a step further by articulating interim goals for inclusion, including

- Reduction in dropout rates;
- Significant increase in the number of students receiving a regular high school diploma;
- Significant gain in the number of students successfully participating in postsecondary opportunities;
- Significant increase in the number of students successfully participating in criterion-referenced testing programs;
- Significant increase in the number of students in instructional setting with students who do not have disabilities. (p. 11)

The elements of transition planning are not addressed directly but are implied through the need for higher graduation rates, the decrease in dropout rates, participation in postsecondary opportunities, and participation in a variety of settings with nondisabled peers. Again, however, even with the mandate for transition planning, little is specified in support of a holistic approach to transition. Educators may work hard at keeping students with learning disabilities in inclusive settings, but at the same time they may not be providing for students' overall transition needs, which include occupational training, social skills development, leisure time activities, and so forth. Therefore, although the inclusion movement is the focus for reform in special education, it may not effectively address students' transition needs. Simply requiring the inclusion of students with disabilities may even make effective transition programming difficult.

Standards-based Education

Goals 2000, the Educate America Act, does not directly address the transition of students with disabilities from high school to postschool environments. However, for teachers of students with learning disabilities, it does represent a powerful tool for strengthening the transition planning process. The act is applicable to all students, including those with disabilities, and must be enforced in accordance with other laws. For students with disabilities, this includes IDEA, Section 504, and the Americans with Disabilities Act. Of the eight national goals included in Goals 2000, at least five have direct application to students with learning disabilities and the transition planning process:

- All children will be ready to learn.

- The high school graduation rate will increase to at least 90%.

- Every adult will be literate and will possess the knowledge and skills to compete in a global economy.

- The teaching force will have access to programs for the continued improvement of their professional skills.

- Every school will promote partnerships that will increase parental involvement and participation.

What Goals 2000 does that other documents have not done is to provide the means by which states can accomplish reforms. States wishing to receive Goals 2000 funds must establish statewide plans that include the establishment of standards and a means for the evaluation of student growth (Council for Exceptional Children, 1994). Included in the standards must be content, performance, and occupational skills. Also included are "opportunities to learn" (OTL) standards, which will vary from state to state. These standards are to be used in conjunction with the content, performance, and occupational standards and reflect the needs of special populations, including students with disabilities, students at risk for school failure, and students with cultural and language differences. Goals 2000 also mandates parent and community involvement in the development of the state plan and subsequent standards development.

Standards-based education can be highly problematic for students with learning disabilities if the standards reflect solely academic achievement, without regard to alternative performance outcomes or occupational skills. However, with the addition of the opportunities to learn, educators are able to use the standards, the OTLs, and performance outcomes to make a relevant and significant contribution to transition planning for students with learning disabilities.

Transition planning for students with learning disabilities can vary tremendously; one student may require preparation for postsecondary training whereas another prepares for employment. One student may need strong remedial academic study, whereas another needs consistent social skills training and training in independent living skills. The use of OTLs and performance standards as components of transition planning will help to provide individualized attention while allowing students to participate with their nondisabled peers and as members of the community at large. Parents and families can also fulfill the dual role of being mandated participants in their child's IEP process and contributing members to standards recommendations.

A number of states are already responding to the flexibility incorporated in Goals 2000. In Colorado, for example, opportunities to learn have been crafted for 24 special populations, with individuals with learning disabilities constituting one of the largest constituencies. The OTLs have been drafted by parents, educators, medical and ancillary personnel, administrators, consumers, and other interested persons. More than 150 people have contributed statewide. The OTLs will help provide educators and parents with a compendium of the resources, practices, and conditions necessary for the appropriate education of individuals with learning disabilities, including transition services.

The result of Goals 2000 and other reform efforts in education will be a positive step for the transition of many students with disabilities. However, reform efforts may also result in problems for this group of students. One of the changes that resulted from some early attempts at secondary school reform was the increased requirements for graduation. Unfortunately, most of these new requirements focus on completion of more academic courses, such as more math and language requirements. The obvious result for many students with learning disabilities is a lessened likelihood of successful completion of graduation requirements. Along with the increased number of academic courses required, some states have mandated that all students have to successfully pass basic academic skills tests before they can graduate. Unless accommodations and modifications are made during this testing process, many students with learning disabilities will not be able to pass.

The unfortunate result for many students with learning disabilities unable to pass graduation examinations or complete more academic courses required for a diploma has been that they exit high school without a regular diploma. Students with learning disabilities without a regular diploma will have a much more difficult time than those with diplomas in making the transition from public schools to adulthood. Alternative curricular requirements for students (not only those with learning disabilities) that could still lead to a regular diploma, appropriate modifications and accommodations in high school graduation exams, and a more comprehensive curriculum for all students must be adopted to ensure that reforms do not prove detrimental to students' successful graduation.

When reform movements emphasize a return to basic skills and stricter graduation requirements, students with learning disabilities find it more difficult to graduate from high school with a regular diploma, and thus more difficult to compete in postsecondary education opportunities and employment. On the other hand, when reform movements emphasize an equal educational opportunity for all students, or programs that are designed to help all students achieve adequate employment skills, students with learning disabilities may receive more appropriate transition efforts and end up achieving more success as adults. Reform efforts, therefore, can have both positive and negative consequences for students with learning disabilities.

The reform movement in education will likely continue unabated over the next several years. Policymakers, advocates for students with learning disabilities, and professionals must influence these reforms to ensure that students with learning disabilities are provided with adequate transition services. Without this attention, reformers are likely to implement changes in the educational system that will have a negative impact on the successful transition of students with learning disabilities from school to postschool settings.

RECOMMENDATIONS FOR THE FUTURE

Students with learning disabilities may well be the last group of students classified as disabled to receive appropriate transition services. Traditionally, students with sensory or more severe cognitive disorders have been appropriately supported via work study programs, linkages with adult service agencies, models for independent living, and instruction in social skills and family relationships. It has long been considered that students with learning disabilities could make successful transitions because they had the cognitive skills to do so. However, as professionals began to realize that learning disabilities do not disappear with age, but are in fact chronic and lifelong in nature (National Joint Committee on Learning Disabilities, 1990), transition efforts were begun for this group of students. This has resulted in educators' moving from providing only academic remediation to including social skill acquisition, career awareness and exploration, vocational training, postsecondary linkages, and such adult domains as independent living and financial responsibility in their programming efforts.

There is perhaps no other disability category that contains such a broad range of strengths and needs as learning disabilities. Some students may have mild learning disabilities in only one or two areas while other students have severe and multiple learning disabilities that require intensive, ongoing support across a number of domains. Because learning disabilities are considered "invisible" disabilities, the tendency has been to lump *all* students with learning disabilities together for assessment and intervention. Currently, most students with learning disabilities are placed primarily in inclusive settings, receive the same type of social skills instruction, receive an emphasis in academic remediation in resource settings, and find jobs by themselves without the assistance of work study or supported employment services.

As Sitlington (chapter 3 of this book) articulated so well in her final comments, educators must look beyond the services that have traditionally been provided for students with learning disabilities, and also use care in providing services across the spectrum of abilities experienced by this group of students. For example, it is obvious now that many students with learning disabilities can choose postsecondary education and succeed in a wide range of professions. Transition planning for these students should include careful general education course selection in addition to strong special education support in these classes. Students who will not attend college may require vocational training and on-the-job experience to attain postschool employment goals. Transition planning for these students will be very different than it is for college-bound students, and must provide increased access to vocational courses as well as requiring increased time spent in community-based activities. Still other students with learning disabilities may need to establish linkages with adult service providers in order to receive training, equipment, or counseling for adult life.

Transition planning must be tailored to fit the unique needs of each student with learning disabilities. Although academic goals may still be appropriate for many of these students, others will require a range of options (Trapani, 1990). Students with learning disabilities are more than able to participate in their education and transition planning, to articulate goals for their future, and to work with significant others to systematically design their future. They should be included from the outset in future planning, IEP staffings, and the design and implementation of transition goals (Dowdy & Smith, 1991).

Finally, the emergence of standards-based education through Goals 2000 can provide the framework by which to emphasize and implement effective transition planning for students with learning disabilities. The process of drafting a state plan must include acknowledgment of differing needs, family involvement, evolving professional practice, and alternatives to demonstration of competencies. Now, in the current mood of reform, is surely the time to "seize the moment," to move aggressively toward the transition of individuals with learning disabilities to the whole of adult life in a systematic and positive way.

Appendix: Position Statements

The Transition of Youth with Disabilities to Adult Life

A Position Statement of the Division on Career Development and Transition, The Council for Exceptional Children

ANDREW S. HALPERN

In 1987, the Division on Career Development of the Council for Exceptional Children published its first position paper on the topic of transition from school to adult life for youth with disabilities. This statement marked the culmination of 3 years of effort, under the leadership of Jane Razeghi, Charles Kokaska, Kathleen Gruenhagen, and George Fair. Since that time, we have witnessed substantial growth and development in the *concept* of transition, its *legislative* foundation, and *service delivery programs* that support the concept. This activity has been encouraged at the federal level through a vast array of ad hoc projects focusing on one or more particular dimensions of transition, and more recently, through a network of *statewide systems change projects* which at the time of this writing were being implemented in 30 states throughout the country.

Perhaps symbolic of this substantial effort, the Division on Career Development has also changed its name to the Division on Career Development *and Transition* (DCDT). The purpose of this new position paper is to regain our bearings on where we have moved during the past 7 years under the banner of "transition," and also to lay a course for continuing

Reprinted from "The transition of youth with disabilities to adult life: A position statement of the Division on Career Development and Transition, The Council for Exceptional Children," by Andrew S. Halpern, *Career Development for Exceptional Individuals*, Vol. 17, Fall 1994, pp. 115–124. Copyright © 1994 by the Division on Career Development and Transition. Reprinted by permission.

to work in this area as we move into the 21st century. No attempt will be made to review the voluminous literature that has emerged in this field; DCDT will only attempt to identify and describe some important markers that summarize where we have been and point the way to the future.

A Brief Review of the Concept

Webster defines transition as "the process of changing from one form, state, activity or place to another." When applying this term to human development, we tend to think of transitions from one "phase of life" into another: from infancy into childhood, from childhood into adolescence, from adolescence into adulthood. It is interesting to note that the field of special education, during the past 10 years, has appropriated the term "transition" to apply to the movement of adolescents with disabilities from school into their next environment as young adults in the community. There are certainly other transitions that also present meaningful challenges and opportunities as we pass through different stages in our lives.

Even within the specific transition timeframe between adolescence and young adulthood, our focus of concern within special education has included some interesting variations. Well before the term "transition" became popular in the early 1980s, we had other ways of describing and addressing similar issues and concerns. The so-called "work/study" programs of the 1960s addressed the inadequacies of high school programs for students with mental retardation, from the perspective of *preparing these students to obtain jobs and enjoy a satisfactory level of "community adjustment" after leaving school.* These programs involved collaborations between special education, vocational education and vocational rehabilitation, and they flourished for more than a decade throughout the country.

During the 1970s, work/study programs became less prevalent throughout the country, but the needs reflected by these programs emerged under the banner of "career education." The federal efforts in this area actually began as a *general education* initiative and provided an impetus for the formation of CEC's Division of Career Development in 1976. Two years later, this new division published a position paper on career education for people with disabilities which included the following statement:

Career education provides the opportunity for children to learn, in the least restrictive environment possible, the academic, daily living, personal-social and occupational knowledge and specific vocational work skills necessary for attaining their highest levels of economic, personal and social fulfillment.

The demise of career education as a *federal* initiative occurred in 1982, which set the stage for the emergence of the term "transition" as a descriptor for a "new" federal initiative in this area. Such an initiative did in fact emerge in 1984, when the U.S. Office of Special Education and Rehabilitation Services (OSERS) published its now famous position paper on transition, including the following definition of transition:

> Transition is an outcome-oriented process encompassing a broad array of services and experiences that lead to employment.

Unlike the earlier initiatives, which construed the goal of postschool adaptation to be multifaceted, the OSERS transition initiative was concerned primarily, although not exclusively, with employment.

During the next 6 years, as substantial attention was focused on the development of transition programs, the concept was slowly broadened to encompass a broader array of desired outcomes than simply employment. This broader focus was incorporated into Public Law 101-476, the Individuals with Disabilities Education Act, which defined transition in the following manner:

> Transition services means a coordinated set of activities for a student, designed within an outcome-oriented process, which promotes movement from school to postschool activities, including postsecondary education, vocational training, integrated employment (including supported employment), continuing and adult education, adult services, independent living or community participation (Section 300.18).

In subsequent sections of the act, a requirement is stipulated that transition planning *as part of the Individualized Education Program* must occur for *all* students with disabilities no later than age 16.

A Definition of Transition

Taking into consideration the growth and development over the past 3 decades of both the concept of transition and supporting programs, the Division of Career Development and Transition adopts the following definition as a framework for guiding future work in this area.

> Transition refers to a change in status from behaving primarily as a student to assuming emergent adult roles in the community. These roles include employment, participating in postsecondary education, maintaining a home, becoming appropriately involved in the community, and experiencing satisfactory personal and social relationships. The process of enhancing transition involves the participation and coordination of school programs, adult

agency services, and natural supports within the community. The foundations for transition should be laid during the elementary and middle school years, guided by the broad concept of career development. Transition planning should begin no later than age 14, and students should be encouraged, to the full extent of their capabilities, to assume a maximum amount of responsibility for such planning.

Transition Planning

The best way to address the various dimensions of transition encompassed in this definition is to focus our attention on the process of transition *planning*. This process includes four major components:

- an emerging sense of student empowerment which eventually enhances student *self-determination* within the transition planning process;

- student *self-evaluation*, as a foundation for transition planning;

- student *identification of postschool transition goals* that are consistent with the outcomes of their self-evaluations; and

- student *selection of appropriate educational experiences* to pursue during high school, both in school and within the broader community, that are consistent with their self-evaluations and their postschool goals.

The impact of transition programs and services will be beneficial only to the extent that interventions are implemented that are congruent with these four components of transition planning.

Empowerment and Self-Determination.   When a person is labeled as having a disability, it is not uncommon for parents, service providers and family members to regard such people as being unable to learn how to take responsibility for their own lives. Such an attitude is especially prevalent when the disability being considered is a cognitive disability. When such attitudes are overly and inappropriately "protective" of the person with a disability, the consequence is to diminish that person's ability and opportunity for assuming responsibility with respect to important life decisions.

A school setting does not always provide students with good opportunities to learn self-determination skills. Resource limitations often constrain the availability of instructional programs that are desired by students. Opportunities for students to express preferences are sometimes constrained by a planning process that is directed primarily by professionals. When this happens students have very limited opportunities to explore options and take responsibility for choices, either for their present or their future lives. *If the transition process is to be successful, it must begin with helping students to gain a sense of empowerment with respect to their own transition planning.*

Self-Evaluation.   Because traditional assessment practices in special education have often treated the *subject* of assessment as an *object* of assessment, there have not been very many opportunities for people with disabilities to take charge and ownership of their own evaluations within the context of customary assessment activities. In response to this disenfranchisement, students with disabilities and their families often feel intimidated by the assessment process and its outcomes, which then defeats the very possibility of using assessment information as a foundation for transition planning.

New options must be explored. Students must be taught, whenever possible, how to examine and evaluate their own academic, vocational, independent living, and personal/social skills. Sources of information should include a variety of assessment techniques including tests, ratings, and observations. The idea of self-evaluation does not imply that we should discard the rigor of traditional assessments, but rather that we should dramatically alter the *locus of interpretation* from the examiner to the person being assessed. *Unlike typical evaluation procedures where people are told by others how well or how poorly they perform, the assessment procedures that accompany transition planning should involve teaching students with disabilities how to evaluate themselves, taking into consideration a variety of assessment areas and findings.* In those instances where the student's cognitive disability is too severe to permit this, the locus of control should still be shifted to the parent whenever possible.

Postschool Goals.   There is little disagreement now that employment is only one *among several* goals of transition. As indicated in the definition stated above, this goal structure should be expanded to also include participating in postsecondary education, maintaining a home, becoming involved in the community, and experiencing satisfactory personal and social relationships. *Student needs and interests should be the primary determinant in selecting those goals for the future that will guide the transition planning process.*

Employment, when students choose this goal, should be construed whenever possible as paid competitive employment in the community, including such variations as supported employment for people with severe disabilities. Issues surrounding *financial security* should also be addressed, including the possible need for income subsidies, such as Supplemental Security Income payments, food stamps, or housing subsidies. Job benefits, especially health insurance, should also be considered when selecting transition programs and services that pertain to this goal.

For many young adults with disabilities, some form of *postsecondary education* is an important transition goal. Several options are possible, including attendance at a 4-year college, a community college, a vocational/technical center, or a vocational training program in the private sector. Within such settings, a vast array of potentially relevant opportunities is available for postsecondary education. These possibilities include 4-year college degrees, 2-year degrees with the goal of transferring to a 4-year college, 2-year vocational specialization degrees, vocational licensure programs with or without a degree, vocational training programs without a degree or licensure, high school completion opportunities, courses in remedial academics and study skills, and individual courses, often described as opportunities for "life-long education," tapping a multitude of adult interests. All of these options should be carefully considered, *in addition to employment,* since advanced education often creates opportunities, both vocational and avocational, that would not otherwise be available.

Maintaining one's own home becomes an issue at some point during the transition years, when most young adults with disabilities, as all young adults, will leave the home of their parents or guardians. A wide variety of skills is needed in order to make this transition effectively, including finding a home, arranging for utility services, maintaining a home, and preparing food. As part of the transition planning process, students should consider whether or not they need assistance in learning these skills as a foundation for eventually moving into their own home.

Preparation for *community involvement* is another dimension of the goal structure that needs to be examined during transition planning. A person's community can be either a resource or a barrier, depending upon how well that person becomes involved in the community. The starting point for such access is almost always the ability to use some form of *transportation* effectively, which is often necessary for a person to get to work, to engage in many leisure activities, and to use a wide array of community services, such as stores, banks, or medical clinics, that one needs to live interdependently. Citizenship is also a relevant component of this goal, including volunteer activities, participation in the political process, and conformity with social laws.

The establishment of effective *personal and social relationships* may be the *most important* of all the transition goals. Over the years, both research findings and common sense would certainly support this proposition. Relationships with family members, especially parents, have a tremendous potential to either help or hinder the transition process. The presence or absence of a *network of friends* will often exercise a profound influence on a person's sense of well-being as well as the opportunities that will be available for both leisure and work activities. The opportunity to experience effective *intimate relationships* is also frequently a critical component of both personal and social adjustment. These needs to relate effectively with family, friends, and lovers are both common and strong for *all* people, with and without disabilities. The issue that must be addressed within transition planning is the extent to which any given person needs assistance in learning and practicing those skills that enhance the development of effective interpersonal relationships.

Delivering Transition Services

If the components just described for doing transition *planning* are properly addressed, a firm foundation will be laid for identifying and delivering good transition *services* in support of the transition plan. Many exemplary programs, services and materials have been developed over the years. These include specific approaches for doing transition planning, innovative instructional programs that address transition goals, effective collaborations between special education, vocational education and adult agency programs and the development of outstanding curriculum materials and technological supports for teaching students important transition skills. *Although DCDT does not recommend any particular approach for delivering transition services, DCDT does recommend that whatever approach is selected for any given individual should be evaluated in terms of how well it conforms to the criteria for effective transition planning that are described above.* The approaches that are selected for delivering transition services should *also* be sensitive to the following five issues:

- the extent to which an instructional program is based on student skills, interests, and preferences,
- inclusion of the student within the regular school program,
- provision of community-based learning opportunities when appropriate,
- involvement of adult service agencies as needed, and
- involvement of community organizations, as contrasted with service agencies, in helping students with their transition.

Instructional Programs. The high drop-out rate among students with disabilities is a well-documented phenomena. One reason why many of these students decide to drop out is their realization that available instructional programs are not congruent with their interests, their abilities, or their current levels of achievement. When left with a choice between sticking it out in a program that seems irrelevant or dropping out, many students choose the latter road.

When a student believes that a current program is not meeting his or her needs, *a satisfactory alternative must be developed* as part of transition planning if the student is to become motivated to remain in school. In essence, the *relevance* and *feasibility* of a school program for attaining a student's *long-range transition goals* must be evident, if the student is to remain motivated to stay in school. In some states where different types of exit document are available, such as a regular diploma, a modified diploma, or a certificate of attendance, the decision to remain in school or drop out is often highly related to the student's ability and willingness to make a realistic choice concerning which exit document to pursue.

Inclusion. Educating students with and without disabilities *together* has been a major concern of special education ever since the passage of Public Law 94-142 in 1975. The issue has emerged under various banners, including least restrictive environment, mainstreaming, regular education initiative, and most recently, inclusion. If inclusion is to work effectively, it must be possible for the student with a disability to actually benefit from the experience, and those without disabilities should also benefit from the experience or, at the very least, not find it to be detrimental.

In order for this mutually beneficial experience to emerge, it is usually necessary for *both the student with a disability and the regular education teacher* to receive some sort of appropriate special education services. Depending on the specific situation, these services might include tutoring the student by the special education teacher, arranging peer tutoring for the student, teaching the student study skills and learning strategies, and/or helping the regular education teacher to modify his or her instruction in order to accommodate the needs of the student with a disability, including such areas as the learning of life skills. When such inclusionary efforts are successful in a high school environment, this can also lay a firm foundation for inclusionary environments to emerge in post-school community environments.

Community-based Learning Opportunities. The classroom is an inappropriate environment for many of the transition-oriented skills that students with disabilities need to learn during the high school years. For example, although the school campus may be acceptable for some job experience placements, in most instances, it is more appropriate for this type of experience to occur in the general community. Similarly, many independent living skills, such as banking, shopping, leisure activities, and learning how to use public transportation, must be learned and practiced in the community. Although this can present some logistical difficulties in arranging for instruction, the alternative of attempting to create a simulated environment within the classroom for learning such skills is usually not acceptable or effective.

Involvement of Adult Service Agencies.   Many students with disabilities will need some sort of additional services after leaving school in order to achieve a successful transition. Depending on the school leavers' particular needs, it is possible for a wide array of agencies to become involved, including colleges and universities, health or mental health agencies, developmental disabilities agencies, the Social Security Administration, the state public assistance agency, the state employment agency, and the state vocational rehabilitation agency.

As transition plans begin to emerge during the school years, it often becomes possible to identify the need for services from such agencies while the student is still in school. Whenever such a possibility exists, it is imperative that the appropriate agencies participate in the student's transition planning activities. The current laws pertaining to both special education (Public Law 101-476) and vocational rehabilitation (Public Law 102-569) require such collaboration. The ultimate goal of any such collaboration is interagency linkage to produce a seamless transition of *agency responsibilities,* providing whatever services the student needs and is entitled to, with minimum disruption of services that are due only to agency administrative inefficiencies.

Community Organizations vs. Service Agencies.   We sometimes have the tendency to think that all needs of people with disabilities should be addressed within the context of agency programs and services, accompanied by family supports. When we view the societal context of our efforts in such a fashion, this results in ignoring a huge arena of opportunity: namely, the wide variety of community organizations that exist for the benefit of *all* people and which often are underutilized as potential resources for people with disabilities. Agencies provide *services* to students, clients, or patients, usually delivered by someone who is paid. Community organizations provide opportunities for social and sometimes *caring interactions* between people who join the organization on a relatively equal footing.

Some such organizations, like churches and community recreation facilities, can be found in almost any community. Conversely, almost any community will contain at least one such organization, reflecting the needs and interests of people in that community. A rural community may have granges or local chapters of the Future Farmers Association. An urban or suburban community may have a wide array of special interest groups, like community service organizations or team sports, providing people with similar interests some opportunities to do things together.

Part of the transition planning process should include teaching people with disabilities to learn the landscape of these community organizations and then help them to gain access to such organizations.

Looking Toward the Future

Most of the recommendations stated above view transition from the perspective of a person with a disability. The issues that we address, however, have relevance for a much wider segment of the population than simply those with disabilities. In the broadest sense of the term, transition from school to postsecondary life is a concern and potentially turbulent period of time for *every adolescent,* with or without a disability.

Under the rubric of *general* education reform, new initiatives are being developed that focus on *transition* programs and services for *all* those high school leavers who are not college bound but are looking instead to join the work force immediately. This underlying context is very important for us to consider as we position ourselves to improve transition programs for people with disabilities. As we move toward the future, we must attempt whenever possible to address the problems and opportunities surrounding transition from a *general perspective,* attending to the needs of people with and without disabilities. We must not only advocate to *benefit from* any broad transition efforts that may emerge from the initiatives for general educational reform, we must also offer to *assist* in such efforts, drawing upon our past 3 decades of experience in this arena. If we take such a stance, the future will hold great promise of creating an environment in which people with and without disabilities can work together to address transition issues and concerns of common interest. Such an environment could be truly inclusionary, helping to break down the barriers that are often experienced by people with disabilities simply because they are viewed as being different from those who are not disabled.

Life Skills Instruction: A Necessary Component for All Students with Disabilities

A Position Statement of the Division on Career Development and Transition

GARY M. CLARK, SHARON FIELD, JAMES R. PATTON,

DONN E. BROLIN, AND PATRICIA L. SITLINGTON

The Division on Career Development and Transition affirms the notion that every student with a disability has the right to an appropriate education in the least restrictive environment. Inherent in this affirmation is the absolute necessity for appropriate education to be individually determined, documented in the Individualized Education Program (IEP), and delivered through effective instructional practice. Although there should be no reason to compromise what is agreed as "appropriate" education, it is important to acknowledge that it is not easy to reach agreement on what constitutes appropriate education when appropriateness depends on the choices dictated by the location of instruction. Nor is it easy when curriculum choice is limited to traditional academic content, regardless of the nature or location of the instructional delivery system.

A growing body of literature suggests that appropriateness of education must be determined in terms of individual needs for dealing with the demands of adulthood. Brolin (1988, 1992, 1993) referred to these challenges of adulthood as "life centered career education competen-

Reprinted from "Life skills instruction: A necessary component for all students with disabilities. A position statement of the Division on Career Development and Training," by Gary M. Clark, Sharon Field, James R. Patton, Donn E. Brolin, and Patricia L. Sitlington, *Career Development for Exceptional Individuals*, Vol. 17, Fall 1994, pp. 125–134. Copyright © 1994 by the Division on Career Development and Training. Reprinted by permission.

cies"; Cronin & Patton (1993) used the term "major life demands"; Mithaug, Martin, and Agran (1987) described "adaptability" skills; Clark (1991, 1994) used the common "functional skills" term. In all cases, there is a clear intent to speak to life skills that relate to functioning as a family member, good neighbor and citizen, worker, and functioning participant in the community. These are the same focus areas that have been advocated in career education and career development for students with disabilities since the 1970s. Since there is some ambiguity in different terminology among professionals, the terms "life skills instruction" and "life skills curriculum approach" will be used in this position statement.

What Is a Life Skills Instruction Approach?

A life skills instruction approach is a commitment to providing a set of goals, objectives, and instructional activities designed to teach concepts and skills needed to function successfully in life. This curriculum approach should be begun as early as possible for all students with disabilities (Clark, Carlson, Fisher, Cook, & D'Alonzo, 1991). Curricular content should emphasize instruction in such areas as personal responsibility, social competence, interpersonal relationships, health (physical and mental), home living, employability, occupational awareness, job skills, recreation and leisure skills, consumer skills, and community participation. Individual goals and objectives for life skills on the IEP should be determined on the basis of current level of functioning in these areas, taking into account individual students' specific needs, interests, and preferences, as well as their next expected environments.

Why Is Life Skills Instruction Important?

The Division on Career Development and Transition affirms the importance of life skills instruction for *all* students in schools today. Students with disabilities are especially in need of life skills instruction in light of the predominance of evidence that indicates, for whatever reasons, a large percentage of them find adult living demands outside their skill range (Valdes, Williamson, & Wagner, 1990). The fact remains, there are other students within the educational system who find adult demands just as difficult when they leave school and have similar problems of adjustment—socially, vocationally, and in independent living. A life skills instruction approach should be a part of (i.e., included within existing coursework) or a recognized and approved option (i.e., alternative coursework) to every school curriculum for all students at all grade levels.

Only then can all students and their families have the opportunity to make life-related decisions with regard to individual educational outcomes they view as important.

The importance of life skills as major outcomes of education is clearly demonstrated in The Individuals with Disabilities Education Act (P.L. 101-476). Congress mandated the inclusion of needed transition services in the IEP and required consideration of transition needs related to instruction, community experiences, employment, and other post-school objectives for all students 16 years of age and older and strongly encouraged it for students at an earlier age when appropriate. The legislation made it clear that appropriate programs and services provided to a student should be determined individually and not based solely on the availability and nature of existing programs and services. The provisions apply to *all* students with disabilities regardless of classification of disability or level of severity. The implications of this broad mandate for the population classified as having mild learning or behavioral disabilities (including speech and language disorders) are tremendous and highlight the importance of a fresh look at the nature and content of existing programs in both general and special education.

The importance of life skills is clearly supported also in the Rehabilitation Act Amendments of 1992 (P.L. 102-569) with the historically significant statement:

> Congress finds that . . .
> Disability is a natural part of the human experience and in no way diminishes the right of an individual to—
> A. Live independently;
> B. Enjoy self-determination;
> C. Make choices;
> D. Contribute to society;
> E. Pursue meaningful careers;
> F. Enjoy full inclusion and integration in the economic, political, social, cultural, and educational mainstream of American society . . . (Section 2. Findings; Purpose; Policy)

This statement of Congressional values presents a strong emphasis on rights for certain outcomes, with the implication that public institutions should provide appropriate programs designed to teach the knowledge and skills required to be able to exercise those rights. The statement presents a paradox in the juxtaposition of the first five outcomes (A–E) with the final outcome (F). The apparent contradiction is seen by those who are alarmed by the term "full inclusion and integration in the . . . educational mainstream of American society," believing that the current mainstream of education is not conducive for or supportive of the attainment of life skills needed to celebrate their empowerment to live independently, enjoy self-determination, contribute to society, or pursue meaningful careers. The right of making choices is key to understanding the paradox of the statement and is at the heart of the decision for a student and his or her family as to whether life skills should be a part of the student's IEP as well as where life skills can be learned. Choices imply alternatives, so it is important for educators to create the opportunity for choice by addressing both issues of curriculum options and options within instructional settings where life skills will be taught.

Polloway, Patton, Epstein, and Smith (1989) laid a conceptual foundation that highlighted the importance of providing a comprehensive curriculum to students, from which current and future options and choices can be addressed. Cronin and Patton (1993) refined this conceptualization by examining the major features and the functional relevance of the following curricular themes that can be identified in special education programs:

- Academic content coverage (reading, math, science, etc.)

- Remedial programming (remediation of basic skills, social skills remediation)

- Regular class support (tutorial assistance, compensatory tactics, learning strategies, cooperative teaching, etc.)

- Adult outcomes programming (vocational training, life skill preparation)

While each of these curricular orientations may be appropriate for students for certain goals and objectives, it is clear that the two primary learning content areas are academic content and adult outcomes (life skills) content. Given our current knowledge of existing programs and the need for addressing adult outcomes, it is difficult to imagine that academic content programming would be provided as the *only* option for many students. Three guiding principles for considering the curriculum needs of any student with a disability before limiting a student's options in any instructional delivery system are suggested:

- Utilize the notion of "subsequent environment as attitude" (Polloway, Patton, Smith, & Rodrique, 1991).

- Consider for each individual the notion that time for learning is short and that school time cannot afford to be wasted or taken lightly.

- Re-evaluate what we are doing with students on a regular basis.

Where Should Life Skills Be Taught?

The Division on Career Development and Transition supports the concept that the potential benefits of inclusive education are the stripping away of stigma, the building of self-esteem, and the developing of social skills and interpersonal relationships within an inclusive environment. Given this, the first consideration for where life skills should be taught should be general education settings and the community. Like any other instructional content area, it should be assumed that unless the student is unable to learn the needed life skills within an inclusive, general education setting, even with every provision of support and reasonable accommodations, no move to separate the student from his or her peers should be made. Many of the same strategies and procedures that are recommended for accommodating students with disabilities in academic content settings can be applied to life skills instructional content (Peterson, Leroy, Field, & Wood, 1992; Field, LeRoy, & Rivea, 1994). Among these include (a) outcomes based education including life skills goals; (b) curriculum matrixing including life skills; (c) cooperative learning on applied problems; (d) peer tutoring on specific life skills; (e) mastery learning of life skills content; (f) specialized curriculum materials; (g) infusion of life skills topics into existing curriculum materials, (h) learning strategies on life skills tasks, (i) collaborative teaching on life skills applications, and (j) collaborative planning among general and special education teachers and families on specific life skills content.

Vocational education is a mainstream example of a specialized, direct instruction program for teaching students with and without disabilities very specific life skills content in the area of employment. This separate, specialized instructional alternative has been a legitimate part of general education for decades. The field of vocational education has demonstrated its capacity to respond to many students' interests and preferences and continues to be an alternative for students to acquire critical vocational skills within an integrated setting. Although barriers to full access to vocational and applied technology programs still exist and the need continues for a wider range of vocational training choices, vocational education is a model for secondary schools to use in providing pertinent life skills instructional options for all students in other areas besides employment.

Least restrictive instructional alternatives must always be given first consideration after the decision is made that the instruction in life skills content is not feasible or is inadequate in a general education setting. If it is determined through experience in general education settings, with accommodations and support, that it is not possible to meet a student's life skills curriculum needs, it is not only appropriate but necessary to consider some other service delivery alternatives. There is a strong precedent for separate pull-out programs for teaching certain functional skills such as mobility and orientation, speech and language, speech reading, manual communication, and employability skills. Even in these types of programs, it is possible to provide integration by including students without disabilities (Beck, Broers, Hogue, Shipstead, & Knowlton, 1994), although the instruction is provided outside of a general education classroom. Community-based instruction has been demonstrated to be highly effective in employment training, consumer education, and various kinds of community participation skills training. Instructional activities provided in community settings and in competitive employment are highly inclusive settings and provide an ideal situation for promoting inclusion and teaching life skills.

Who Is Responsible for Life Skills Instruction?

Until such time as there is only one education system and the divisions between general education and special education are indistinguishable, responsibilities for ensuring appropriate education for students with disabilities must be targeted. First, it is the responsibility of general educators at the elementary and middle school levels to ensure the applicability of basic skills education to the functional demands of independent living for students at school, at home, and the community. This means that curriculum and adopted textbook series must relate to the needs of a highly diverse student population, and that schools need to consider new strategies for instructional delivery. Full service schools with "wraparound" services that are in operation year round may become the models for how to provide the time and opportunity to go beyond the traditional focus on basic academic skills instruction. For example, many schools provide breakfast meals for students which could be structured to offer students learning opportunities for social skills, nutrition, health, or even small group guidance on a variety of topics of interest to students. School nurses or social workers in a full-service school can be used for individuals or small group instruction in life skills content rather than just crisis intervention.

Second, it is the responsibility of general educators at the secondary level to ensure the applicability and generalization of subject matter areas to the demands of employment, postsecondary education, and independent living. In doing this, they should shape curriculum content for the current demands of adolescence and the anticipated demands of young adulthood. The goals of secondary education are not the same as for elementary and middle school education. Basic skills are assumed for a majority of secondary students and the goal is to move them to higher levels of performance to prepare them for postsecondary education demands or for advanced levels of skills needed for employment. Given the increasing discrepancy between students' achievement in basic skills and grade level expectations as they move up the grade-level hierarchy, secondary educators must provide for a much more diverse population than in the past. They should acknowledge also that most students, with or without disabilities, who are capable of grade-level achievement still have some specific functional life skills needs in independent living and interpersonal relationships for being successful in an increasingly complex world. One appealing alternative is for secondary schools to provide more options among core or required courses that emphasize transferability of academic content to life demands, as well as more elective courses in life skills areas. These options should be open to all students who choose to take them and monitored like any other course in the school's curriculum.

Third, it is the responsibility of both general and special educators to advocate for the functional needs of all students with disabilities and of those who are at risk of being classified as having disabilities if they do not receive appropriate instruction. It is imperative that all educators expand their repertoire of assessment procedures to include methods for identifying the interests, preferences, and functional needs of each student in terms of current and future functioning. Teachers and related services staff who provide instruction or support for students in inclusive settings must share their observations of students relative to these areas. Functional life skills are not likely to emerge as priorities in a student's individualized education program planning process without a more direct approach to determining functional skill needs. This is where functional assessment of knowledge and performance levels in life skills becomes a critical part of the planning and instructional process.

Both general and special educators in collaborative teaching situations should consider the functional applications of the general education curriculum content and make accommodations whenever possible. The Secretary's Commission on Achieving Necessary Skills (Department of Labor, 1991) provided a framework for targeting specific competencies and basic skills needed in work environments for all individuals. Most of the competencies and skills are generic and apply to home and community environments as well. The special educator may need to take the lead in providing the functional applications for all students in the class and in collaborating with the general education teacher on individualizing assignments and curriculum-based assessment with life skills applications.

Finally, it is the responsibility of special educators to provide specialized or direct instruction in functional skill areas at a level of such quality that there can be no question of commitment to meeting students' needs. Students who spend part of their instructional day in special education settings should have been removed from general education settings only when the nature of the instruction demands a different setting and when every reasonable accommodation has been made and the students' needs still have not been met. When a separate setting is determined to be the most appropriate option for specific instructional content, it must be delivered at such a level of quality that the student's learning is not compromised. Separate, specialized instructional settings cannot be justified as belonging on the educational continuum of service delivery options if *relevant, quality instruction* is not ensured and the educational benefits do not outweigh the disadvantages associated with separation from the general education environment. Without such quality and relevance, the result is worse than Edgar's (1987) "equally appalling alternatives"—". . . integrated mainstreaming in a nonfunctional curriculum . . . or separate, segregated programs for an already devalued group. . ." (p. 560).

Conclusion

Until acceptable alternatives for appropriate education with regard to life skills instruction is available in some form in all instructional settings, the challenge of P.L. 94-142 and its amendments is still before us. The Division on Career Development and Transition renews its commitment to the need for providing life career development and transition programming beginning in early childhood and continuing through adulthood. It recognizes that the individual needs of students with disabilities will sometimes differ from the needs of other students in the type of direct instruction that may be required in a life skills approach. One major difference in needs occurs in some students' abilities to use basic skills and academic content as sufficient preparation for coping with life demands. The Division recognizes that meeting the personal–social, daily living, and occupational adjustment demands that students currently have, as well as those demands they will have in the future, will not occur for many students with disabilities through a traditional academic approach. Response to this concern must involve curriculum considerations and not just an instructional environment or instructional strategy response.

When the individual life skill needs of students with disabilities vary significantly from those of other students in general education after accommodations for their needs have been provided, meeting their needs in an alternative fashion becomes a critical responsibility and should not be compromised. A clear commitment to a life skills approach in both general and special education is an appropriate long-term goal for achieving both curriculum and inclusive education goals for students with special needs.

References

CHAPTER 1

Affleck, J. Q., Edgar, E., Levine, P., & Kottering, L. (1990). *Postschool status of students classified as mildly retarded, learning disabled, or nonhandicapped: Does it get better with time?* Education and Training in Mental Retardation, 25, 315–324.

Benz, M. R., & Halpern, A. S. (1993). Vocational and transition services needed and received by students with disabilities during their last year of high school. *Career Development for Exceptional Individuals, 16, 197–211.*

Blalock, G., Brito, C., Chenault, B., Detwiler, B., Hessmiller, R., Husted, D., Oney, D., Putnam, P., & Van Dyke, R. (1994). *Life span transition planning in New Mexico: A technical assistance document.* Santa Fe, NM: State Board of Education.

Clark, G. M., & Patton, J. R. (in press). *Transition planning inventory.* Austin, TX: PRO-ED.

Cronin, M. E., & Patton, J. R. (1993). *Life skills instruction for all students with special needs: A practical guide for integrating real-life content into the curriculum.* Austin, TX: PRO-ED.

Edgar, E. (1988). Employment as an outcome for mildly handicapped students: Current status and future directions. *Focus on Exceptional Children, 21(1), 1–8.*

Halloran, W. (1989). Foreword. In D. E. Berkell & J. M. Brown (Eds.), *Transition from school to work for persons with disabilities* (pp. xiii–xvi). New York: Longman.

Halpern, A. S. (1985). Transition: A look at the foundations. *Exceptional Children, 51, 479–486.*

Halpern, A. S. (1993). Quality of life as a conceptual framework for evaluating transition outcomes. *Exceptional Children, 59, 486–498.*

Halpern, A. S. (1994). The transition of youth with disabilities to adult life: A position statement of the Division on Career Development and Transition, The Council for Exceptional Children. *Career Development for Exceptional Individuals, 17, 115–124.*

Halpern, A. S., Doren, B., & Benz, M. R. (1993). Job experiences of students with disabilities during their last two years of school. *Career Development for Exceptional Individuals, 16, 63–73.*

Hasazi, S. B., Gordon, L. B., & Roe, C. A. (1985). Factors associated with the employment status of handicapped youth exiting from high school from 1979 to 1983. *Exceptional Children, 51, 455–469.*

Karge, B. D., Patton, P. L., & de la Garza, B. (1992). Transition services for youth with mild disabilities: Do they exist, are they needed? *Career Development for Exceptional Individuals, 15, 47–68.*

Lewis, K., & Taymans, J. M. (1992). An examination of autonomous functioning skills of adolescents with learning disabilities. Career Development for Exceptional Individuals, 15, 37–46.

Mithaug, D. E., Horiuchi, C. N., & Fanning, P. N. (1985). A report on the Colorado statewide follow-up survey of special education students. Exceptional Children, 51, 397–404.

Patton, J. (1995). Transition from school to adult life for students with special needs: Basic concepts and recommended practices. Austin, TX: Learning for Living.

Polloway, E. A., Patton, J. R., Smith, J. D., & Roderique, T. W. (1991). Issues in program design for elementary students with mild retardation: Emphasis on curriculum development. Education and Training in Mental Retardation, 26, 142–150.

Scott, P., & Raborn, D. T. (1995). Realizing the gift of diversity among students with learning disabilities. Unpublished manuscript, University of New Mexico, Albuquerque.

Sitlington, P., Frank, A., & Carson, R. (1992). Adult adjustment among graduates with mild disabilities. Exceptional Children, 59, 221–233.

Wagner, M., Blackorby, J., Cameto, R., Hebbeler, K., & Newman, L. (1993). The transition experiences of young people with disabilities: A summary of findings from the National Longitudinal Transition Study of special education students. Menlo Park, CA: SRI International.

Wagner, M., Newman, L., D'Amico, R., Jay, E. D., Butler-Nalin, P., Marder, C., & Cox, R. (1991). Youth with disabilities: How are they doing? The first comprehensive report from the National Longitudinal Transition Study of special education students. Menlo Park, CA: SRI International.

Wehman, P. (1995). Individual transition plans: The teacher's curriculum guide for helping youth with special needs. Austin, TX: PRO-ED.

Will, M. (1984). OSERS programming for the transition of youth with disabilities: Bridges from school to working life. Washington, DC: Office of Special Education and Rehabilitative Services.

CHAPTER 2

Alley, G. R., Deshler, D., Clark, F., Schumaker, J., & Warner, M. (1983). Learning disabilities in adolescent and adult populations: Research implications (Part II). Focus on Exceptional Children, 15(9), 1–4.

Ariel, A. (1992). Education of children and adolescents with learning disabilities. New York: Merrill.

Aune, E. (1991). A transition model for postsecondary-bound students with learning disabilities. Learning Disabilities Research and Practice, 6, 177–187.

Bates, P. (1993). Administrative considerations in transition planning. In B. Haugh (Ed.), Transition from school to adult life for pupils with disabilities: Best practices in planning and programming transition to adult life. Proceeding of the 1991 and 1992 Summer Institutes (pp. 21–28). Trenton: New Jersey Department of Education.

Bingham, G. (1978). Career attitudes among boys with and without specific learning disabilities. Exceptional Children, 44, 341–342.

Blalock, J. (1981). Persistent problems and concerns of young adults with learning disabilities. In W. Cruickshank & A. Silver (Eds.), Bridges to tommorow (Vol. 2, 35–55). Syracuse, NY: Syracuse University Press.

Browning, P., Brown, C., & Dunn, C. (1993). Another decade of transition for secondary students with disabilities. The High School Journal, 76, 187–194.

Browning, P., & Nave, G. (1993). Teaching social problem solving to learners with mild disabilities. Education and Training in Mental Retardation, 28, 309–317.

Chelser, B. (1982, July–August). ACLD committee survey on LD adults. ACLD Newsbrief, 145, 1, 5.

Cronin, M., & Gerber, P. J. (1982). Preparing the learning disabled adolescent for adulthood. Topics in Learning and Learning Disabilities, 2, 55–68.

Cronin, M. E., & Patton, J. R. (1993). Life skills instruction for all students with special needs: A practical guide for integrating real-life content into the curriculum. Austin, TX. PRO-ED.

Cummings, R., & Maddux, C. (1987). Holland personality types among learning disabled and non–learning disabled high school students. Exceptional Children, 54, 167–170.

Dalke, C., & Franzene, J. (1988). Secondary–postsecondary collaboration: A model of shared responsibility. Learning Disabilities Focus, 4(1), 38–45.

DeStefano, L., & Wermuth, T. R. (1992). IDEA (P.L. 101–476): Defining a second generation of transition services. In F. Rusch, L. DeStefano, J. Chadsey-Rusch, L. A. Phelps, & E. Szymanski (Eds.), Transition from school to adult life: Models, linkages, and policy (pp. 537–549). Sycamore, IL: Sycamore.

Durlak, C. M., Rose, E., & Bursuck, W. D. (1994). Preparing high school students with learning disabilities for the transition to postsecondary education: Teaching the skills of self-determination. Journal of Learning Disabilities, 27, 51–59.

Edgar, E. (1988, March). Secondary education programs for learning disabled students: The need for multiple options. Paper presented at the annual meeting of the Council for Exceptional Children, Washington, DC.

Geist, C. S., & McGrath, C. (1983). Psychosocial aspects of the adult learning disabled person in the world of work: A vocational rehabilitation perspective. Rehabilitation Literature, 44, 210–213.

Gerber, P. J., Ginsberg, R., & Reiff, H. B. (1992). Identifying alterable patterns in employment success for highly successful adults with learning disabilities. Journal of Learning Disabilities, 25, 475–487.

Getzel, E. E., & Gugerty, J. J. (1992). Applications for youth with learning disabilities. In P. Wehman (Ed.), Life beyond the classroom (pp. 301–355). Baltimore: Brookes.

Greenan, J. P. (1983). Identification of generalizable skills in secondary vocational programs. (Executive summary). Urbana–Champaign: Illinois State Board of Education.

Greenan, J. P. (1984). The construct of generalizable skills for assessing the functional learning abilities of students in vocational–technical programs. Journal of Studies in Technical Careers, 2, 91–104.

Halloran, W. D. (1993). Transition services requirement: Issues, implications, challenge. In R. C. Eaves & P. J. McLaughlin (Eds.), Recent advances in special education and rehabilitation (pp. 210–224). Boston: Andover.

Halpern, A. (1985). Transition: A look at the foundations. Exceptional Children, 57, 479–486.

Hoffman, F. J., Sheldon, K. L., Minskoff, E. H., Sautter, S. W., Steidle, E. F., Baker, D. P., Bailey, M. B., & Echols, L. D. (1987). Needs of learning disabled adults. Journal of Learning Disabilities, 20, 43–52.

Houck, C. K., Engelhard, J., & Geller, C. (1989). Self-assessment of learning disabled and nondisabled college students: A comparative study. Learning Disabilities Research, 5, 61–67.

Individuals with Disabilities Education Act of 1990, Public Law 101–476. (October 30, 1990). Title 20, U.S.C. 1400–1485: U.S. Statutes at Large, 104, 1103–1151.

Izzo, M. V., Pritz, S. G., & Ott, P. (1990). Teaching problem solving skills: A ticket to a brighter future. The Journal for Vocational Special Needs Education, 13, 23–26.

Karge, B. D., Patton, P. L., & de la Garza, B. (1992). Transition services for youth with mild disabilities: Do they exist, are they needed? Career Development of the Exceptional Individual, 15, 47–68.

Kohler, P. D. (1993). Best practices in transition: Substantiated or implied? Career Development for Exceptional Individuals, 16, 107–121.

Levin, E. K., Zigmond, N., & Birch, J. (1985). A follow-up study of 52 learning disabled adolescents. Journal of Learning Disabilities, 18, 2–7.

Lewis, K., & Taymans, J. (1992). An examination of autonomous functioning skills of adolescents with learning disabilities. Career Development for Exceptional Individuals, 15, 37–46.

Lichtenstein, S. (1993). Transition from school to adulthood: Case studies of adults with learning disabilities who dropped out of school. Exceptional Children, 59, 336–347.

Martin, J., Marshall, L., & Maxson, L. (1993). Transition policy: Infusing self-determination and self-advocacy into transition programs. Career Development and Exceptional Individuals, 16, 53–61.

Mercer, C. (1991). Students with learning disabilities (4th ed.). New York: Merrill.

Miller, R., Snider, B., & Rzonca, C. (1990). Variables related to the decision of young adults with learning disabilities in postsecondary education. Journal of Learning Disabilities, 23, 349–354.

Minskoff, E. H., & DeMoss, S. (1993). Facilitating successful transition: Using the TRAC model to assess and develop academic skills needed for vocational competence. Learning Disability Quarterly, 16, 161–170.

Minskoff, E., Sautter, S., Sheldon, K., Steidle, E., & Baker, D. (1988). A comparison of learning disabled adults and high school students. Learning Disabilities Research, 3, 115–123.

National Transition Network. (1993, Winter). IDEA: Its impact on transition regulations. Policy Network, pp. 1–4.

National Transition Network. (n.d.). Overview of the National Transition Network (NTN). Minneapolis, MN: Author.

Neubert, D. A., Tilson, G. P., Jr., & Ianacone, R. N. (1989). Postsecondary transition needs and employment patterns of individuals with mild disabilities. Exceptional Children, 55, 494–500.

Okolo, C.M., & Sitlington, P. (1988). The role of special education in LD adolescents' transition from school to work. Learning Disability Quarterly, 11, 292–306.

Patton, J. D., & Polloway, E. A. (1982). The learning disabled: The adult years. Topics in Learning & Learning Disabilities, 2, 79–88.

Peraino, J. M. (1992). Post-21 follow-up studies: How do special education graduates fare? In P. Wehman (Ed.), Life beyond the classroom (pp. 21–70). Baltimore: Brookes.

Peters, M. T., & Heron, T. E. (1993). When the best is not good enough: An examination of best practice. The Journal of Special Education, 26, 371–385.

Polloway, E. A., Patton, J. R., Epstein, M. H., & Smith, T. (1989). Comprehensive curriculum for students with mild handicaps. Focus on Exceptional Children, 21(8), 1–12.

Polloway, E. A., Smith, J. D., & Patton, J. R. (1984). Learning disabilities: An adult development perspective. Learning Disability Quarterly, 7, 179–186.

Price, L. A., Johnson, J. M., & Evelo, S. (1994). When academic assistance is not enough: Addressing the mental health issues of adolescents and adults with learning disabilities. Journal of Learning Disabilities, 27, 82–90.

Reiff, H. B., & deFur, S. (1992). Transition for youths with learning disabilities: A focus on developing independence. Learning Disability Quarterly, 15, 237–249.

Rhoades, C., Browning, P., & Thorin, E. (1986). A self-help advocacy movement: A promising peer support system for mentally handicapped people. Rehabilitation Literature, 47, 2–7.

Rojewski, J. W. (1992). Key components of model transition services for students with learning disabilities. Learning Disability Quarterly, 15, 135–150.

Ryan, A. G., & Price, L. (1992). Adults with learning disabilities in the 1990s. Intervention in School and Clinic, 28, 6–20.

Saracoglu, B., Minden, H., & Wilchesky, M. (1989). The adjustment of students with learning disabilities to university and its relationship to self-esteem and self-efficacy. Journal of Learning Disabilities, 22, 590–592.

Schloss, P., Alper, S., & Jayne, D. (1993). Self-determination for persons with disabilities: Choice, risk, and dignity. Exceptional Children, 60, 215–255.

Seidenberg, P. L., & Koenigsberg, E. (1990). A survey of regular and special education high school teachers and college faculty: Implications for program development for secondary learning disabled students. Learning Disabilities Research, 5, 110–117.

Siperstein, G. N. (1988). Students with learning disabilities in college: The need for a programmatic approach to critical transitions. Journal of Learning Disabilities, 21, 431–436.

Sitlington, P. (1981). Vocational and special education in career programming for the mildly handicapped adolescent. Exceptional Children, 47, 592–598.

Sitlington, P. L., Frank, A. R., & Carson, R. (1992). Adult adjustment among high school graduates with mild disabilities. Exceptional Children, 59, 221–233.

Smith, T. E. C., Finn, D. M., & Dowdy, C. A. (1993). Teaching students with mild disabilities. Fort Worth, TX: Holt, Rinehart & Winston.

Stowitschek, J. J. (1992). Policy and planning in transition programs at the state agency level. In F. Rusch, L. DeStefano, J. Chadsey-Rusch, L. A. Phelps, & E. Szymanski (Eds.), Transition from school to adult life: Models, linkages, and policy (pp. 519–536). Sycamore, IL: Sycamore.

Texas Rehabilitation Commission. (n.d.). Vocational rehabilitation process for specific learning disabilities. Dallas: Author.

U.S. Office of Special Education Programs. (1994). Sixteenth annual report to Congress on the implementation of the Individuals with Disabilities Education Act. Washington, DC: Office of Special Education and Rehabilitative Services.

Valenti, R. A. (1989). Developing self-advocacy: A practical guide and workbook for preparing high school learning disabled students for postsecondary school success. Columbia, MO: Hawthorne Educational Services.

Wagner, M. (1990). The school programs and school performance of secondary students classified as learning disabled: Findings from the National Longitudinal Transition Study of Special Education Students. Menlo Park, CA: SRI International.

Wagner, M. (1993). The school programs and school performance of secondary students classified as learning disabled: Findings from the National Longitudinal Transition Study of Special Education Students. Menlo Park, CA: SRI International.

Wagner, M., Blackorby, J., Cameto, R., Hebbeler, K., & Newman, L. (1993). The transition experiences of young people with disabilities: A summary of findings from the National Longitudinal Transition Study of Special Education Students. Menlo Park, CA: SRI International.

Ward, M. (1988). The many facets of self-determination. Transition Summary, 5, 2–3. Washington, DC: National Information Center for Children and Youth with Disabilities.

Wehmeyer, M. (1992). Self-determination and the education of students with mental retardation. Education and Training in Mental Retardation, 27, 302–314.

Wehmeyer, M. (1993). Self-determination as an educational outcome. Impact, 6(4), 6–7.

White, W. J., Deshler, D., Schumacker, J. B., Warner, M., Alley, R., & Clark, F. L. (1983). The effects of learning disabilities on postschool adjustment. Journal of Rehabilitation, 49, 46–50.

Will, M. (1984). Bridges from school to working life. Washington, DC: Office of Special Education and Rehabilitative Services.

Chapter 3

Ariel, A. A. (1992). Education of children and adolescents with learning disabilities. New York: Merrill.

Brolin, D. E. (1991). Life-centered career education: A competency-based approach. Reston, VA: Council for Exceptional Children.

Bryan, T., Werner, M., & Pearl, R. (1981). Learning disabled students' conformity responses to prosocial and antisocial situations. Learning Disability Quarterly, 5, 344–352.

Chesler, B. (1982, July–August). ACLD committee survey on LD adults. ACLD Newsbrief, 145, 1, 5.

Clark, G. M., Field, S., Patton, J. R., Brolin, D. E., & Sitlington, P. L. (1994). Life skills instruction: A necessary component for all students with disabilities. A position statement of the Division on Career Development and Transition. Career Development for Exceptional Individuals, 17, 125–134.

Clark, G. M., & Kolstoe, O. P. (1990). Career development and transition education for adolescents with disabilities. Boston: Allyn & Bacon.

Cronin, M. E., & Patton, J. R. (1993). Life skills instruction for all students with special needs: A practical guide for integrating real-life content into the curriculum. Austin, TX: PRO-ED.

Darrow, M. A., & Clark, G. M. (1992). Cross-state comparisons of former special education students: Evaluation of a follow-along model. Career Development for Exceptional Individuals, 15, 83–99.

Derr, A. M. (1986). How learning disabled adolescent boys make moral judgements. Journal of Learning Disabilities, 19, 160–164.

Deshler, D. D., Schumaker, J. B., Alley, G. R., Warner, M. M., & Clark, F. L. (1982). Learning disabilities in adolescent and young adult populations: Research implications. Focus on Exceptional Children, 15(1), 1–12.

Deshler, D. D., Schumaker, J. B., & Lenz, B. K. (1984). Academic and cognitive interventions for LD adolescents: Part I. Journal of Learning Disabilities, 17, 108–117.

Dever, R. B. (1988). Community living skills. A taxonomy. Washington, DC: American Association on Mental Retardation.

Edgar, E. (1987). Secondary programs in special education: Are many of them justifiable? Exceptional Children, 53, 555–561.

Edgar, E., & Levine, P. (1987). Special education students in transition: Washington state data 1976–1986. Unpublished manuscript.

Edgar, E., Levine, P., Levine, R., & Dubey, M. (1988). Washington state follow-along studies 1983–87: Students in transition (final report). Unpublished manuscript.

Fine, E., & Zeitlin, S. (1984). Coping means survival for learning disabled adolescents. In W. M. Cruickshank & J. M. Kliebhan (Eds.), The best of ACLD: Early adolescence to early adulthood (Vol. 5, pp. 39–48). Syracuse, NY: Syracuse University Press.

Frank, A., & Sitlington, P. (1994). Iowa transition project post–high school interview form and in-school data form. Unpublished manuscript.

Graves, A., Landers, M., Lokerson, J., Luchow, J., Horvath M., & Garnett, K. (1992). The DLD competencies for teachers of students with learning disabilities. Reston, VA: Division for Learning Disabilities, Council for Exceptional Children.

Gray, R. A. (1981). Services for LD adults: A working paper. Learning Disability Quarterly, 4, 426–434.

Halpern, A. (1985). Transition: A look at the foundations. Exceptional Children, 51, 479–486.

Halpern, A. (1990). A methodological review of follow-up and follow-along studies tracking school leavers from special education. Career Development for Exceptional Individuals, 13, 13–27.

Halpern, A. (1993). Quality of life as a conceptual framework for evaluating transition outcomes. Exceptional Children, 59, 486–498.

Halpern, A. (1994). The transition of youth with disabilities to adult life: A position statement of the Division on Career Development and Transition, The Council for Exceptional Children. Career Development for Exceptional Individuals, 17, 115–124.

Haring, K., Lovett, D., & Smith, D. (1990). A follow-up study of recent special education graduates of learning disabilities programs. Journal of Learning Disabilities, 23, 108–113.

Hartzell, H., & Compton, C. (1984). Learning disability: 10-year follow-up. Pediatrics, 74, 1058–1064.

Hasazi, S., Gordon, L., & Roe, C. (1985). Factors associated with the employment status of handicapped youth exiting high school from 1979 to 1983. Exceptional Children, 51, 455–469.

Hawaii Transition Project. (1987). Honolulu: Department of Special Education, University of Hawaii.

Hoffman, F. J., Sheldon, K. L., Minskoff, E. M., Sautter, S. W., Steidel, E. F., Baker, D. P., Bailey, M. B., & Echols, L. D. (1987). Needs of learning disabled adults. Journal of Learning Disabilities, 20, 43–53.

Hunt, P., Farron-Davis, F., Beckstead, S., Curtis, D., & Goetz, L. (1994). Evaluating the effects of placement of students with severe disabilities in general education versus special classes. The Journal of the Association for Persons with Severe Handicaps, 19, 200–214.

Kennedy, C., & Itkenen, T. (1994). Some effects of regular class participation on the social contacts and social networks of high school students with severe disabilities. The Journal of the Association for Persons with Severe Handicaps, 19, 1–10.

Knowles, M. (1990). The adult learner: The neglected species. Houston: Gulf.

Kokaska, C. J., & Brolin, D. E. (1985). Career education for handicapped individuals (2nd ed.). Columbus, OH: Merrill.

McKinney, J. D. (1984). The search for subtypes of specific learning disability. Journal of Learning Disabilities, 17, 19–26.

National Center on Educational Outcomes. (1993). Education outcomes and indicators for individuals at the post-school level. Minneapolis: University of Minnesota.

Okolo, C., & Sitlington, P. (1988). The role of special education in LD adolescents' transition from school to work. Learning Disability Quarterly, 11, 292–306.

Polloway, E. A., & Patton, J. R. (1993). Strategies for teaching learners with special needs (5th ed.). New York: Macmillan.

Roessler, R., Brolin, D., & Johnson, J. (1990). Factors affecting employment success and quality of life: A one year follow-up of students in special education. Career Development for Exceptional Individuals, 13, 95–107.

Rosenthal, I. (1985). A career development program for learning disabled college students. Journal of Counseling and Development, 63, 308–310.

Schalock, R., Wolzen, B., Ross, I., Elliott, B., Werbel, G., & Peterson, K. (1986). Postsecondary community placement of handicapped students: A five-year follow-up. Learning Disability Quarterly, 9, 295–303.

Scuccimarra, D., & Speece, D. (1990). Employment outcomes and social integration of students with mild handicaps: The quality of life two years after high school. Journal of Learning Disabilities, 23, 213–219.

Sitlington, P., & Frank, A. (1990) Are adolescents with learning disabilities successfully crossing the bridge into adult life? Learning Disability Quarterly, 13, 97–111.

Sitlington, P., & Frank, A. (1993). Iowa statewide follow-up study: Adult adjustment of individuals with learning disabilities three vs. one year out of school. Des Moines: Iowa Department of Education.

Sitlington, P., Frank, A., & Carson, R. (1993). Adult adjustment among graduates with mild disabilities. Exceptional Children, 59, 221–233.

Smith, M. A., & Schloss, P. J. (1988). Teaching to transition. In P. J. Schloss, C. A. Hughes, & M. A. Smith (Eds.), Community integration for persons with mental retaration (pp. 1–16). Austin, TX: PRO-ED.

Thompson, R. J. (1986). Behavior problems in children with developmental and learning disabilities (Monograph No. 3). Ann Arbor: University of Michigan Press.

Torgesen, J. K. (1980). Conceptional and educational implications of the use of efficient task strategies by learning disabled children. Journal of Learning Disabilities, 13, 364–371.

Wagner, M., D'Amico, R., Marder, C., Newman, L., & Blackorby, J. (1992). What happens next? Trends in postschool outcomes of youth with disabilities: The second comprehensive report from the National Longitudinal Transition Study of Special Education Students. Menlo Park, CA: SRI International.

Wagner, M., Newman, L., D'Amico, R., Jay, E., Butler-Nalin, P., Marder, C., & Cox, R. (1991). Youth with disabilities: How are they doing? The first comprehensive report from the National Longitudinal Transition Study of Special Education Students. Menlo Park, CA: SRI International.

Wanant, P. E. (1983). Social skills: An awareness program with learning disabled adolescents. Journal of Learning Disabilities, 16, 35–38.

White, W., Alley, G., Deshler, D., Schumaker, J., Warner, M., & Clark, F. (1982). Are there learning disabilities after high school? Exceptional Children, 48, 273–274.

White, W., Schumaker, J., Warner, M., Alley, G., & Deshler, D. (1980). The current status of young adults identified as learning disabled during their school career (Research Rep. No. 21). Lawrence: University of Kansas Institute for Research in Learning Disabilities.

Wiederholt, J. L., & McEntire, B. (1980). Educational options for handicapped adolescents. Exceptional Education Quarterly, 1(2), 1–10.

Wiens, J. W. (1983). Metacognition and the adolescent passive learner. Journal of Learning Disabilities, 16, 144–149.

Will, M. (1984). OSERS programming for the transition of youth with disabilities: Bridges from school to working life. Washington, DC: Office of Special Education and Rehabilitative Services.

Zigmond, N., & Sansone, J. (1986). Designing a program for the learning disabled adolescent. Remedial and Special Education, 7(5), 13–17.

CHAPTER 4

Abery, B. (1994). A conceptual framework for enhancing self-determination. In M. F. Hayden & B. H. Abery (Eds.), Challenges for a service system in transition (pp. 345–380). Baltimore: Brookes.

Abery, B., & McGrew, K. (1992). Research on the self-determination of individuals with disabilities. Unpublished manuscript, University of Minnesota, Minneapolis.

Adelman, H. S., & Taylor, L. (1993). Learning problems and learning disabilities: Moving forward. Pacific Grove, CA: Brooks/Cole.

American Heritage Dictionary. (1992). Boston: Houghton Mifflin.

Bandura, A. (1986). *Social foundations of thought and action: A social cognitive theory.* Englewood Cliffs, NJ: Prentice Hall.

Brinckerhoff, L. C. (1994). Developing effective self-advocacy skills in college bound students with learning disabilities. *Intervention in School and Clinic, 29,* 229–237.

Brinckerhoff, L. C., Shaw, S. F., & McGuire, J. M. (1992). Promoting access, accommodations, and independence for college students with learning disabilities. *Journal of Learning Disabilities, 25,* 417–429.

Brolin, D. E. (1991). *Life centered career education.* Reston, VA: Council for Exceptional Children.

Campeau, P., & Wolman, J. (1993). *Research on self-determination in individuals with disabilities.* Palo Alto, CA: American Institutes for Research.

Cornell Empowerment Group. (1990). *Empowerment through family support.* Ithaca, NY: Author.

Deci, E. L., Connell, J. P., & Ryan, R. M. (1989). Self-determination in a work organization. *Journal of Applied Psychology, 74,* 580–590.

Deci, E. L., & Ryan, R. M. (1985). *Intrinsic motivation and self-determination in human behavior.* New York: Plenum.

Durlak, C. M., Rose, E., & Bursuck, W. D. (1994). Preparing high school students with learning disabilities for the transition to postsecondary education: Teaching the skills of self-determination. *Journal of Learning Disabilities, 27,* 51–59.

Dyer, W. W. (1976). *Your erroneous zones.* New York: Avon Books.

Eichelberger, R. T. (1989). *Disciplined inquiry: Understanding and doing educational research.* New York: Longman.

Erikson, E. (1975). *Life history and the historical moment.* New York: Norton.

Federal Register. (1992, January 28). 57(18). Washington, DC: U.S. Government Printing Office.

Field, S., & Hoffman, A. (1994). Development of a model for self-determination. *Career Development for Exceptional Individuals, 17(2),* 159–169.

Field, S., & Hoffman, A. (in press-a). Increasing the ability of educators to support youth self-determination. In L. E. Powers, G. H. S. Singer, & J. Sowers (Eds.), *Making our way: Building self-competence among youth with disabilities.* Baltimore: Brookes.

Field, S., & Hoffman, A. (in press-b). *Steps to self-determination.* Austin, TX: PRO-ED.

Field, S., Hoffman, A., & Sawilowsky, S. (1994). *Research in self-determination: Interim research report.* Detroit, MI: Wayne State University.

Field, S., Hoffman, A., St. Peter, S., & Sawilowsky, S. (1992). *Skills and knowledge for self-determination: Interim research report.* Detroit, MI: Developmental Disabilities Institute/College of Education, Wayne State University.

Gordon, R. L. (1977). *Unidimensional scaling of social variables: Concepts and procedures.* New York: The Free Press.

Harris, C., & McKinney, D. (1993). *Project PARTnership: Instructional kit.* Washington, DC: USA Educational Services.

Hoffman, A., & Field, S. (1995). Promoting self-determination through effective curriculum development. *Intervention in School and Clinic, 30,* 134–141.

Hoffman, A., Field, S., & Sawilowsky, S. (1995). *Self-determination assessment battery.* Detroit, MI: Wayne State University.

Hoffman, A., Field, S., & Sawilowsky, S. (in press). *Self-determination knowledge scale.* Austin, TX: PRO-ED.

Johnson, D., & Johnson, R. (1986). Mainstreaming and cooperative learning strategies. Exceptional Children, 52, 553–561.

Johnson, D., Johnson, R., Holubec, E., & Roy, P. (1984). Circles of learning. Alexandria, VA: Association for Supervision and Curriculum Development.

Johnson, D. W., Johnson, R. T., & Maruyama, G. (1983). Interdependence and interpersonal attraction among heterogeneous and homogeneous individuals: A theoretical formulation and a meta-analysis of the research. Review of Educational Research, 53(1), 5–54.

Koestner, R., Ryan, R. M., Bernieri, R., & Holt, K. (1984). The effects of controlling versus information limit-setting styles on children's intrinsic motivation and creativity. Journal of Personality, 52, 233–248.

Lehmann, J. (1993). Sharing the journey. Fort Collins: Colorado State University.

Lewis, D. T., Erickson, R. N., Johnson, D. R., & Bruininks, R. H. (1991). Using multi-attribute utility evaluation techniques in special education: A participatory planning and decision-making model. Minneapolis, MN: Institute on Community Integration.

Lovitt, T. C. (1989). Introduction to learning disabilities. Boston: Allyn & Bacon.

Martin, J. E., & Marshall, L. H. (1994a). Choicemaker self-determination transition curriculum matrix. Colorado Springs: University of Colorado at Colorado Springs Center for Educational Research.

Martin, J. E., & Marshall, L. H. (1994b). Choicemaker self-determination transition assessment. Colorado Springs: University of Colorado at Colorado Springs Center for Educational Research.

Martin, J. E., & Marshall, L. H. (1994c). Choicemaker: A comprehensive self-determination transition program. Manuscript submitted for publication.

Mithaug, D. (1993). Self-regulation theory: How optimal adjustment maximizes gain. Westport, CT: Praeger.

Mithaug, D., Campeau, P., & Wolman, J. (1992). Research on self-determination in individuals with disabilities. Unpublished manuscript.

Mithaug, D., Campeau, P., & Wolman, J. (1994). Self-determination assessment. Unpublished manuscript.

Murtaugh, M., & Zetlin, A. G. (1990). The development of autonomy among learning handicapped and nonhandicapped adolescents: A longitudinal perspective. Journal of Youth and Adolescence, 19, 245–255.

Powers, L. E., Sowers, J., Turner, A., Nesbitt, M., Matuszewski, J., Phillips, A., & Ellison, R. (in press). TAKE CHARGE: A model for promoting self-determination among adolescents with challenges. In L. E. Powers, G. H. S. Singer, & J. Sowers (Eds.), Making our way: Building self-competence among youth with disabilities. Baltimore: Brookes.

Rehabilitation Act Amendments of 1992, 2,29, U.S.C. 701.

Sachs, J. J., Iliff, V. W., & Donnelly, R. F. (1987). Oh, ok I'm LD! Journal of Learning Disabilities, 20, 92–93.

Shulman, S., & Rubinroit, C. (1987). The second individuation process in handicapped adolescents. The Journal of Adolescence, 10, 373–384.

Smith, D. D. (1989). Teaching students with learning and behavior problems (2nd ed.). Englewood Cliffs, NJ: Prentice Hall.

Snow, J. H. (1992). Mental flexibility and planning skills in children and adolescents with learning disabilities. Journal of Learning Disabilities, 25, 265–270.

VanReusen, A. K., & Bos, C. S. (1990). IPLAN: Helping students communicate in planning conferences. Teaching Exceptional Children, 22(4), 30–32.

Wagner, M., D'Amico, R., Marder, C., Newman, L., & Blackorby, J. (1992). What happens next? Trends in postschool outcomes of youth with disabilities. Menlo Park, CA: SRI International.

Ward, M. J. (1988). The many facets of self-determination. Transition Summary, 5, 2–3.

Ward, M. J. (1991). Self-determination revisited: Going beyond expectations. Transition Summary, 7, 2–4, 12.

Ward, M. J. (1992). Introduction to secondary special education and transition issues. In F. R. Rusch, L. DeStefano, J. Chadsey-Rusch, L. A. Phelps, & E. Szymanski (Eds.), Transition from school to adult life: Models, linkages and policy (pp. 387–389). Sycamore, IL: Sycamore.

Wehmeyer, M. L. (1992). Self-determination and the education of students with mental retardation. Education and Training in Mental Retardation, 27, 302–314.

Wehmeyer, M. L. (in press). Self-directed learning and self-determination. In M. Agran (Ed.), Student-directed learning: A handbook of self-management. Pacific Grove, CA: Brooks/Cole.

Wehmeyer, M. L., & Berkobien, R. (1991). Self-determination and self-advocacy: A case of mistaken identity. The Association for Persons with Severe Handicaps Newsletter, 17(7), 4.

Wehmeyer, M. L., & Brolin D. E. (in press). Using the Life Centered Career Education Curriculum to promote self-determination. In D. E. Brolin (Ed.), Life centered career education, competency units for personal social skills. Reston, VA: Council for Exceptional Children.

Wehmeyer, M. L., Kelchner, K., & Richards, S. (1994). Essential characteristics and component elements of self-determined behavior for individuals with mental retardation. Manuscript submitted for publication.

Will, M. (1984). OSERS programming for the transition of youth with disabilities: Bridges from school to working life. Washington, DC: Office of Special Education and Rehabilitative Services.

CHAPTER 5

Alberto, P. A., & Troutman, A. C. (1995). Applied behavior analysis for teachers (4th ed.). Englewood Cliffs, NJ: Prentice Hall.

Bender, M., & Valletutti, P. J. (1982). Teaching functional academics: A curriculum guide for adolescents and adults with learning problems. Austin, TX: PRO-ED.

Bigge, J. (1988). Curriculum-based instruction for special education students. Mountain View, CA: Mayfield.

Bingham, G. (1981). Exploratory process in career development: Implications for learning disabled students. Career Development for Exceptional Individuals, 4(2), 77–80.

Brolin, D. E. (1983). Career education: Where do we go from here? Career Development for Exceptional Individuals, 6(1), 3–14.

Brolin, D. E. (1991). Life-centered career education: A competency-based approach (3rd ed.). Reston, VA: Council for Exceptional Children.

Brolin, D. E. (1995). *Career education: A functional life skills approach (3rd ed.)*. Columbus, OH: Merrill.

Brolin, D. E., & D'Alonzo, B. J. (1979). Critical issues in career education for handicapped students. *Exceptional Children, 45*, 246–255.

Buchanan, D. W. (1975). Two versions of literacy. *English Quarterly, 10*, 73–75.

Bucher, D. E., Brolin, D. E., & Kunce, J. T. (1987). Importance of Life-Centered Career Education for special education students: The parent's perspective. *Journal of Career Development, 13(4)*, 63–69.

Bullock, L. (1992). *Exceptionalities in children and youth*. Boston: Allyn & Bacon.

Chadsey-Rusch, J., Rusch, F. R., & O'Reilly, M. F. (1991). Transition from school to integrated communities. *Remedial and Special Education, 12(6)*, 23–33.

Cipani, E. (1988). Functional skills and behavioral technology: Identifying what to train and how to train it. *Child & Youth Services, 10(2)*, 83–103.

Clark, G. M. (1974). Career education for the mildly handicapped. *Focus on Exceptional Children, 5(9)*, 1–10

Clark, G. M. (1979). *Career education for the handicapped child in the elementary school*. Denver: Love.

Clark, G. M. (1980). Career preparation for handicapped adolescents: A matter of appropriate education. *Exceptional Education Quarterly, 1(2)*, 11–17.

Clark, G. M. (1991, October). *Functional curriculum and its place in the Regular Education Initiative*. Paper presented at the meeting of the Division on Career Development, Council for Exceptional Children, Kansas City, MO.

Clark, G. M. (1994). Is a functional curriculum approach compatible with an inclusive education model? *Teaching Exceptional Children, 26(2)*, 36–39.

Clark, G. M., Field, S., Patton, J., Brolin, D., & Sitlington, P. (1994). Life skill instruction: A necessary component for all students with disabilities. *Career Development for Exceptional Individuals, 17(2)*, 125–134.

Clark, G. M., & Kolstoe, O. P. (1995). *Career development and transition education for adolescents with disabilities*. Boston: Allyn & Bacon.

Cook, W. (1977). *Adult literacy education in the U.S.* Newark, DE: International Reading Association.

Cooper, C. (1988). We're in business. *Academic Therapy, 24*, 43–56.

Cronin, M. E. (1988). Applying curriculum for the instruction of life skills. In G. A. Robinson, J. R. Patton, E. A. Polloway, & L. Sargent (Eds.), *Best practices in mild mental disabilities*. (Vol. 2, pp. 39–52). Des Moines, IA: Department of Public Instruction.

Cronin, M. E., Lord, D., & Wendling, K. (1991). Learning for life: The life skills curriculum. *Intervention in School and Clinic, 26*, 306–311.

Cronin, M. E., & Patton, J. R. (1993). *Life skills instruction for all students with special needs: A practical guide for integrating real-life content into the curriculum*. Austin, TX: PRO-ED.

Cronin, M. E., Wendling, K., Lord, D., & Palmisano, D. (1991). Community vocational training: Transition to employment. *Intervention in School and Clinic, 27*, 52–55, 59.

D'Alonzo, B. J., Faas, L. A., & Crawford, D. (1988). School to work transition: Project M.E.A.L.—Model for employment and adult living. *Career Development for Exceptional Individuals, 11*, 126–140.

Dennis, R. E., Williams, W., Giangreco, M. F., & Cloninger, C. J. (1993). *Quality of life as context for planning and evaluation of services for people with disabilities.* Exceptional Children, 59, 499–512.

Drake, G. A., & Witten, B. J. (1986). *Facilitating learning disabled adolescents' successful transition from school to work.* Journal of Applied Rehabilitation Counseling, 17(1), 34–37.

Edgar, E. (1987). *Secondary programs in special education: Are many of them justifiable?* Exceptional Children, 53, 555–561.

Edgar, E. (1988). *Employment as an outcome for mildly handicapped students: Current status and future direction.* Focus on Exceptional Children, 21(1), 1–8.

Fafard, M. B., & Haubrich, P. A. (1981). *Vocational and social adjustment of learning disabled young adults: A follow-up study.* Learning Disability Quarterly, 4, 122–130.

Ferguson, D. (1995). *Celebrating diversity: A response.* Remedial and Special Education, 16, 199–202.

Field, S., LeRoy, B., & Rivera, S. (1994). *Meeting functional curriculum needs in middle school general education classrooms.* Teaching Exceptional Children, 26(2), 40–43.

Fisher, S., & Clark, G. (1992). *Validating occupational awareness vocabulary words for middle school students with mild disabilities.* Career Development for Exceptional Individuals, 15, 189–204.

Gajar, A. (1992). *Adults with learning disabilities: Current and future research priorities.* Journal of Learning Disabilities, 25, 507–519.

Gerber, P. (1994). *Researching adults with learning disabilities from an adult-development perspective.* Journal of Learning Disabilities, 27, 6–9.

Gerber, P., Ginsberg, R., & Reiff, H. (1992). *Identifying alterable patterns in employment success for highly successful adults with learning disabilities.* Journal of Learning Disabilities, 25, 475–487.

Gillet, P. (1980). *Career education and the learning disabled student.* Career Development for Exceptional Individuals, 3, 67–73.

Ginsberg, R., Gerber, P., & Reiff, H. (1994). *Employment success for adults with learning disabilities.* In P. Gerber & H. Reiff (Eds.), *Learning disabilities in adulthood: Persisting problems and evolving issues* (pp. 204–213). Austin, TX: PRO-ED.

Grattan, C. (1959). *American ideas about adult education.* New York: Teachers College, Columbia University Press.

Greenan, J. P., Miller, S. R., & White, M. (1985). *Research and development problems in the delivery of career development programs for exceptional individuals.* Career Development for Exceptional Individuals, 8, 33–41.

Hallahan, D. P., & Kauffman, J. M. (1994). *Exceptional children.* Boston: Allyn & Bacon.

Halpern, A. S. (1979). *Adolescents and young adults.* Exceptional Children, 45, 518–523.

Halpern, A. S. (1990). *A methodological review of follow-up and follow-along studies tracking school leavers from special education.* Career Development for Exceptional Individuals, 13, 13–27.

Halpern, A. S. (1993). *Quality of life as a conceptual framework for evaluating transition outcomes.* Exceptional Children, 59, 486–498.

Halpern, A. S., & Benz, M. R. (1987). A statewide examination of secondary special education for students with mild disabilities: Implications for the high school curriculum. *Exceptional Children, 54*, 122–129.

Haring, K. A., & Lovett, D. L. (1990). A follow-up study of special education graduates. *The Journal of Special Education, 23*, 463–477.

Haring, K. A., Lovett, D. L., & Smith, D. D. (1990). A follow-up study of recent special education graduates of learning disabilities programs. *Journal of Learning Disabilities, 23*, 108–113.

Hastings, F. L., Raymond, G., & McLaughlin, T. F. (1989). Speed counting money: The use of direct instruction to train learning disabled and mentally retarded adolescents to count money efficiently. *British Columbia Journal of Special Education, 13(2)*, 137–146.

Heller, H. W., & Schilit, J. (1979). Career education for the handicapped: Directions for the future. *Career Development for Exceptional Individuals, 2*, 91–96.

Helmke, L. M., Havekost, D. M., Patton, J. R., & Polloway, E. A. (1994). Life skill programming. Development of a high school science course. *Teaching Exceptional Children, 26(2)*, 49–53.

Hittleman, D. R. (1988). Using literature to develop daily-living literacy: Strategies for students with learning difficulties. *Reading, Writing, and Learning Disabilities, 4*, 1–12.

Hunt, N., & Marshall, K. (1994). *Exceptional children and youth*. Boston: Houghton Mifflin.

Kohler, P. (1994). On-the-job training: A curricula approach to employment. *Career Development for Exceptional Individuals, 17*, 91–96.

Kranstover, L. L., Thurlow, M. L., & Bruininks, R. H. (1989). Special education graduates versus non-graduates: A longitudinal study of outcomes. *Career Development for Exceptional Individuals, 12*, 153–166.

Lamkin, J. S. (1980). *Getting started: Career education activities for exceptional children (K–9)*. Reston, VA: Council for Exceptional Children.

Lewis, K., & Taymans, J. (1992). An examination of autonomous functioning skills of adolescents with learning disabilities. *Career Development for Exceptional Individuals, 15*, 37–46.

Mannix, D. (1992). *Life skills activities for special children*. West Nyack, NY: The Center for Applied Research in Education.

Mannix, D. (1995). *Life skills activities for secondary students with special needs*. West Nyack, NY: Center for Applied Research in Education.

Marchand-Martella, N. E., Smith, M. A. H., & Agran, M. (1992). Food preparation and meal planning for persons with disabilities: A review of the literature. *British Columbia Journal of Special Education, 16(1)*, 13–28.

Mastropieri, M. A., & Scruggs, T. E. (1994). *Effective instruction for special education*. Austin, TX: PRO–ED.

McClure, L., Cook, S. C., & Thompson, V. (1977). *Experienced-based learning: How to make the community your classroom*. Portland, OR: Northwest Regional Educational Laboratory.

Meese, R. L. (1994). *Teaching students with mild disabilities*. Pacific Grove, CA: Brooks/Cole.

Miller, D. E. (1994). "On your own": A functional skills activity for adolescents with mild disabilities. *Teaching Exceptional Children, 26(3)*, 29–32.

Miller, G. (1973). Linguistic communication: Perspectives for research. Newark, DE: National Reading Council.

Minskoff, E. H. (1982). Training LD students to cope with the everyday world. Academic Therapy, 17, 311–316.

Minskoff, E. H., Sautter, S. W., Sheldon, K. L., Steidle, E. F., & Baker, D. P. (1988). A comparison of learning disabled adults and high school students. Learning Disabilities Research, 3(2), 115–123.

Moats, L. C., & Lyon, G. R. (1993). Learning disabilities in the United States: Advocacy, science, and the future of the field. Journal of Learning Disabilities, 26, 282–294.

Montague, M. (1988). Job-related social skills training for adolescents with handicaps. Career Development for Exceptional Individuals, 11, 26–41.

Moore, S. C., Agran, M., & McSweyn, C. A. (1990). Career education: Are we starting early enough? Career Development for Exceptional Individuals, 13, 95–108.

Parent, W. (1993). Quality of life and consumer choice. In P. Wehman (Ed.), The ADA mandates for social change (pp. 19–44). Baltimore: Brookes.

Patton, J. R., Cronin, M. E., Polloway, E. A., Hutchinson, D., & Robinson, G. (1989). Curricular considerations: A life skills orientation. In G. A. Robinson, J. R. Patton, E. A. Polloway, & L. Sargent (Eds.), Best practices in mild mental retardation (pp. 21–38). Reston, VA: Division on Mental Retardation, Council for Exceptional Children.

Peters, M. T., & Heron, T. E. (1993). When the best is not enough: An examination of best practice. The Journal of Special Education, 26, 371–385.

Posthill, S. M., & Roffman, A. J. (1990). Issues of money management for the learning disabled adolescent in transition to adulthood. Academic Therapy, 25, 321–332.

Public Law 101-476, Individuals with Disabilities Education Act. (1990). Federal Register, 54, 35210–35271.

Reid, D. K., & Bunsen, T. D. (Eds.). (1995). Research in special education: Expanding our options [Special Issue]. Remedial and Special Education, 16(3).

Reid, D. K., Robinson, S. J., & Bunsen, T. D. (1995). Empiricism and beyond: Expanding the boundaries of special education. Remedial and Special Education, 16, 131–141.

Reiff, H., Gerber, P., & Ginsberg, R. (1993). Definitions of learning disabilities from adults with learning disabilities: The insiders' perspective. Learning Disability Quarterly, 16, 114–125.

Reiff, H., Ginsberg, R., & Gerber, P. (1995). New perspectives on teaching from successful adults with learning disabilities. Remedial and Special Education, 16, 29–37.

Reynolds, C. R., & Fletcher-Janzen, E. (1990). Concise encyclopedia of special education. New York: Wiley.

Roessler, R. T. (1988). Implementing career education: Barriers and potential solutions. Career Development Quarterly, 37, 22–30.

Roessler, R. T. (1991). A problem-solving approach to implementing career education. Career Development for Exceptional Individuals, 14, 59–66.

Roessler, R. T., Brolin, D. E., & Johnson, J. M. (1990). Factors affecting employment success and quality of life: A one year follow-up of students in special education. Career Development for Exceptional Individuals, 13, 95–107.

Roessler, R. T., & Lewis, F. D. (1984). Conversation skill training with mentally retarded and learning disabled sheltered workshop students. Rehabilitation Counseling Bulletin, 27, 161–171.

Roessler, R. T., Loyd, R. J., & Brolin, D. E. (1990). Implementing life-centered career education: Contextual barriers and implementation recommendations. Academic Therapy, 25, 523–533.

Roth, G. S. (1990). An integrated approach to special education and vocational training. Illinois Schools Journal, 70(1), 27–30.

Rule, S., Fiechtl, B. J., & Innocenti, M. S. (1990). Preparation for transition to mainstreamed post-preschool environments: Development of a survival skills curriculum. Topics in Early Childhood Special Education, 9(4), 78–90.

Schalock, R. L., Holl, C., Elliott, B., & Ross, I. (1992). A longitudinal follow-up of graduates from a rural special education program. Learning Disability Quarterly, 15, 29–38.

Schalock, R. L., Wolzen, B., Ross, I., Elliott, B., Werbel, G., & Peterson, K. (1986). Postsecondary community placement of handicapped students: A five-year follow-up. Learning Disability Quarterly, 9, 295–303.

Scheibe, J., & Tolonen, H. (1973). SERVE and Project ISU offer new career options. Teaching Exceptional Children, 5(3), 142–145.

Schirmer, T. A., & George, M. P. (1982). Practical help for the long-term learning disabled adolescent. Teaching Exceptional Children, 15, 97–101.

Schumaker, J. B., Hazel, J. S., & Deshler, D. D. (1985). A model for facilitating postsecondary transitions. Techniques: A Journal for Remedial Education and Counseling, 1, 437–446.

Scuccimarra, D. J., & Speece, D. L. (1990). Employment outcomes and social integration of students with mild handicaps: The quality of life two years after high school. The Journal of Special Education, 23, 213–219.

Siegel, S., Robert, M., & Gaylord-Ross, R. (1992). A follow-along study of participants in a longitudinal transition program for youths with mild disabilities. Exceptional Children, 58, 346–356.

Siegel, S., Robert, M., Greener, K., Meyer, G., Halloran, W., & Gaylord-Ross, R. (1993). Career ladders for challenged youths in transition from school to adult life. Austin, TX: PRO-ED.

Sitlington, P. L. (1981). Vocational and special education in career programming for the mildly handicapped adolescent. Exceptional Children, 47, 592–599.

Sitlington, P., & Frank, A. R. (1990). Are adolescents with learning disabilities successfully crossing the bridge into adult life? Learning Disability Quarterly, 13, 97–111.

Sitlington, P., & Frank, A. R. (1993). Dropouts with learning disabilities: What happens to them as young adults? Learning Disabilities Research and Practice, 8(4), 244–252.

Sitlington, P., Frank, A. R., & Carson, R. (1993). Adult adjustment among high school graduates with mild disabilities. Exceptional Children, 59, 221–233.

Smith, D. D., & Luckasson, R. (1995). Introduction to special education: Teaching in an age of challenge. Boston: Allyn & Bacon.

Swanson, H. L. (1993). Selecting a research program in special education: Some advice and generalizations from published research. Remedial and Special Education, 14(3), 7–20, 27.

Trach, J. S., & Rusch, F. R. (1988). Research and trends in employment of adolescents with handicaps. Child and Youth Services, 10(2), 183–200.

U.S. Office of Special Education Programs. (1994). Sixteenth annual report to Congress on the Implementation of the Individuals with Disabilities Education Act. Washington, DC: Office of Special Education and Rehabilitative Services, Department of Education.

Vasa, S. F., & Steckelberg, A. L. (1980). Parent programs in career education for the handicapped. Career Development for Exceptional Individuals, 3, 74–82.

Wagner, M., Blackorby, J., Cameto, R., Hebbeler, K., & Newman, L. (1993). The transition experiences of young people with disabilities: A summary of findings from the National Longitudinal Transition Study of Special Education Students. Menlo Park, CA: SRI International.

Wagner, M., D'Amico, R., Marder, C., Newman, L., & Blackorby, J. (1992). What happens next? Trends in post-school outcomes of youth with disabilities. Menlo Park, CA: SRI International.

Wagner, M., Newman, L., D'Amico, R., Joy, E. D., Butler-Nalin, P., Marder, C., & Cox, R. (Eds.). (1991). Youth with disabilities: How are they doing? The first comprehensive report from the National Longitudinal Transition Study of Special Education Students. Menlo Park, CA: SRI International.

Weaver, R., Landers, M. F., & Adams, S. (1991). Making curriculum functional: Special education and beyond. Intervention in School and Clinic, 26, 306–311.

White, W. (1983). The validity of occupational skills in career education: Fact or fantasy? Career Development for Exceptional Individuals, 6, 3–14.

Wiederholt, J. L., Cronin, M. E., & Stubbs, V. (1980). Measurement of functional competencies and the handicapped: Constructs, assessment, and recommendations. Exceptional Education Quarterly, 1(3), 59–73.

Wimmer, D. (1981). Functional learning curricula in the secondary schools. Exceptional Children, 47, 610–617.

Wimmer, D., & Sitlington, P. A. (1981). A survey of research priorities in career education for the handicapped. Career Development for Exceptional Individuals, 4, 50–58.

Wolery, M., & Haring, T. G. (1994). Moderate, severe, and profound disabilities. In N. G. Haring, L. McCormick, & T. G. Haring (Eds.), Exceptional children and youth (pp. 261–298). Columbus, OH: Merrill.

Wong, B. Y. L. (1994). The relevance of longitudinal research to learning disabilities. Journal of Learning Disabilities, 27, 270–274.

Zigmond, N., & Thornton, H. (1985). Follow-up of postsecondary age learning disabled graduates and drop-outs. Learning Disabilities Research, 1(1), 50–55.

CHAPTER 6

America 2000: An education strategy. Washington, DC: Author.

Benz, M. R., & Halpern, A. S. (1986). Vocational preparation for high school students with mild disabilities: A statewide study of administrator, teacher, and parent perceptions. Career Development for Exceptional Individuals, 9, 3–15.

Benz, M. R., & Halpern, A. S. (1993). Vocational and transition services needed and received by students with disabilities during their last year of high school. Career Development for Exceptional Individuals, 16, 197–211.

Brown, J. M., Asselin, S. B., Hoerner, J. L., Daines, J., & Clowes, D. A. (1992). Should special needs learners have access to Tech-Prep programs? The Journal for Vocational Special Needs Education, 14(2/3), 21–26.

Cawley, J. F., Kahn, H., & Tedesco, A. (1989). Vocational education and students with learning disabilities. Journal of Learning Disabilities, 22, 630–640.

Claxton, S. B. (1986). Determining attitudes of trade and industrial teachers toward handicapped students. Journal of Industrial Teacher Education, 23, 55–63.

Cline, B. V., & Billingsley, B. S. (1991). Teachers' and supervisors' perceptions of secondary learning disabilities programs: A multistate survey. Learning Disabilities Research & Practice, 6, 158–165.

Cobb, R. B., & Neubert, D. A. (1992). Vocational education models. In F. R. Rusch, L. DeStefano, J. Chadsey-Rusch, L. A. Phelps, & E. Szymanski (Eds.), Transition from school to adult life (pp. 93-113). Sycamore, IL: Sycamore.

Congress blocks ED changes to Perkins rules. (1994, September 29). Vocational Training News, p. 1.

Council for Exceptional Children. (1994). Summary of the School-To-Work Opportunities Act. Reston, VA: Author.

D'Amico, R. (1991). The working world awaits: Employment experience during and shortly after secondary school. In M. Wagner, L. Newman, R. D'Amico, E. D. Jay, P. Butler-Nalin, C. Marder, & R. Cox (Eds.), Youth with disabilities: How are they doing? The first comprehensive report for the National Longitudinal Transition Study of special education students (pp. 8-1–8-55). Menlo Park, CA: SRI International.

Denny, R. K., Epstein, M. H., & Rose, E. (1992). Direct observation of adolescents with serious emotional disturbance and their nonhandicapped peers in mainstream vocational educational classrooms. Behavior Disorders, 8, 33–41.

Deshler, D. D., Putnam, M. L., & Bulgren, J. A. (1985). Academic accommodations for adolescents with behavior and learning problems. In S. Braaten, R. B. Rutherford, Jr., & C. A. Kardash (Eds.), Programming for adolescents with behavioral disorders (Vol. 2, pp. 22–30). Reston, VA: Council for Exceptional Children.

DeStefano, L., & Wermuth, T. R. (1992). Chapter 29: IDEA (P.L. 101-476): Defining a second generation of transition services. In F. R. Rusch, L. DeStefano, J. Chadsey-Rusch, L. A. Phelps, & E. Szymanski (Eds.), Transition from school to adult life (pp. 537–549). Sycamore, IL: Sycamore.

Edgar, E. (1987). Secondary programs in special education: Are many of them justifiable? Exceptional Children, 53, 555–561.

Edgar, E. (1988). Employment as an outcome for mildly handicapped students: Current status and future directions. Focus on Exceptional Children, 21, 1–8.

Elrod, G. F. (1987). Academic and social skills pre-requisite to success in vocational training. The Journal for Vocational Special Needs Education, 10(1), 17–21.

Eschenmann, K. K. (1989). A follow up study of certification requirements for trade and industrial teachers with disadvantaged and handicapped students. The Journal for Vocational Special Needs Education, 12(1), 17–20.

Eschenmann, K. K., & O'Reilly, P. A. (1980). *Certification requirements for trade and industrial teachers working with disadvantaged and handicapped students.* The Journal for Vocational Special Needs Education, 2(2), 27–28.

Evers, R. B., & Bursuck, W. B. (1993). *Teacher ratings of instructional and setting demands in vocation education classes.* Learning Disability Quarterly, 16, 82–92.

Evers, R. B., & Bursuck, W. B. (1994). *Literacy demands in secondary technical vocational education programs: Teacher interviews.* Career Development for Exceptional Individuals, 17, 135–143.

Gartner, A., & Lipsky, D. K. (1987). *Beyond special education: Toward a quality system for all students.* Harvard Educational Review, 57, 367–395.

Gersten, R., & Woodward, J. (1990). *Rethinking the Regular Education Initiative: Focus on the classroom teacher.* Remedial and Special Education, 11(3), 7–16.

Green, J. E., & Weaver, R. A. (1994). *Tech Prep: A strategy for school reform.* Bloomington, IN: Phi Delta Kappa Educational Foundation.

Greenan, J. P. (1982). *State planning for vocational/special education personnel development.* Teacher Education and Special Education, 5, 69–76.

Greenan, J. P. (1983). *Identification of generalizable skills in secondary vocational programs: Executive summary.* Springfield: Illinois State Board of Education.

Greenan, J. P., & Larkin, D. J. (1983). *Vocational/special education certification: State of the art.* Career Development for Exceptional Individuals, 6, 45–50.

Greenan, J. P., & Phelps, L. A. (1982). *Delivering vocational education to handicapped learners.* Exceptional Children, 48, 408–411.

Greenbaum, B., Graham, S., & Scales, W. (1995). *Adults with learning disabilities: Educational and social experiences during college.* Exceptional Children, 61, 460–471.

Hasazi, S. B., Johnson, R. E., Hasazi, J. E., Gordon, L. R., & Hull, M. (1989). *Employment of youth with and without handicaps following high school: Outcomes and correlates.* The Journal of Special Education, 23, 243–255.

Honaker, K., & Henderson, J. L. (1989). *Attitudes of vocational horticulture teachers towards students with handicaps: Implications for integration.* The Journal for Vocational Special Needs Education, 12(1), 27–30.

House, Senate may kill off longtime Voc Ed law. (1995, March 16). *Vocational Training News*, p. 1.

Humes, C. W., & Brammer, G. (1985). *LD career success after high school.* Academic Therapy, 21, 171–176.

Jenkins, J. R., Pious, C. G., & Jewell, M. (1990). *Special education and the Regular Education Initiative: Basic assumptions.* Exceptional Children, 56, 479–491.

Johnson, W. B., & Packer, A. E. (1987). *Workforce 2000: Work and workers for the 21st century.* Indianapolis, IN: Hudson Institute.

Kerr, M. M., Zigmond, N., Harris, A., & Brown, G. (1985). *What's important to high school teachers? A look at successful and unsuccessful high school students.* Unpublished manuscript.

Kochhar, C.A., & Deschamps, A. B. (1992). *Policy crossroads in preserving the right of passage to independence for learners with special needs: Implications of recent changes in national vocational and special education policies.* The Journal for Vocational Special Needs Education, 14(2/3), 9–19.

Majsterek, D., Wilson, R., & Southern, W. T. (1988). The "Regular Education Initiative" in secondary schools: Deterrents and directions. High School Journal, 72(1), 30–35.

Marder, C. (1992). Education after secondary school. In M. Wagner, R. D'Amico, C. Marder, L. Newman, & J. Blackorby (Eds.), What happens next? The second comprehensive report for the National Longitudinal Transition Study of Special Education Students (pp. 3-1–3-39). Menlo Park, CA: SRI International.

Mithaug, D. E., Horiuchi, C. N., & Fanning, P. N. (1985). A report on the Colorado statewide follow-up survey of special education students. Exceptional Children, 51, 397–404.

Okolo, C. M. (1988). Instructional environments in secondary vocational education programs: Implications for LD adolescents. Learning Disability Quarterly, 11, 136–148.

Okolo, C. M., & Sitlington, P. (1986). The role of special education in LD adolescents' transition from school to work. Learning Disability Quarterly, 9, 292–306.

Okolo, C. M., & Sitlington, P. L. (1988). Mildly handicapped learners in vocational education: A statewide survey. The Journal of Special Education, 22, 220–230.

Orlich, D. C. (1989). Educational reforms: Mistakes, misconceptions, miscues. Phi Delta Kappan, 70, 512–517.

Passmore, D. L. (1989). Economics of transition. In D. E. Berkell & J. M. Brown (Eds.), Transition from school to work for persons with disabilities (pp. 42–63). New York: Longman.

Rojewski, J. W., & Greenan, J. P. (1992). Teacher certification policies and practices for vocational education personnel: A national study. Teacher Education and Special Education, 15, 194–210.

Rojewski, J. W., Pollard, R. R., & Meers, G. D. (1990). Grading mainstreamed special needs students: Determining practices and attitudes of secondary vocational educators using a qualitative approach. Remedial and Special Education, 12(1), 7–15.

Rojewski, J. W., Pollard, R. R., & Meers, G. D. (1992). Grading secondary vocational education students with disabilities: A national perspective. Exceptional Children, 59, 68–76.

Schell, J. W., & Babich, A. M. (1993). Tech-Prep and the development of higher-order thinking skills among learners with special needs. The Journal for Vocational and Special Needs Education, 16(1), 6–13.

Schumaker, J. B., & Deshler, D. (1988). Implementing the Regular Education Initiative in secondary schools: A different ball game. Journal of Learning Disabilities, 21, 36–42.

Schwarz, S. L., & Taymans, J. M. (1991). Urban vocational/technical program completers with learning disabilities: A follow-up study. The Journal for Vocational Special Needs Education, 13(3), 15–20.

Shapiro, E. S., & Lentz, F. E. (1991). Vocational–technical programs: Follow-up of students with learning disabilities. Exceptional Children, 58, 47–59.

Sitlington, P. L., & Frank, A. R. (1990). Are adolescents with learning disabilities successfully crossing the bridge into adult life? Learning Disability Quarterly, 13, 97–111.

Sitlington, P., & Frank, A. (1993). Dropouts with learning disabilities: What happens to them as young adults? Learning Disabilities Research & Practice, 8, 244–252.

Sitlington, P. L., Frank, A. R., & Carson, R. (1993). *Adult adjustment among high school graduates with mild disabilities.* Exceptional Children, 59, 221–233.

Sitlington, P. L., & Goh, S. R. (1984). *The relationship of years of experience and special educators' concern regarding cooperation with vocational education.* Teacher Education and Special Education, 7(4), 221–227.

Sitlington, P. L., & Okolo, C. M. (1987). *Statewide survey of vocational educators: Attitudes, training, and involvement with handicapped learners.* Journal of Career Development, 13, 21–29.

Stern, S., & Gathercoal, F. (1986, January). *Working with handicapped students.* School Shop, pp. 13–14.

U.S. Department of Education. (1994a). *Sixteenth annual report to Congress on the implementation of the Individuals with Disabilities Education Act.* Washington, DC: Office of Special Education Programs.

U.S. Department of Education. (1994b). *Public secondary school teacher survey on vocational education: Contractor report.* Washington, DC: National Center for Education Statistics.

Wagner, M. (1989). *Youth with disabilities during transition: An overview of descriptive findings from the National Longitudinal Transition Study.* Menlo Park, CA: The National Longitudinal Study of Special Education Students.

Wagner, M. (1991, April). *The benefits of secondary vocational education for young people with disabilities: Findings from the National Longitudinal Transition Study of Special Education Students.* Paper presented at the Vocational Special Interest Group/American Educational Research Association, Chicago.

Weisenstein, G. R., Stowitschek, J. J., & Affleck, J. Q.(1991). *Integrating students enrolled in special education into vocational education.* Career Development for Exceptional Individuals, 14, 131–144.

Will, M. (1986). *Educating students with learning problems: A shared responsibility.* Washington, DC: U.S. Department of Education.

York, J., & Vandercook, T. (1990). *Strategies for achieving an integrated education for middle school students with severe disabilities.* Remedial and Special Education, 11(5), 6–16.

Zigmond, N. (1990). *Rethinking secondary school programs for students with learning disabilities.* Focus on Exceptional Children, 21, 1–22.

Zigmond, N., & Sansone, J. (1986). *Designing a program for the learning disabled adolescent.* Remedial and Special Education, 7(5), 13–17.

Zigmond, N., & Thorton, H. (1985). *Follow-up on postsecondary age learning disabled graduates and drop-outs.* Learning Disabilities Research, 1(1), 50–55.

CHAPTER 7

Brigance, A. H. (1995a). *Employability skills inventory.* North Billerica, MA: Curriculum Associates.

Brigance, A. H. (1995b). *Life skills inventory.* North Billerica, MA: Curriculum Associates.

Brolin, D. E. (1989). *Life-centered career education: A competency-based approach* (3rd ed.). Reston, VA: The Council for Exceptional Children.

Brolin, D. E. (1992). *Life centered career education (LCCE) knowledge and performance batteries*. Reston, VA: The Council for Exceptional Children.

Brolin, D. E. (1993). *Life-centered career education: A competency-based approach* (4th ed.). Reston, VA: The Council for Exceptional Children.

Clark, G. M., Carlson, B. C., Fisher, S., Cook, I. D., & D'Alonzo, B. J. (1991). Career development for students with disabilities in elementary schools: A position statement of the Division on Career Development. *Career Development for Exceptional Individuals, 14,* 109–120.

Clark, G. M., Field, S., Patton, J. R., Brolin, D. E., & Sitlington, P. L. (1994). Life skills instruction: A necessary component for all students with disabilities. A position statement of the Division on Career Development and Transition. *Career Development for Exceptional Individuals, 17,* 125–134.

Clark, G. M., & Kolstoe, O. P. (1995). *Career development and transition education for adolescents with disabilities* (2nd ed.). Needham Heights, MA: Allyn & Bacon.

Clark, G. M., & Patton, J. R. (in press). *Transition planning inventory.* Austin, TX: PRO-ED.

Council for Exceptional Children. (1994). *CEC IDEA reauthorization testimony before the House Select Subcommittee on Education and Civil Rights.* Reston, VA: Author.

Cronin, M. E., & Patton, J. R. (1993). *Life skills instruction for all students with special needs: A practical guide for integrating real-life content into the curriculum.* Austin, TX: PRO-ED.

Dever, R. B. (1988). *Community living skills: A taxonomy.* Washington, DC: American Association on Mental Retardation.

Enderle, J., & Severson, S. (1991). *Enderle-Severson transition rating scale.* Moorehead, MN: Practical Press.

Halpern, A. S. (1985). Transition: A look at the foundations. *Exceptional Children, 51,* 479–486.

Halpern, A. S., Irvin, L., & Landman, J. J. (1979). *Tests for everyday living.* Monterey, CA: CTB/McGraw-Hill.

Halpern, A. S., Irvin, L., & Munkres, J. (1986). *Social and prevocational information battery—Revised.* Monterey, CA: CTB/McGraw-Hill.

Halpern, A. S., Raffeld, P., Irvin, L., & Link, R. (1975). *Social and prevocational information battery.* Eugene: University of Oregon, Rehabilitation Research and Training Center.

Hammill, D. D. (1987). Assessing students in the schools. In J. L. Wiederholt & B. R. Bryant (Eds.), *Assessing the reading abilities and instructional needs of students* (pp. 1–32). Austin, TX: PRO-ED.

Keith, K. D., & Schalock, R. L. (1995). *Quality of student life questionnaire.* Worthington, OH: IDS.

Knowles, M. (1990). *The adult learner: The neglected species.* Houston: Gulf.

Kokaska, C. J., & Brolin, D. E. (1985). *Career education for handicapped individuals* (2nd ed.). Columbus, OH: Merrill.

McBride, J. W., & Forgnone, C. (1985). Emphasis of instruction provided LD, EH, and EMR students in categorical and cross-categorical programming. *Journal of Research and Development in Education, 18*(4), 50–54.

McCarney, S. B. (1989). *Transition behavior scale.* Columbia, MO: Hawthorne Educational Service.

National Joint Committee on Learning Disabilities. (1990). Providing appropriate education for students with learning disabilities in regular education classrooms: A position paper by the National Joint Committee on Learning Disabilities. In National Joint Committee on Learning Disabilities (Ed.), Collective perspectives on issues affecting learning disabilities: Position papers and statements (pp. 67–73). Austin, TX: PRO-ED.

National Joint Committee on Learning Disabilities. (1994). Secondary to postsecondary education transition planning for students with disabilities: A position paper of the National Joint Committee on Learning Disabilities. In National Joint Committee on Learning Disabilities (Ed.), Collective perspectives on issues affecting learning disabilities: Position papers and statements (pp. 97–104). Austin, TX: PRO-ED.

Perske, R. (1988). Circles of friends: People with disabilities enrich the lives of one another. Nashville, TN: Abingdon Press.

Reiman, J., & Bullis, M. (1993). Transition competence battery for deaf adolescents and young adults. Santa Barbara, CA: James Stanfield.

Schalock, R. L., & Keith, K. D. (1993). Quality of life questionnaire. Worthington, OH: IDS.

Smith, M. A., & Schloss, P. J. (1988). Teaching to transition. In P. J. Schloss, C. A. Hughes, & M. A. Smith (Eds.), Community integration for persons with mental retardation (pp. 1–16). Austin, TX: PRO-ED.

Smith, S. (1990). Comparison of IEPs of students with behavioral disorders and learning disabilities. The Journal of Special Education, 24, 85–99.

Vandercook, T., & York, J. (1989). The McGill Action Planning System (M.A.P.S.): A strategy for building vision. Journal of the Association for the Severely Handicapped, 14, 205–215.

Weller, C., & Strawser, S. (1981). Weller-Strawser scales of adaptive behavior for the learning disabled. Novato, CA: Academic Therapy.

CHAPTER 8

Aase, S., & Price, L. (1987). Building the bridge: LD adolescents' and adults' transition from secondary to postsecondary settings. In D. Knapke & C. Lendman (Eds.), Capitalizing on the future (pp. 126–149). Columbus, OH: Association on Handicapped Student Service Programs in Postsecondary Education.

Alley, G. R., Deshler, D. D., Clark, F. L., Schumaker, J. B., & Warner, M. M. (1983). Learning disabilities in adolescent and young adult populations: Research implications (part II). Focus on Exceptional Children, 15(9), 1–14.

Anderson, P. A. (1993). Issues in assessment and diagnosis. In L. Brinckerhoff, S. Shaw, & J. McGuire (Eds.), Promoting postsecondary education for students with learning disabilities: A handbook for practitioners (pp. 89–136). Austin, TX: PRO-ED.

Anderson, P. A., & Brinckerhoff, L. C. (1989). Interpreting LD diagnostic reports for appropriate service delivery. In J. J. vander Putten (Ed.), Proceedings of the 1989 AHSSPPE national conference (pp. 92–100). Columbus, OH: Association on Handicapped Student Service Programs in Postsecondary Education.

Aune, E. (1991). A transition model for post-secondary-bound students with learning disabilities. Learning Disabilities Research and Practice, 6, 177–187.

Aune, E., & Ness, J. (1991). Tools for transition: Preparing students with learning disabilities for postsecondary education. Circle Pines, MN: American Guidance Service.

Barnett, L. (1993). Disability support practices in community colleges: Selected examples. Washington, DC: American Association of Community Colleges.

Biller, E. (1985). Understanding and guiding the career development of adolescents and young adults with learning disabilities. Springfield, IL: Thomas.

Block, L. (1993). Students with learning disabilities. In S. Kroeger & J. Schuck (Eds.), Responding to disability issues in student affairs (pp. 69–78). San Francisco: Jossey-Bass.

Brinckerhoff, L. C. (1993a). Establishing learning disability support services with minimal resources. In M. Farrell (Ed.), Support services for students with learning disabilities in higher education: A compendium of readings (Vol. 3, pp. 54–63). Columbus, OH: AHEAD.

Brinckerhoff, L. C. (1993b). Self-advocacy: A critical skill for college students with learning disabilities. Journal of School and Community Health, 16(3), 23–33.

Brinckerhoff, L. C. (1994). Developing effective self-advocacy skills in college-bound students with learning disabilities. Intervention in School and Clinic, 29, 229–237.

Brinckerhoff, L. C., & Eaton, H. (1991). Developing a summer orientation program for college students with learning disabilities. Postsecondary LD Network News, 12, 1–3, 6.

Brinckerhoff, L. C., Shaw, S. A., & McGuire, J. M. (1992). Promoting access, accommodations, and independence for college students with learning disabilities. Journal of Learning Disabilities, 25, 417–429.

Brinckerhoff, L. C., Shaw, S. F., & McGuire, J. M. (1993). Promoting postsecondary education for students with learning disabilities: A handbook for practitioners. Austin, TX: PRO-ED.

Bursuck, W. D. (1991). Learning strategies: Module Two. Specific intervention strategies. DeKalb: Northern Illinois University.

Bursuck, W. D., & Jayanthi, M. (1993). Programming for independent study skills usage. In S. A. Vogel & P. B. Adelman (Eds.), Success for college students with learning disabilities (pp. 177–205). New York: Springer-Verlag.

Bursuck, W. D., & Rose E. (1992). Community college options for students with mild disabilities. In F. R. Rusch, L. DeStefano, J. Chadsey-Rusch, L. A. Phelps, & E. Szmanski (Eds.), Transition from school to adult life (pp. 71–92). Sycamore, IL: Sycamore.

Bursuck, W. D., Rose, E., Cowen, S., & Yahaya, A. (1989). Nationwide survey of postsecondary education services for students with learning disabilities. Exceptional Children, 56, 236–245.

Clark, G. M., & Patton, J. R. (1994). The transition planning inventory. Austin, TX: PRO-ED.

Cordoni, B. (1987). Living with a learning disability. Carbondale: Southern Illinois Press.

Cowen, S. (1990). The LINKS college transition planning guide. Unpublished manuscript, Northern Illinois University, DeKalb.

Cowen, S. (1991). How to choose a college: Helpful strategies for students with learning disabilities. Unpublished manuscript.

Cowen, S. (1993). Transition planning for LD college-bound students. In S. A. Vogel & P. B. Adelman (Eds.), Success for college students with learning disabilities (pp. 39–56). New York: Springer-Verlag.

Dalke, C. (1991). Support programs in higher education for students with disabilities: Access for all. Gaithersburg, MD: Aspen.

Dalke, C. (1993). Programming for independent study skills usage. In S. A. Vogel & P. B. Adelman (Eds.), Success for college students with learning disabilities (pp. 177–205). New York: Springer-Verlag.

Dalke, C., & Franzene, J. (1988). Secondary–postsecondary collaboration: A model of shared responsibility. Learning Disabilities Focus, 4, 38–45.

Dalke, C., & Schmitt, S. (1987). Meeting the transition needs of college-bound students with learning disabilities. Journal of Learning Disabilities, 20, 176–180.

Day, N. (1994, October). Straight A's don't cut it. Boston Magazine, 86(10), 53–55, 92–95.

Decker, K., Spector, S., & Shaw, S. A. (1992). Teaching study skills to students with mild handicaps: The role of the classroom teacher. The Clearing House, 65, 280–284.

Deshler, D. D., & Schumaker, J. B. (1986). Learning strategies: An instructional alternative for low-achieving adolescents. Exceptional Children, 52, 583–590.

Deshler, D., Schumaker, J., Lenz, K., & Ellis, J. (1984). Academic and cognitive interventions for LD adolescents: Part II. Journal of Learning Disabilities, 17, 170–179.

Dowdy, C. A., & McCue, M. (1994). Crossing service systems: From special education to vocational rehabilitation. In C. A. Michaels (Ed.), Transition strategies for persons with learning disabilities (pp. 53–78). San Diego: Singular.

DuChossois, G., & Michaels, C. (1994). Postsecondary education. In C. A. Michaels (Ed.), Transition strategies for persons with learning disabilities (pp. 79–118). San Diego: Singular.

DuChossois, G., & Stein, E. (1992). Choosing the right college: A step-by-step system to aid the student with learning disabilities in selecting the suitable college setting for them. New York: New York University.

Educational Testing Service. (1991). SIGI plus. Princeton, NJ: Author.

Ellis, E. S. (1990). What's so strategic about teaching teachers to teach strategies? Teacher Education and Special Education, 13, 56–62.

Goldhammer, R., & Brinckerhoff, L. C. (1992). Self-advocacy for college students. Their World, 94–97.

Hartman, R. C. (1992). Foreword. In C. T. Mangrum & S. S. Strichart (Eds.), Peterson's guide to colleges with programs for students with learning disabilities (pp. v–vi). Princeton, NJ: Peterson's Guides.

Hartman, R. C. (1993). Transition to higher education. In S. Kroeger & J. Schuck (Eds.), Responding to disability issues in student affairs (pp. 31–43). San Francisco: Jossey-Bass.

Haugh, R., & McDonald, R. (1994). Transition from school to adult life for students with disabilities. Piscataway: New Jersey Office of Special Education Programs.

HEATH Resource Center. (1993). How to choose a college: A guide for the student with a disability. Washington, DC: American Council on Education.

Henderson, C. (1992). College freshmen with disabilities: A statistical profile. Washington, DC: American Council on Education.

Heyward, Lawton, & Associates. (1991). Compliance with both the Education of the Handicapped Act (EHA) and Section 504: Mission impossible? Disability Accommodation Digest, 1(1), 5, 7.

Holland, J. (1971). The self-directed search. Odessa, FL: Psychological Assessment Resources.

Johnson, J. (1989). The LD academic support group manual. Columbus, OH: Association on Handicapped Student Service Programs in Postsecondary Education.

Kincaid, J. M. (1992, July). Compliance requirements of the ADA and Section 504. Paper presented at the annual meeting of the Association on Handicapped Student Service Programs in Postsecondary Education, Long Beach, CA.

Kravets, M., & Wax, I. (1991). The K & W guide to colleges for the learning disabled: A resource book for students, parents, and professionals, New York: HarperCollins.

Kuperstein, J. S., & Kessler, J. M. (1991). Building bridges: A guide to making the high school-college transition for students with learning disabilities. Edison, NJ: Middlesex County College.

Lipkin, M. (1993). Guide to college with programs or services for students with learning disabilities. Belmont, MA: Schoolsearch Press.

Mangrum, C. T., & Strichart, S. S. (1988). College and the learning disabled student (2nd ed.). Orlando, FL: Grune & Stratton.

Mangrum, C. T., & Strichart, S. S. (Eds.). (1995). Peterson's colleges with programs for students with learning disabilities (4th ed.). Princeton, NJ: Peterson's Guides.

McGuire, J. M., Hall, D., & Litt, V. A. (1991). A field based study of the direct service needs of college students with learning disabilities. Journal of College Student Development, 32, 101–108.

McGuire, J. M., Norlander, K. A., & Shaw, S. F. (1990). Postsecondary education for students with learning disabilities: Forecasting challenges for the future. Learning Disabilities Focus, 5, 69–74.

McGuire, J. M., & Shaw, S. F. (1986a). McGuire–Shaw postsecondary selection guide and manual for learning disabled college students. Storrs: The University of Connecticut.

McGuire, J. M., & Shaw, S. F. (1986b). A decision-making process for the college-bound student: Matching the learner, institution, and support programs. Learning Disability Quarterly, 10, 106–111.

Michaels, C. A. (1994). Curriculum ideology in the secondary special education transition planning process. In C. A. Michaels (Ed.), Transition strategies for persons with learning disabilities (pp. 23–52). San Diego: Singular.

Michaels, C. A., Thaler, R., Zwerlein, R., Gioglio, M., & Apostoli, B. (1988a). From high school to college: Keys to success for students with learning disabilities. Albertson, NY: Human Resources Center.

Michaels, C. A., Thaler, R., Zwerlein, R., Gioglio, M., & Apostoli, B. (1988b). How to succeed in college: A handbook for students with learning disabilities. Albertson, NY: Human Resources Center.

National Joint Committee on Learning Disabilities. (1994). Secondary to postsecondary education transition planning for students with learning disabilities. Collective perspectives on issues affecting learning disabilities: Position papers and statements (pp. 97–104). Austin, TX: PRO-ED.

Patton, J. R., & Polloway, E. A. (1992). Learning disabilities: The challenges of adulthood. Journal of Learning Disabilities, 25, 410–415.

Phillips, P. (1990). *A self-advocacy plan for high school students with learning disabilities: A comparative case analysis of students', teachers', and parents' perceptions of program effectiveness. Journal of Learning Disabilities, 23, 466–471.*

Price, L. (1988). *Support groups work! The Journal of Counseling and Human Services Professions, 2, 35–46.*

Price, L. (1993). *Psychosocial characteristics and issues of adults with learning disabilities. In L.C. Brinckerhoff, S. F. Shaw, & J. M. McGuire (Eds.), Promoting postsecondary education for students with learning disabilities: A handbook for practitioners (pp. 137–167). Austin, TX: PRO-ED.*

Rolfe, J. (1989). *College interview preparation form. Unpublished manuscript.*

Rose, E., & Bursuck, W. D. (1989). *A survey of college transition planning for students with learning disabilities. In D. Knapke & C. Lendman (Eds.), Support services for LD students in postsecondary education: A compendium of readings (Vol. 2, pp. 43–50). Columbus, OH: AHSSPPE.*

Rose, E., & Bursuck, W. D. (1992). *College transition planning guide. Unpublished manuscript, Northern Illinois University.*

Rubenstone, S., & Dalby, S. (1994). *College admissions: A crash course for panicked parents. New York: Macmillan.*

Ryan, A., & Price, L. (1992). *Adults with LD in the 1990s: Addressing the needs of students with learning disabilities. Intervention in School and Clinic, 28, 6–20.*

Scheiber, B., & Talpers, J. (1987). *Unlocking potential: College and other choices for learning disabled people: A step-by-step guide. Bethesda, MD: Alder & Alder.*

Scott, S. S. (1991). *A change in legal status: An overlooked dimension in the transition to higher education. Journal of Learning Disabilities, 24, 459–466.*

Seidenberg, P. (1986). *Curriculum-based assessment procedures for secondary learning disabled students: Student centered and programmatic implications. Greenvale, NY: Long Island University Press.*

Shaw, S. F., Brinckerhoff, L. C., Kistler, J. K., & McGuire, J. M. (1991). *Preparing students with learning disabilities for postsecondary education: Issues and future needs. Learning Disabilities: A Multidisciplinary Journal, 1, 21–26.*

Siperstein, G. N. (1988). *Students with learning disabilities in college: The need for a programmatic approach to critical transitions. Journal of Learning Disabilities, 21, 431–436.*

Sitlington, P. L. (1986). *Transition, special needs, and vocational education. Columbus, OH: National Center for Research in Vocational Education. (ERIC Document Reproduction Service No. ED 272 769)*

Sitlington, P. L., & Frank, A. (1990). *Are adolescents with learning disabilities successful crossing the bridge to adult life? Learning Disability Quarterly, 13, 97–111.*

Spector, C., Decker, K., & Shaw, S.F. (1991). *Independence and responsibility: An LD resource room at South Windsor High School. Intervention in School and Clinic, 26, 159–167.*

Straughn, C. T. (1992). *Lovejoy's college guide for the learning disabled (3rd ed.). New York: Monarch.*

Trapani, C. (1990). *Transition goals for adolescents with learning disabilities. Austin, TX: PRO-ED.*

U.S. Department of Education. (1994). *Sixteenth annual report to Congress on the implementation of the Education of the Handicapped Act. Washington, DC: Government Printing Office.*

Vogel, S. A. (1982). On developing LD college programs. Journal of Learning Disabilities, 15, 518–528.

Vogel, S. A. (1993). Postsecondary decison-making for students with learning disabilities. Pittsburgh, PA: Learning Disabilities Association of America.

Vogel, S. A., & Adelman, P. B. (1992). The success of college students with learning disabilities: Factors related to educational attainment. Journal of Learning Disabilities, 25, 430–441.

Wade, S. E., & Reynolds, R. E. (1989). Developing students' metacognitive awareness may be essential to effective strategy instruction. Journal of Reading, 33, 6–15.

Wang, M. C., & Palincsar, A. S. (1989). Teaching students to assume an active role in their learning. In M. C. Reynolds (Ed.), Knowledge base for the beginning teacher. Elmsford, NY: Pergamon.

Wehman, P. (1992). Life beyond the classroom: Transition strategies for young people with disabilities. Baltimore: Brookes.

West, L., Corbey, S., Boyer Stephens, A., Jones, B., Miller, R., & Sarkees-Wircenksi, M (1992). Integrating transition planning into the IEP process. Reston, VA: The Council for Exceptional Children.

Wilson, G. L. (1994). Self-advocacy skills. In C. A. Michaels (Ed.), Transition strategies for persons with learning disabilities (pp. 153–184). San Diego: Singular Publishing.

Wong, B. Y. (1987). How do the results of metacognitive research impact on the learning disabled individual? Learning Disability Quarterly, 10, 189–195.

Wong, B. Y., & Jones, W. (1992). Increasing metacomprehension in learning disabled and normally achieving students through self-questioning training. Learning Disability Quarterly, 5, 228–238.

Zigmond, N., & Thornton, H. (1985). Follow-up on postsecondary age learning disabled graduates and drop-outs. Learning Disabilities Research, 1(1), 50–55.

CHAPTER 9

Abbott, J. (1987, February) Accessing vocational rehabilitation training and employment programs. Paper presented at the annual meeting of the ACLD, San Antonio, TX.

American Psychiatric Association. (1994). Diagnostic and statistical manual of mental disorders (4th ed.). Washington, DC: Author.

Berkeley Planning Associates. (1989). Evaluation of services provided for individuals with specific learning disabilities (Contract No. 300-87-0112). Washington, DC: Office of Rehabilitation Services Administration.

Dowdy, C. A. (1992). Identification of characteristics of specific learning disabilities as a critical component in the vocational rehabilitation process. Journal of Rehabilitation 58(3), 51–54.

Dowdy, C. A. (1994). Rating scale of functional limitations. In M. McCue, S. L. Chase, C. A. Dowdy, M. Pramuka, J. Petrick, S. Aitken, & P. Fabry (Eds.), Functional assessment of individuals with cognitive disabilities: A desk reference for rehabilitation (pp. 115–117). Pittsburgh, PA: Center for Applied Neuropsychology Associates.

Dowdy, C. A., Carter, J., & Smith, T. E. C. (1990). Differences in traditional needs of high school students with and without learning disabilities. Journal of Learning Disabilities 23, 343–348.

Dowdy, C. A., & McCue, M. (1994). Crossing service systems: From special education to vocational rehabilitation. In C. A. Michaels (Ed.), Transition strategies for persons with learning disabilities (pp. 53-78). San Diego: Singular.

Dowdy, C. A., & Smith, T. E. C. (1994). Serving individuals with specific learning disabilities in the vocational rehabilitation system. In P. J. Gerber & H. B. Reiff (Eds.), Learning disabilities in adulthood: Persisting problems and evolving issues (pp. 171–178). Boston: Andover Medical.

Dowdy, C. A., Smith, T. E. C., & Nowell, C. H. (1992). Learning disabilities and vocational rehabilitation. Journal of Learning Disabilities, 25, 442–447.

Federal Register (1977, December). Washington, DC: U.S. Government Printing Office.

Gerber, P., & Ginsberg, R. J. (1990) Identifying alterable patterns of success in highly successful adults with learning disabilities (Report No. H133G80500). Washington, DC: National Institute on Disability and Rehabilitation Research, ED/OSERS.

Individuals with Disabilities Education Act Amendments of 1990 (P.L. 104-476). Washington, DC: U.S. Government Printing Office.

McCue, M. (1994). Clinical, diagnostic, and functional assessment of adults with learning disabilities. In P. J. Gerber & H. B. Reiff (Eds.), Learning disabilities in adulthood: Persisting problems and evolving issues (pp. 55–71). Boston: Andover Medical.

McCue, M., Chase, S. L., Dowdy, C. A., Pramuka, M., Petrick, J., Aitken, S., & Fabry, P. (1994) Functional assessment of individuals with cognitive disabilities: A desk reference for rehabilitation. Pittsburgh, PA: Center for Applied Neuropsychology Associates.

Michaels, C. (1994). Transition, adolescents, and learning disabilities. In C. A. Michaels (Ed.), Transition strategies for persons with learning disabilities (pp. 1–22). San Diego: Singular.

Michaels, C. A., & Dowdy, C. A. (1995). Parental perceptions of vocational rehabilitation services for individuals with learning disabilities. Unpublished manuscript.

Pramuka, M. (1994). Facilitating empowerment in students with learning disabilities: Guidelines for teachers. Unpublished manuscript.

The Rehabilitation Act of 1973 as amended by the Rehabilitation Act Amendments of 1992. Washington, DC: United States Department of Education.

Rehabilitation Services Administration. (1985, March 5). Program policy Directive (RSA-PPD 85-7). Washington, DC: U.S. Office of Special Education and Rehabilitation Service.

Rehabilitation Services Administration. (1990, September 28). Program assistance circular (90-7). Washington, DC: U.S. Office of Special Education and Rehabilitation Service.

Smith, J. O. (1992). Falling through the cracks: Rehabilitation services for adults with learning disabilities. Exceptional Children. 58, 451–460.

Smith, T. E. C., Finn, D. M., & Dowdy, C. A. (1993) Teaching students with mild disabilities. Ft. Worth, TX: Holt, Rinehart.

U.S. Department of Health and Human Services. (1980). The international classification of diseases (9th ed.). Washington, DC: U.S. Government Printing Office.

Van Reusen, A. K., Bos, C. S., Schumaker, J. B., & Deshler, D. D. (1995). The self-advocacy strategy. Lawrence, KS: Excell Enterprises.

Wilson, G. L. (1994). Self-advocacy skills. In C. A. Michaels (Ed.), Transition strategies for persons with learning disabilities (pp. 153–184). San Diego: Singular.

CHAPTER 10

Akridge, R. L. (1992). *Jobs rally: Marketing a community development project using peer support strategies. Fayetteville: University of Arkansas Research and Training Center in Vocational Rehabilitation.* (ERIC Document Reproduction Service No. ED 352 796)

Bates, P. E., Bronkema, J., Ames, T., & Hess, C. (1992). State-level interagency planning models. In F. R. Rusch, L. DeStefano, J. Chadsey-Rusch, L. A. Phelps, & E. Szymanski (Eds.), *Transition from school to adult life: Models, linkages, and policy* (pp. 115–129). Sycamore, IL: Sycamore.

Benz, M., & Halpern, A. (1986). Vocational preparation for high school students with mild disabilities: A statewide study of administrator, teacher, and parent perceptions. *Career Development for Exceptional Individuals, 9*, 3–15.

Benz, M., & Halpern, A. (1987). Transition services for secondary students with mild disabilities: A statewide perspective. *Exceptional Children, 53*, 507–514.

Benz, M. R., Lindstrom, L. E., Halpern, A. S., & Rothstrom, R. S. (1991). *Community transition team model facilitator's manual.* Eugene: University of Oregon Press.

Blalock, G., Brito, C., Chenault, B., Detwiler, B., Hessmiller, R., Husted, D., Oney, D., Putnam, P., & Van Dyke, R. (1994). *Life span transition planning in New Mexico: A technical assistance document.* Santa Fe: New Mexico State Board of Education and State Department of Education.

Blalock, G., Hessmiller, R., Webb, K., & Schlee, C. (1995). *Community-level outcomes of the New Mexico Transition Specialist Training Project.* Unpublished manuscript.

Bracey, G. W. (1991). Educational change (Research column). *Phi Delta Kappan, 72*, 557–560.

Carl, J. (no date-a). *Networking: A training unit in support of the Iowa Transition Initiative Transition Process Model.* Des Moines: Iowa Transition Initiative.

Carl, J. (no date-b). *Team building: A training unit in support of the Iowa Transition Initiative Transition Process Model.* Des Moines: Iowa Transition Initiative.

CIRCLE of Life Transition Project. (1994, August). Transition knocks. *Information/ Action Alert*, pp. 1–2. (New Mexico State Department of Education and the Division of Vocational Rehabilitation)

Coombe, E. (1993). Planning transition to employment in rural areas for students with disabilities: Start with a good local fit. *Rural Special Education Quarterly, 12(3)*, 3–7.

DeFur, S., & Reiff, H. B. (1994). Transition of youths with learning disabilities to adulthood: The secondary education foundation. In P. J. Gerber & H. B. Reiff (Eds.), *Learning disabilities in adulthood: Persisting problems and evolving issues* (pp. 99–110). Boston: Andover.

Halloran, W. (1995). Multi-district outreach projects: School-to-work transition initiatives. *InterChange, 13*, 1–6.

Halpern, A., & Benz, M. (1987). A statewide examination of secondary special education for students with mild disabilities: Implications for the high school curriculum. *Exceptional Children, 54*, 122–129.

Halpern, A. S., Benz, M. R., & Lindstrom, L. E. (1992). A systems change approach to improving secondary special education and transition programs at the community level. *Career Development for Exceptional Individuals, 15(1)*, 109–120.

Halpern, A. S., Lindstrom, L. E., Benz, M. R., & Nelson, D. J. (1991). Community transition team model team leader's manual. Eugene: University of Oregon Press.

Halpern, A. S., Lindstrom, L. E., Benz, M. R., & Rothstrom, R. S. (1991). Community transition team model needs assessment instrument. Eugene: University of Oregon Press.

Helge, D. (1984). The state of the art of rural special education. Exceptional Children, 50, 294–305.

Iowa Transition Initiative. (1993). Iowa transition model. Des Moines, IA: Author.

LaRue, S. (1994). Systems changing to better serve youth in transition. Counterpoint, 14(4), 1, 14.

Lindsey, P., & Blalock, G. (1993). Transition to work programs in rural areas: Developing collaborative ethic. Career Development for Exceptional Individuals, 16(2), 159–170.

Lyon, C. P. (1994). Think globally, act locally. Vocational Education Journal, 69(7), 6.

McAlonan, S. J. (1992). Colorado transition manual. Denver: Colorado Department of Education.

Minnesota Department of Education. (1990). Interagency planning for transition in Minnesota: A resource guide. Minneapolis: Author.

National Council on Disability. (1989). The education of students with disabilities: Where do we stand? Washington, DC: Author.

Okolo, C. M., & Sitlington, P. (1988). The role of special education in LD adolescents' transition from school to work. Learning Disability Quarterly, 9, 141–155.

Palace, D., & Whitmore, W. (1988). Collaborative transition planning systems in Los Angeles County. Sacramento: California State Department of Education Transition Center. (ERIC Document Reproduction Service No. ED 302 006)

Phillips, V., & McCullough, L. (1990). Consultation-based programming: Instituting the collaborative ethic in schools. Exceptional Children, 56, 291–304.

Rusch, F. R., DeStefano, L., Chadsey-Rusch, J., Phelps, L. A., & Szymanski, E. M. (Eds.). (1992). Transition from school to adult life: Models, linkages, and policy. Sycamore, IL: Sycamore.

Rusch, F. R., Kohler, P. D., & Hughes, C. (1992). An analysis of OSERS-sponsored secondary special education and transitional services research. Career Development for Exceptional Individuals, 15(1), 121–143.

Sitlington, P., & Frank, A. (1993). Dropouts with learning disabilities: What happens to them as young adults? Learning Disabilities Research and Practice, 8, 244–252.

Sitlington, P., Frank, A., & Carson, R. (1990). Iowa statewide follow-up study: Adult adjustment of individuals with mild disabilities one year after leaving school. Des Moines: Iowa Department of Education.

Smith, G., & Edelen-Smith, P. (1993). Restructuring secondary special education Hawaiian style. Intervention in School and Clinic, 28, 248–252, 247.

Stodden, R. A., & Leake, D. W. (1994). Getting to the core of transition: A re-assessment of old wine in new bottles. Career Development for Exceptional Individuals, 17(1), 65–76.

Vermont Department of Education (n.d.). Team building and facilitating effective teams. In Building capacity for effective transition. Montpelier: Vermont Department of Education Transition Systems Change Project.

Wagner, M. (1989). The transition experiences of youth with disabilities: A report from the National Longitudinal Transition Study (USDOE, OSEP Contract No. 300-87-0054). Menlo Park, CA: SRI International.

Wehman, P. (1990). School-to-work: Elements of successful programs. Teaching Exceptional Children, 23(1), 40–43.

CHAPTER 11

Carnegie Forum on Education and the Economy. (1986). A nation prepared: Teachers for the 21st century. Washington, DC: Author.

Council for Exceptional Children (1994). What is Goals 2000: The Educate America Act? Teaching Exceptional Children, 27, 78–80.

Dowdy, C. A., & Smith, T. E. C. (1991). Future-based assessment and intervention. Intervention in School and Clinic, 27, 101–106.

Haring, K. A., Lovett, D. L., & Smith, D. D. (1990). A follow-up study of recent special education graduates of learning disabilities programs. Journal of Learning Disabilities, 23, 108–113.

Murray, F. B. (1986). Goals for the reform of teacher education: An executive summary of the Holmes Group Report. Phi Delta Kappan, 87, 28–32.

National Association of State Boards of Education. (1992). Winners all: A call for inclusive schools. Alexandria, VA: Author.

National Association of State Directors of Special Education. (1993). Leading and managing for performance: An examination of challenges confronting special education. Alexandria, VA: Author.

National Joint Committee on Learning Disabilities. (1990). Learning disabilities: Issues on definition. Austin, TX: PRO-ED.

Renaissance Group. (1989). Teachers for a new world: A statement of principles. Cedar Falls, IA: University of Northern Iowa.

Smith, T. E. C. (1990). Introduction to education (2nd ed). St. Paul, MN: West.

Smith, T. E. C., Finn, D. F., & Dowdy, C. A. (1993). Teaching students with disabilities. Ft. Worth, TX: Harcourt and Brace.

Smith, T. E. C., Price, B. J., & Marsh, G. E. (1986). Mildly handicapped children and adults. St. Paul, MN: West.

Trapani, C. (1990). Transition goals for adolescents with learning disabilities. Austin, TX: PRO-ED.

Wehman, P., Moon, M. S., Everson, J. M., Wood, W., & Barcus, J. M. (1988). Transition from school to work. Baltimore: Brookes.

APPENDIX

Beck, J., Broers, J., Hogue, E., Shipstead, J., & Knowlton, H. E. (1994, Winter). Strategies for functional community-based instruction and inclusion for elementary-aged children with mental retardation. Teaching Exceptional Children, 26(2), 44–48.

Brolin, D. E. (1988). Life centered career education: A competency based approach (3rd ed.). Reston, VA: The Council for Exceptional Children.

Brolin, D. E. (1993). Life centered career education: A competency based approach (4th ed.). Reston, VA: The Council for Exceptional Children.

Brolin, D. E. (1992). Life centered career education (LCCE) curriculum program. Reston, VA: The Council for Exceptional Children.

Clark, G. M. (1991, October). Functional curriculum and its place in the regular education initiative. Paper presented at the Seventh International Conference of the Division on Career Development, Council for Exceptional Children, Kansas City, MO.

Clark, G. M. (1994, Winter). Is a functional curriculum approach compatible with an inclusive education model? Teaching Exceptional Children, 26(2), 36–39.

Clark, G. M., Carlson, B. C., Fisher, S. L., Cook, I. D., & D'Alonzo, B. J. (1991). Career development for students with disabilities in elementary schools: A position statement of the Division on Career Development. Career Development for Exceptional Individuals, 14, 109–120.

Cronin, M. E., & Patton, J. R. (1993). Life skills instruction for all students with special needs: A practical guide for integrating real-life content into the curriculum. Austin, TX: PRO-ED.

Department of Labor. (1991, June). What work requires of schools: A SCANS report for America 2000. Washington, DC: Department of Labor, The Secretary's Commission on Achieving Necessary Skills.

Edgar, E. (1987). Secondary programs in special education: Are many of them justifiable? Exceptional Children, 53, 555–561.

Field, S., LeRoy, B., & Rivera, S. (1994, Winter). Meeting functional curriculum needs in middle school general education classrooms. Teaching Exceptional Children, 26(2), 40–43.

Mithaug, D., Martin, J. E., & Agran, M. (1987). Adaptability instruction: The goal of transitional programming. Exceptional Children, 53, 500–505.

Peterson, M., LeRoy, B., Field, S., & Wood, P. (1992). Community referenced learning in inclusive schools: Effective curriculum for all students. In S. Stainback & W. Stainback (Eds.), Curriculum considerations in inclusive classrooms. Baltimore: Paul H. Brookes.

Polloway, E. A., Patton, J. R., Epstein, M. H., & Smith, T. (1989). Comprehensive curriculum for students with mild handicaps. Focus on Exceptional Children, 21(8), 1–12.

Polloway, E. A., Patton, J. R., Smith, J. D., & Rodrique, T. W. (1991). Issues in program design for elementary students with mild mental retardation: Emphasis on curriculum development. Education and Training in Mental Retardation, 26, 142–150.

The Rehabilitation Act Amendments of 1992 (P.L. 102-569).

Valdes, K. A., Williamson, C. L., & Wagner, M. (1990, July). National Longitudinal Transition Study of Special Education Students Statistical Almanac. Volume 1: Overview. Menlo Park, CA: SRI International.

Contributors

 Diane S. Bassett, PhD, University of Northern Colorado. Address: Division of Special Education, McKee 325, Greeley, CO 80639.

 Ginger Blalock, PhD, University of New Mexico. Address: Special Education Program, University of New Mexico, Mesa Vista Hall, 3rd Floor, Albuquerque, NM 87131.

 Loring C. Brinckerhoff, PhD, Tufts University. Address: 17 Rich Valley Road, Wayland, MA 01778.

 Gary M. Clark, EdD, University of Kansas. Address: Department of Special Education, 3001 Robert Dole Human Development Center, University of Kansas, Lawrence, KS 66045.

 Mary E. Cronin, PhD, University of New Orleans. Address: Department of Special Education and Habilitative Services, University of New Orleans, New Orleans, LA 70148.

Carol A. Dowdy, EdD, University of Alabama at Birmingham. Address: Room 214, 901 13th St. South, Birmingham, AL 35294-1250.

Caroline Dunn, PhD, Auburn University. Address: Department of Rehabilitation and Special Education, 1228 Haley Center, Auburn University, Auburn, AL 36849-5226.

Rebecca B. Evers, EdD, Winthrop University. Address: 304 Withers Hall, School of Education, Winthrop University, Rock Hill, SC 29733.

Sharon Field, EdD, Wayne State University. Address: Office of the Dean, 469 Education Building, College of Education, Wayne State University, Detroit, MI 48202.

James R. Patton, EdD, PRO-ED, Inc. Address: 8700 Shoal Creek Blvd., Austin, TX 78757-6897.

Patricia L. Sitlington, PhD, University of Northern Iowa. Address: Department of Special Education, University of Northern Iowa, Cedar Falls, IA 50614-0601.

Tom E. C. Smith, PhD, University of Arkansas at Little Rock. Address: Department of Teacher Education, University of Arkansas at Little Rock, 2801 S. University, Little Rock, AR 72204.

Author Index

Gerber, P. J. 23, 40, 94, 206
Gersten, R. 127
Getzel, E. E. 23, 39, 41
Giangreco, M. F. 85
Ginsberg, R. 40, 94, 206
Gioglio, M. 158, 172, 173, 174, 183
Goetz, L. 57
Goh, S. R. 123
Goldhammer, R. 157, 165, 172
Gordon, L. B. 2, 44
Gordon, R. L. 65
Graham, S. 115
Grattan, C. 87
Graves, A. 57
Green, J. E. 117
Greenan, J. P. 38, 122, 124
Greenbaum, B. 115
Gugerty, J. J. 23, 39, 41

Hall, D. 166, 167
Halloran, W. D. 13, 28, 215, 216
Halpern, A. S. 3, 5, 7, 8, 21, 44, 45, 51,
    56, 85, 86, 92, 94, 96, 97, 120, 131,
    133, 136, 215, 220, 222, 223, 224, 225,
    226, 227, 228, 229
Hammill, D. D. 134
Haring, K. A. 45, 48, 86, 92, 94, 96, 237
Harris, A. 126
Harris, C. 74
Hartman, R. C. 158, 162, 175
Hartzell, H. 47, 48
Hasazi, S. B. 2, 44
Haubrich, P. A. 92, 96
Haugh, R. 162, 170
Havekost, D. M. 96
HEATH Resource Center 175
Hebbeler, K. 9, 20, 21, 33, 34, 35, 36, 92
Helmke, L. M. 96
Henderson, C. 161
Henderson, J. L. 123
Heron, T. E. 31, 98
Hess, C. 220
Hessmiller, R. 13, 215, 221, 224, 225, 227,
    231
Heyward, Lawton, & Associates 166
Hoerner, J. L. 117
Hoffman, A. 62, 65, 66, 69, 70, 71, 72, 73,
    76, 78, 80, 81, 82
Hoffman, F. J. 23, 24, 40, 49
Holl, C. 92
Holland, J. 173
Holubec, E. 76
Holt, K. 63, 78

Honaker, K. 123
Horiuchi, C. N. 2
Horvath, M. 57
Houck, C. K. 40
Hughes, C. 215
Hunt, P. 57
Husted, D. 13
Hutchinson, D. 85

Ianacone, R. N. 19
Iliff, V. W. 62, 75
Irvin, L. 136
Itkenen, T. 57
Izzo, M. V. 41

Jay, E. D. 2, 46
Jayanthi, M. 168, 171
Jenkins, J. R. 127
Jewell, M. 127
Johnson, D. R. 70
Johnson, D. W. 76
Johnson, J. M. 40, 45, 85, 91, 166, 172
Johnson, R. T. 76
Johnson, W. B. 127
Jones, B. 170
Jones, W. 167
Joy, E. D. 86, 92

Kahn, H. 118
Karge, B. D. 8, 15, 38
Keith, K. D. 137, 138
Kelchner, K. 67
Kennedy, C. 57
Kerr, M. M. 126
Kessler, J. M. 181, 182, 184
Kincaid, J. M. 166
Kistler, J. K. 161, 166, 167
Knowles, M. 133
Kochhar, C. A. 128
Koenigsberg, E. 39
Koestner, R. 63, 78
Kohler, P. D. 31, 33, 215
Kokaska, C. J. 51, 133
Kolstoe, O. P. 51, 132
Kottering, L. 2
Kranstover, L. L. 92, 96
Kravets, M. 175
Kuperstein, J. S. 181, 182, 184

Landers, M. F. 57, 86, 96
Landman, J. J. 136
Larkin, D. J. 122

Subject Index